Central Bank Governance and Oversight Reform

The Hoover Institution gratefully acknowledges the following individuals and foundations for their significant support of the **Working Group on Economic Policy** *and this publication:*

Lynde and Harry Bradley Foundation

Preston and Carolyn Butcher

Stephen and Sarah Page Herrick

Michael and Rosalind Keiser

Koret Foundation

William E. Simon Foundation

John A. Gunn and Cynthia Fry Gunn

Central Bank Governance and **Oversight Reform**

EDITED BY
John H. Cochrane
John B. Taylor

CONTRIBUTING AUTHORS
Michael D. Bordo
Alex Nikolsko-Rzhevskyy
David H. Papell
Charles I. Plosser
Ruxandra Prodan
George P. Shultz
Paul Tucker
Carl E. Walsh
Kevin M. Warsh
John C. Williams

HOOVER INSTITUTION PRESS
STANFORD UNIVERSITY   STANFORD, CALIFORNIA

www.hoover.org

Hoover Institution Press Publication No. 666
Hoover Institution at Leland Stanford Junior University,
Stanford, California 94305-6003

First printing 2016
24 23 22 21 20 19 18 17 16   9 8 7 6 5 4 3 2 1

Manufactured in the United States of America

The paper used in this publication meets the minimum requirements of the American National Standard for Information Sciences—Permanence of Paper for Printed Library Materials, ANSI/NISO z39.48-1992.♾

Cataloging-in-Publication Data is available from the Library of Congress.
ISBN-13: 978-0-8179-1924-5 (cloth. : alk. paper)
ISBN-13: 978-0-8179-1926-9 (epub)
ISBN-13: 978-0-8179-1927-6 (mobi)
ISBN-13: 978-0-8179-1928-3 (PDF)

Contents

Preface   vii
John H. Cochrane and John B. Taylor

ONE   **How Can Central Banks Deliver Credible
Commitment and Be "Emergency Institutions"?**   1
Paul Tucker
Comments: *John H. Cochrane*
General Discussion: *Michael D. Bordo, John H. Cochrane,
Peter Fisher, Robert Hodrick, Charles I. Plosser, George P.
Shultz, John B. Taylor, Paul Tucker, Kevin M. Warsh*

TWO   **Policy Rule Legislation in Practice**   55
David H. Papell, Alex Nikolsko-Rzhevskyy and Ruxandra Prodan
Comments: *Michael Dotsey*
General Discussion: *John H. Cochrane, Michael Dotsey,
Peter Fisher, Andrew Levin, David H. Papell, Charle I. Plosser,
John B. Taylor, Paul Tucker, Carl E. Walsh, John C. Williams*

THREE **Goals versus Rules as Central Bank
Performance Measures**   109
Carl E. Walsh
Comments: *Andrew Levin*
General Discussion: *John H. Cochrane, Michael Dotsey,
David H. Papell, John B. Taylor, Carl E. Walsh, John C.
Williams*

FOUR   Institutional Design: Deliberations, Decisions,
       and Committee Dynamics   173
       Kevin M. Warsh
         Comments: *Peter Fisher*
         General Discussion: *Binyamin Appelbaum, Michael D. Bordo,*
         John H. Cochrane, Michael Dotsey, Peter Fisher, Andrew Levin,
         Charles I. Plosser, George P. Shultz, Paul Tucker, Kevin M.
         Warsh, John C. Williams

FIVE   Some Historical Reflections on the Governance
       of the Federal Reserve   221
       Michael D. Bordo
         Comments: *Mary H. Karr*
         General Discussion: *Michael D. Bordo, John H. Cochrane,*
         Peter Fisher, Mary H. Karr, Andrew Levin, Charles I. Plosser,
         George P. Shultz, John B. Taylor, Paul Tucker, Kevin M. Warsh,
         John C. Williams

SIX   Panel on Independence, Accountability, and
       Transparency in Central Bank Governance   255
       Charles I. Plosser, George P. Shultz, and John C. Williams
         General Discussion: *Michael J. Boskin, John H. Cochrane,*
         Peter Fisher, Robert Hodrick, Andrew Levin, David Papell,
         Charles I. Plosser, John B. Taylor, Paul Tucker, Kevin M. Warsh,
         John C. Williams

       Conference Agenda   297
       About the Contributors   299
       About the Hoover Institution's Working Group on
          Economic Policy   305
       Index   309

Preface

John H. Cochrane and John B. Taylor

At the time we were organizing this conference, most of the voluminous commentary about the Federal Reserve System centered on what decisions it should take. Should the Fed raise interest rates? How soon? How much?

We thought the conference could make more progress by focusing on a different and deeper set of questions. How should the Fed make decisions? How should the Fed govern its internal decision-making processes? How should Congress, from which the Fed ultimately receives its authority, oversee the Fed? Central bank independence is a great virtue, but independence in a democracy must come with clear limits and a limited scope of action. What should those limits be? What is the trade-off between greater Fed power and less Fed independence? How should Congress manage its fundamental oversight role? Several bills in Congress stipulate more rules-based policy and consequent accountability, along with deeper monetary reforms. Are these bills a good idea? How should they be structured?

The distinguished scholars and policymakers at the conference, whose contributions and commentary are represented in this conference volume, do not disappoint in their analysis of these and related questions.

Paul Tucker's opening paper, "How Can Central Banks Deliver Credible Commitment and be 'Emergency Institutions'?" leads off with a central conundrum: in general, people seem to want central banks to follow rule-based policy in normal times, but people expect banks to take a much more discretionary do-what-it-takes approach to stopping financial crises. Tucker asks if these two hats can be worn at once. He builds up to the basic conclusion: "LOLR [lender of last resort] liquidity reinsurance policy *can* be systematic, and *should* be framed within a regime," just as normal-times monetary policy should be so framed.

Tucker starts by thinking through the limits on the central bank's tools. Should the central bank, even in a crisis, be legally limited to traditional open market operations, exchanging reserves for short-term treasuries? Or should the central bank be free to purchase many different kinds of assets in crises? He notes the many restrictions, including central bank independence, that stand in the way of inflationary finance in normal times, but which may be inappropriate during crises.

Looking at the modern financial system, Tucker concludes that money, credit, and finance are not separable. He advocates an integrated money-credit constitution consisting of "inflation targeting plus a reserves requirement that increased with a bank's leverage plus a liquidity-reinsurance regime plus a resolution regime for bankrupt banks plus constraints on how the central bank is free to pursue its mandate."

Tucker goes on to think about what constraints and governance should apply to the central banks' lender-of-last-resort and liquidity-reinsurance functions. He starts by noting the current status: "nearly all central banks . . . stand ready to lend against a wide variety of collateral, including portfolios of illiquid loans . . ." More contentious is whether central banks should "lend to non-banks or . . . act as a market-maker of last resort."

In this situation, bankers face large moral hazard and pre-commitment problems. Tucker points out that received wisdom says they should lend only to illiquid—not insolvent—firms, but in practice the two are hard to distinguish. He argues therefore that a "regime" is desirable vs. untrammeled discretion, and legislative constraints can overcome the large pre-commitment problem.

Tucker frames the issue within the broader question of what "emergency powers" are appropriate for any government. In practical terms, he approves of arrangements, such as in the Dodd-Frank Act, that allow the Fed to innovate beyond its customary or legislatively limited powers, after getting permission from the president and secretary of the treasury, a view echoed in slightly different form later in the conference by Charles Plosser.

Tucker goes on to consider the question of whether the central bank should be able to exceed its limits in perceived economic (rather than financial) emergencies—by, for example, buying stocks, mortgages, or government-guaranteed mortgage-backed securities in order to stimulate demand, as the Fed did—again concluding that some sort of regime is needed.

John Cochrane's discussion cheers the basic conclusion: untrammeled discretion in crises leads to unlimited moral hazard in the preceding boom. Cochrane emphasizes the pre-commitment problem, that "self-imposed rules, promises, guidance, and tradition are not enough." In the crisis, central bankers will bail out institutions and their creditors, support prices, and lend if they can; knowing that fact, people will take risks and fail to keep enough cash around, making the crisis worse and forcing the bankers to cave. Only legally binding limitations can stop the cycle.

Cochrane takes a dimmer view of current institutions in fulfilling Tucker's vision, opining that there is very little current constraint on central bank actions. He also criticizes the traditional Bagehot rules. Who cares if an institution is illiquid vs. insolvent? The central bank is not there to be a profitable hedge fund—it's there to save the economy. There is little obvious link between systemic danger (whatever that is) and the liquidity vs. solvency line.

Responding to Tucker's call for yet more thinking and research to make the current money-credit constitution work, Cochrane opines that an equity-financed banking system is a much more promising alternative to endless research.

A written record of the general discussion of Tucker's paper follows, with George Shultz's summary of the financial crisis being the highlight.

As with all of the general discussions throughout this book, the commentary is based on a recording made at the conference, from which a transcript was created. Participants then edited their comments for clarity following the conference.

The next paper, "Policy Rule Legislation in Practice," was presented at the conference by David Papell and is coauthored with Alex Nikolsko-Rzhevskyy and Ruxandra Prodan.

The paper carefully evaluates legislation, recently proposed in the US House and Senate, which would require the Fed to describe its monetary policy rule and, if and when the Fed changed or deviated from its rule, explain the reasons. The paper applies formal econometric methods to these legislative proposals. Papell, Nikolsko-Rzhevskyy, and Prodan consider several versions of the Taylor rule to see how often in the past monetary policy deviated from that rule, and thereby assess how often the Fed would have had to explain deviations from its own rule to Congress under the proposed legislation. Their analysis carefully uses real-time data, adheres to the data definitions in use historically, and offers several plausible variations.

All of the versions of the Taylor rule examined in the paper produce extended periods of substantial deviation, including the 1970s inflation (they find that policy was loose), the Volcker disinflation (they find that policy was tight), and in the early 2000s and 2010s. So, if the legislation had been in place starting in the early 1970s, if the Fed had chosen the Taylor rule back then, and if the legislation had not induced the Fed to alter its policy, the Fed would have had either to announce a new rule or to explain its deviations for substantial periods in the 1970s, early 1980s, and more recently.

Michael Dotsey leads a sharp discussion. Though the broad brush of when the Fed was in compliance with the rule is fairly robust, Dotsey notes that "how one measures the output gap, and which inflation rate is used in the rule" matter to whether the Fed is in compliance or not.

The biggest issue Dotsey raises is the difference between the Taylor rule with no lags which Taylor originally proposed (described as a reference rule in the proposed legislation), in which the funds rate depends on output and inflation only, and estimated Taylor rules that include the lagged funds rate and (less important quantitatively) lagged responses to inflation and output gaps. With lags, we obtain a very good fit throughout postwar history: "It is rare to find discrepancies greater than twenty basis points . . . " Dotsey adds that much theoretical literature recommends rules with inertial responses, i.e., lagged funds rates on the right-hand side.

A long and thoughtful general discussion of these ideas follows. Which kind of rule should be used: an "inertial" rule with lags or a simpler rule without lags? The inertial rule fits the data better, but largely says that the Fed should continue doing whatever it was doing, even if that was a mistake. It also fits so well that the Fed would likely never be in violation. Should a rule fit the data well, or is the whole point of legislation in fact to constrain the Fed to do things differently in the future than it has at some times in the past? If there are to be long-lasting deviations from the rule, should Congress get used to routine "explanations" of deviations from a rule? Or will the Fed just announce new "rules"?

John Taylor concludes the discussion, answering many of these questions by emphasizing that the bills envision the rule as a "strategy," not necessarily a mechanical formula. It would be the Fed's job to define and communicate its goals along with the strategy to achieve the goals.

Carl Walsh's contribution considers "Goals versus Rules as Central Bank Performance Measures."

Walsh takes on an issue that pervades much of the discussion in this book: If Congress holds the central bank to a rule, should it be an instrument rule, such as an interest rate rule, telling the Fed how to act? Or should it be a goal, such as an inflation target, setting a narrow objective for the central bank and accountability for that objective, but leaving the bank great discretion in how to achieve the objective?

The heart of Walsh's paper is an evaluation of goal-based vs. instrument-based rules in a simple model. Walsh assumes that the social welfare function is a weighted sum of squared deviations of output and inflation. The central bank's objective, however, adds shocks, so it tries to minimize the weighted sum of output and inflation from these shocked values. The shocks represent temporary political pressures to deviate from the regular rule. The economy follows a standard new-Keynesian intertemporal substitution relation, in which output depends on expected future output and the real interest rate, and a standard new-Keynesian forward-looking Phillips curve.

In this setting, Walsh is able analytically to characterize the social welfare of the resulting equilibrium. He models a rule as an additional term in the central bank's objective that prizes deviations from an inflation target or deviations of the funds rate from the recommended rule.

So which is better? Walsh finds that, in general, an optimal combination includes both an inflation target and a rule. The relative weight depends on the variances of shocks: cost shocks raise the weight on a rule, but demand shocks raise the weight on an inflation target.

In a more complex calibrated model, Walsh finds that "the definition of real activity used in the rule is crucial." A rule based on output deviations from potential receives no weight relative to an inflation target. But a rule based on the gap between output and its efficient level gets weight along with an inflation target.

Naturally, the comments and discussion about Walsh's analysis rage over just how to interpret these results, and which features of the rule vs. goal debate the model captures.

Andrew Levin, the lead discussant, notes that the model has i.i.d. shocks, considers only the discretionary solution (i.e., the Fed cannot commit to policies), and has no learning.

Levin points out that in this model the Fed can perfectly offset aggregate demand shocks but not aggregate supply shocks. As he explains, the inflation target is imperfect—it forces the central bank away from its preference shocks, but only toward desirable inflation, not output. He wonders whether adding an output target as well would restore this balance. Analytically, adding huge costs to deviations from inflation and output, the government could, in this model, make the central bank's objective equal to the social objective.

Similarly, Levin points out that the Taylor rule is imperfect here because the central bank can no longer respond to natural rate or aggregate demand shocks. Well, since these are observable in the model, why not just add them to the rule? The problem with models is that there is always an optimal policy, and then one must think why a simple rule is not just the optimal policy.

Levin continues to say that a large function of the rule is to communicate what the Fed is doing. This communication role is missed in the paper.

Next, Kevin Warsh presents "Institution Design: Deliberations, Decisions, and Committee Dynamics." He focuses on the eternally vexing question: How do you best structure a committee—like the Federal Open Market Committee, which sets interest rates—to make good decisions?

Warsh reviews a lengthy, interesting, and, to economists, largely unknown literature on committee decisions, especially how to foster a genuine deliberation and how to balance inquiry vs. advocacy. Anyone running a faculty meeting, take note.

Warsh then summarizes his conclusions from a comparison of the UK Monetary Policy Committee (MPC), which he was invited to evaluate, and the US Federal Open Market Committee (FOMC).

In Warsh's view, the MPC is set up in a way that is "favorable to genuine deliberation and sound decision-making." It is small and diverse. "Individual contributions can be identified and evaluated, and its members are encouraged to think for themselves."

The first day of an MPC meeting has a free-flowing and open debate, with healthy listening, deliberation, and changing of minds. The second day moves to "advocacy," in which members try to convince each other of the conclusions they have reached.

By contrast, the FOMC suffers "certain institutional aspects . . . which differ somewhat from best practice . . . " The FOMC is much larger: nineteen people convene in the discussion, with about sixty people in the room. Dissents are rare and the chair never loses a vote, in contrast with the UK, in which votes are seldom unanimous and the chair often loses.

Public transcripts, while seemingly useful for transparency, may have the unintended effect that "FOMC participants . . . voice less dissent in the meetings themselves, and [are] less willing to change policy positions over time." The Sunshine Act means that the "real" discussions happen in small groups centered around the chair. The resulting meetings consist of members giving carefully prepared set-piece speeches, in full advocacy mode from the start, and there is little true deliberation.

Peter Fisher, the lead discussant of Warsh's paper, stresses individual vs. group accountability, which covers many issues raised in the general discussion. As Fisher puts it, "I thought I understood the awkwardness of group accountability when more than once I saw the FOMC gravitate toward no one's first choice and virtually no one's second choice, and we ended up with third-best outcomes. But now I'm also worried about individual accountability of a pseudo-nature [speeches for the FOMC record], which I'm afraid is the regime we now have."

Fisher stresses that "effective decision-making bodies tend to practice individual input but collective accountability . . ." After the vote, people don't stress their dissents. He believes that we don't have that now. "The single most important output of monetary policy is the expected path of short-term interest rates, and yet the current FOMC feels free to allow every man and woman to have their own expected path."

Next is Michael Bordo's paper, "Some Historical Reflections on the Governance of the Federal Reserve." The Federal Reserve has a complex structure which has evolved through history. The United States has long distrusted a national central bank, appointed by the central government and close to the financial center, as is the case in many other countries. So the Fed in 1914 started with a degree of autonomy of the regional banks that is surprising even by today's standards. Furthermore, regional banks were owned by member banks and their governors were appointed by local directors. In the early years, regional banks actually conducted "their own monetary policies to influence economic conditions in their own districts." Bordo recounts many instances of regional vs. Board of Governors conflict.

Bordo then chronicles the shift of power from Reserve Banks to the Board of Governors. Most recently, the financial crisis was managed by the Board and the New York Fed, and the Dodd-Frank Act gives the Board great power as part of the Financial Stability Oversight Council. It also weakens the power of local boards to select regional bank chairs.

Bordo focuses on a major controversy, central to the theme of this book: Were the Federal Reserve's many failures primarily due to its governance structure or to mistakes in its understanding of how monetary policy works?

Bordo also recounts some of the history in which regional banks played important roles in developing new ideas, outside the

Washington–New York axis of power and occasional groupthink. In particular, he cites the monetarist influence from St. Louis in the 1960s and the recent concerns by regional presidents—including Jeffrey Lacker of Richmond, Charles Plosser of Philadelphia, Thomas Hoenig of Kansas City, and Richard Fisher of Dallas—over the use of credit policy, bailouts, and large-scale asset purchases.

Bordo concludes that "the federal/regional nature of the Fed is one of its great sources of strength" and that the "federal/regional structure . . . should be preserved."

Mary Karr's lead discussion emphasizes the question of "how best to retain independent voices." She warns that "structural reorganization" usually means "some further centralization of authority in Washington." She also emphasizes the deep question of whether the Fed's mistakes were "structural defects or mistakes in theory." She argues against the "myth that bankers control the Fed and the Fed was created by—and to benefit—bankers," while explaining the "complex scheme for the selection of Reserve Bank directors."

A long, insightful discussion on the value of the regional bank structure follows.

The conference volume closes with a "Panel on Independence, Accountability, and Transparency in Central Bank Governance" with Charles Plosser, George Shultz, and John Williams. Charles Plosser leads off. He first reminds us how important it is to have a "healthy degree of separation between government officials who are in charge of spending and those who are in charge of printing the money," which is the most essential part of good governance. He emphasizes that recent criticisms and the moves in Congress to rethink Fed governance are natural given how much the "Fed has pushed the envelope of traditional monetary policy," including bailouts, six years of zero interest rates, aggressive asset purchases, and purchases of mortgage-backed securities which constitute a credit allocation policy, properly part of fiscal policy.

So how can we balance authority, including independence, with accountability and constraints? Plosser argues, first, that the mandate should be narrower. He advocates price stability as the only mandate. Second, the Fed should be restricted in the type of assets it can buy or sell. And third, a more transparent communication of monetary policy strategy, "where rules can play a vital role," would help to ensure discipline and accountability.

Plosser thinks the public "has come to expect way too much from central banks" to solve "all manner of economic ills." In the end, the demand for constraints on Fed action must derive from the public and be represented in Congress.

Regarding Paul Tucker's conundrum—whether lender of last resort should be less limited and more discretionary—Plosser suggests that emergency lending and bailouts really are fiscal policy. Therefore, there should be a new accord between the Treasury and the Fed. The Treasury takes the responsibility for bailouts or asset purchases to enhance financial stability (ruefully noting, "however they want to define that term"). But the Treasury then asks the Fed to execute the policy.

George Shultz next reminds us that we need to restore a competent government, and trust in that competence. Limiting the purposes of an organization is a key to competence.

He sounds a warning against the siren song of transparency, noting that "the Fed speaks with about a dozen voices . . . people sound off all the time, and it's a little hard to figure out just what is the policy." Bottom line: the Fed, like Ted Williams (or Teddy Roosevelt) should talk less. This is a deep comment in an era when the Fed, under "forward guidance" and at the zero bound, does really little else than talk.

But Shultz reminds us that the administration must support Fed independence. Reagan supported the Fed's anti-inflation efforts, whereas other presidents undermined the Fed.

Last, but certainly not least, John Williams writes about the "independence dilemma," touching on many themes of the conference.

He describes the day's dilemma thus: "Successful monetary policy necessitates both an arm's-length relationship to the political process and oversight by elected officials." Williams reminds us of "operational mandates" of the gold standard, fixed exchange rates, and money growth rules. Each neatly solved the governance problem, but each turned out to produce troubled monetary policy regimes. He contrasts these regimes with "goal mandates" in which the government tells the central bank what it wants to achieve, such as an inflation target, but leaves the bank free to achieve it with much less constraints on the nature and use of tools. He reminds us of the general success of inflation targeting.

Williams closes, however, in favor of a "monetary policy rule such as the Taylor rule." Such a rule includes goals—such as the target 2 percent inflation rate—but also specifies in general terms how the Fed should move its lever, the short-term interest rate, to achieve those goals.

He raises three important issues, however: how to handle variation in the "natural rate" of interest, which is an input to Taylor rules, in a less judgmental and discretionary way; and the lesser issues of the zero bound and just which rule should be followed.

George Shultz concludes the general discussion and the whole conference with "Welcome to California," wry in context but surely expressing how the participants in this conference felt at the end of the long day of fascinating and novel discussion.

CHAPTER ONE

How Can Central Banks Deliver Credible Commitment and Be "Emergency Institutions"?

Paul Tucker

Central banks perform two apparently quite different functions. On the one hand, they are expected to operate monetary policy in a *systematic* manner in order to smooth fluctuations in economic activity without jeopardizing the economy's nominal anchor. On the other hand, in their role as the lender of last resort, they are expected to operate with the *flexibility* of the economy's equivalent of the US cavalry.

Both those propositions invite dissent and are unquestionably contested. On monetary policy, there are those, perhaps not here in Stanford, who will want to shout that monetary policy cannot be tied to rules but must be free to meet circumstances that are hard to fathom in advance. On lender-of-last-resort (LOLR) policy, meanwhile, there are those who stress with no less vehemence that a more rule-like regime is needed in order to keep central banks from straying too far into fiscal territory: liquidity support should be distinct from a solvency bailout.

Nevertheless, I suggest that the dominant views are as I initially expressed them, and not without reason.

Society gives the monetary reins to unelected technocrats in order to mitigate problems of credible commitment. A necessary precondition for delivering on that promise is that policy be

My thanks for exchanges on various of the issues covered here to Alberto Alesina, Eric Beerbohm, Steve Cecchetti, Anil Kashyap, Athanasios Orphanides, Philip Pettit, Jeremy Stein, Adrian Vermeule, and Luigi Zingales.

systematic. Big picture, this is an institution designed for normal circumstances. Having, separately, allowed fractional-reserve banking, society also wants the monetary authority to provide liquidity re-insurance to banks in order to protect it from the social costs consequent upon the private banking system's liquidity-insurance services being abruptly withdrawn. That, by contrast with regular monetary policy, is an institution for economic and financial emergencies.

If a central bank succeeds in building a reputation for operating a systematic monetary policy, is that reputation jeopardized when it reveals its normally hidden innovative side during a crisis? Conversely, might a reputation for rule-like behavior in normal times sap confidence in its ability to ride to the rescue in a crisis? In other words, do central banks need to sustain a rich, multipurpose reputation that faces in two directions?

That is the subject of these remarks. Note that my title is not "*Can* central banks deliver credible commitment and be 'emergency institutions'?" It is "*How* can central banks [do so]?" In other words, I am positing that there is no choice other than to house these two functions, two missions, in a single institution and, further, one that is highly insulated from day-to-day politics: an independent central bank.

It is striking, therefore, that debates about the design of monetary-policy regimes and, when they have occurred at all, debates about the LOLR's role in crisis management have largely existed in parallel universes. The silos might be comfortable, but they hardly help society design and oversee the central banks into which they have placed so much trust.

Signs of this are apparent in current debates about the Federal Reserve and its advanced-economy peers. The "Audit the Fed" and "Taylor Rule" bills in Congress are framed as being about monetary policy, which of course they are. Quite separately, the Dodd-Frank Act materially changed the scope and autonomy of the Fed as a lender of last resort, and fresh proposals have recently been launched in the Senate. My point here is not on the merits or demerits of those or any other substantive provisions, nor is it that all reforms should come via a single piece of jumbo legislation. Rather, the point is that we might do better to think about central bank functions in the round, in terms of one joined-up regime for preserving *monetary stability broadly defined*.

If that is right, we need to step back a bit to think more carefully about what we are dealing with here. As I attempt to do so, we shall bump into some fairly deep questions about the distribution of power in democracies. We will also see the monetary policy/LOLR dichotomy dissolve, but only for it to be replaced by a deeper challenge for the design of robust, legitimate central banks: how to proceed when the fiscal constitution is not pinned down.

What do central banks do? Delegated managers of the consolidated state balance sheet

One way into this is to think of the central bank as conducting financial operations that change the liability structure and, potentially, the asset structure of the consolidated balance sheet of the state. If they buy (or lend against) only government paper, the consolidated balance sheet's liability structure is altered. If they purchase or lend against private-sector paper, the state's balance sheet is enlarged, its asset portfolio changed, and its risk exposures affected. Net losses flow to the central treasury in the form of reduced seigniorage income, entailing either higher taxes or lower spending in the longer run (and conversely for net profits).

The state's risks, taken in the round, might not necessarily increase with such operations. If purchasing private-sector assets helped to revive spending in the economy that might, in principle, reduce the probability of the state paying out larger aggregate welfare benefits and receiving lower taxes later. But the form of the

risk would change and, because the driver was central bank operations, the decision-taker on the state's exposures would switch
from elected fiscal policymakers to unelected central bankers.

Seen in that light, the question is what *degrees of freedom* central
banks should be granted, and to what ends, to change the state's
balance sheet.

A minimalist conception, advanced by Marvin Goodfriend,
among others, would restrict the proper scope of central bank
interventions to open market operations that exchange monetary
liabilities for short-term Treasury bills (in order to steer the overnight money-market rate of interest). On this model, the LOLR
function is conceived of as being to accommodate shocks to the
aggregate demand for base money and plays no role in offsetting
temporary problems in the distribution of reserves among banks.

Arguably, this would get close to abolishing the LOLR function
as traditionally executed. As a governor of the Bank of England
said of the 1820s crisis, when the function was first emerging, "we
lent in modes that we had never adopted before . . . by every possible means consistent with the safety of the Bank."[1]

Perhaps more profoundly, at the zero lower bound the only
instrument available to the central bank would be to talk down
expectations of the future path of the policy rate ("forward guidance"). All other interventions to stimulate aggregate demand—for
example, quantitative and credit easing—would fall to the "fiscal
arm" of government. And that, not a judgment on the merits of the
minimal conception, is my point: what is not within the realm of
the central bank falls to elected policymakers, with the attendant
problems of credible commitment and time-inconsistency.

At the other, *maximalist* end of the spectrum, the central bank
would be given free rein to manage the consolidated balance sheet,
even including writing state-contingent options with different

1. Quoted in David Kynaston, "The City of London," chapter 4, one-volume edition (London: Vintage, 2011).

groups of households and firms. That would get very close to *being* the fiscal authority, and cannot be squared with any mainstream ideas of central banking competencies in democracies.

So in one direction, the state's overall capabilities shrivel; and in the other, its functions are effectively seized by unelected central bankers.

We could try to resolve the question of boundaries through positive economics on the effectiveness of different instruments in responding to the shocks hitting a monetary economy. While that work is obviously essential, it is not the approach I take here, partly because answers are likely to be hedged about with uncertainty; but, more fundamentally, because that approach does not speak to which arm of the state should be delegated which tools. The problem appears to be that we don't know where the welfare advantages of credible commitment are outweighed by the disadvantages of the loss of majoritarian control, because that looks like a trade-off between incommensurable values.

I am going to approach the question of boundaries, therefore, by asking first what purposes a central bank serves and then what constraints are appropriate for independent agencies to have legitimacy in a democratic republic. As we proceed, the tension between commitment technologies and majoritarian legitimacy will resolve itself.

A money-credit constitution

Central banks are the fulcrum of the monetary system: the pivot, as Francis Baring put it two centuries ago when coining the term "dernier resort."

It is usual to think of their independence as being warranted by a problem of credible commitment. That is a necessary condition, but it is not a sufficient condition once wider issues than economic welfare are weighed, such as the loss of democratic control.

The imperative of central bank independence is, I think, political, almost constitutional.

In order to maintain the separation of powers between the executive government and the legislature, the fiscal tool of the inflation tax cannot lie in the hands of an executive striving to stay in power. Otherwise it could avoid, or at least delay, requesting "supply" from the assembly by inflating away the burden of any outstanding state debt or, more generally, by printing money to finance its needs and increase seigniorage income. That society chooses to delegate to an agency rather than rely on tying itself to a commodity standard to meet this problem is, I believe, down to modern full-franchise democracies being unprepared to live with the volatility in jobs and output associated with the nineteenth-century gold standard.

On this view, in a fiat money system the independence of the monetary authority is a corollary of the higher-order, constitutional separation of powers. For the delegation actually to deliver credible commitment, the reputation of the central bank and its policymakers must be strapped to their success in maintaining price stability. That is one reason transparency is so important.

The setup unavoidably becomes richer, however, once we acknowledge that society has chosen, rightly or wrongly, to allow fractional-reserve banking, which brings the social benefits of liquidity insurance for households and firms bundled together with the risks from its inherent fragility and the social costs of systemic crises.

The LOLR function is called into existence to reduce both the probability and the impact of those risks crystallizing. That takes the central bank to the scene of almost any meaningful socially costly financial disaster, whether sourced in economic problems or operational malfunction, as when the Fed lent hugely to the Bank of New York to keep the payments system going in the mid-1980s. In consequence, central banks have a keen interest in the adequacy of regulatory and supervisory regimes, in order to contain the moral hazard costs entailed.

In other words, once private banking (in the economic sense) is permitted, central banks cannot avoid being de facto multiple-mission agencies intimately interested and involved in the functioning of the credit system, since most of the economy's money is the credit-money created by the banking system (broad rather than narrow money). As Paul Volcker said with tragic foresight in his 1989 valedictory Per Jacobsson lecture, "I insist that neither monetary policy nor the financial system will be well-served if a central bank loses interest in, or influence over, the financial system."[2]

Since unelected power needs framing carefully in democracies, the de facto position I have outlined should be recognized de jure.

If that sounds ridiculously banal, remember that the Federal Reserve does not have an overall statutory objective to help preserve the stability of the financial system but only objectives tied to specific powers: for example, safety and soundness for the generality of banks and, since Dodd-Frank, stability for its powers over "systemically important financial institutions." In the United Kingdom, only since 2012 has the Bank of England had macroprudential and microregulatory functions framed in terms of an objective of stability.

The world I am describing requires not a "monetary constitution" of the kind advocated by James Buchanan but a *money-credit constitution*. By that I mean rules of the game for both banking and central banking designed to ensure broad monetary stability, understood as having two components: stability in the value of central bank money in terms of goods and services, and also stability of private-banking-system deposit money in terms of central bank money.

2. Paul Volcker, "The Triumph of Central Banking?" Per Jacobsson Lecture, 1989. The question mark in the title was underlined during the Q&A.

The idea would have been familiar to our nineteenth-century predecessors. Their money-credit constitution comprised the gold standard plus a reserves requirement for private banks (an indirect claim on the central bank's gold pool) plus the lender-of- last-resort function celebrated by Walter Bagehot. That package was deficient insofar as it did not cater explicitly for solvency—as opposed to liquidity—crises. Worse, as our economies moved to embrace fiat money during the twentieth century, policymakers fatally relaxed the connection between the nominal anchor and the binding constraint on bank balance sheets—to the point where, on the eve of the 2007 crisis, they were over-leveraged and horribly illiquid.

At a schematic level, a money-credit constitution for today might have five components: inflation targeting plus a reserves requirement that increased with a bank's leverage plus a liquidity-reinsurance regime plus a resolution regime for bankrupt banks plus constraints on how the central bank is free to pursue its mandate.

Compared with the nineteenth century, all five components of that schema would need fleshing out. Much of the past quarter century has been spent on the first—the nominal anchor—and even that work turns out to be incomplete. But other parts of the money-credit constitution are even more difficult to design. We have learned that regulatory arbitrage is endemic in finance, so that any regime for the economic activity of banking would need to cover "shadow banks"—not only de jure banks—and it would need to be richer and more adaptable than could be delivered solely by a leverage-driven reserves requirement. Nevertheless, that simple conception serves as a useful benchmark and a reminder that constraints on, and supervision of, banking soundness are integral to an economy's money-credit constitution.

To pursue the regulation of banking would be too big a detour from the parts of the money-credit constitution that most concern me here: what central banks must do (their mandate), what they may do, and the constraints on them.

Some of the necessary constraints on central banks are implicit in my earlier derivation of their independence from constitutional principles. Most obviously, rather than simply making the definitional statement that any independent agency must be in control of its instruments, it is specifically important that an independent central bank should be barred from lending to government on the government's direction. (Only the legislature should be able to sanction such lending, and through regular legislation, as with any tax.)

That provides one vitally important element of an answer to our question of where the line should be drawn around the capacity of the central bank to reshape the state's consolidated balance sheet. The outline of other components of the answer emerges from considering the legitimacy of central banks as very powerful, unelected institutions.

Constraints and principles for independent agencies

My broad answer to the general question of conditions for the legitimacy of independent agencies in a democratic, liberal republic comes in three parts.

First, a policy function should not be delegated to an independent agency unless: society has settled preferences; the objective is capable of being framed in a reasonably clear way; delegation would materially mitigate a problem of credible commitment; and the policymaker would not have to make first-order distributional *choices*. Whether those conditions are satisfied in any particular field is properly a matter for public debate and for determination by elected legislators.

Second, the way the delegation is framed should meet five design precepts: (1) the agency's purposes, objectives, and powers should be set clearly by legislators; (2) its decision-making procedures should be set largely by legislators; (3) the agency itself, in this case the central bank, should publish the operating principles that will guide its exercise of discretion within the delegated domain; (4) there should be transparency sufficient to permit accountability for the central bank's stewardship of the regime and, separately, for politicians' framing of the regime; and, (5), crucially for the problem I posed, it should be clear *ex ante* what (if anything) happens, procedurally and/or substantively, when the edges of the regime are reached but the central bank could do more to avert or contain a crisis.

Third, multiple missions should be delegated to a single agency only if: they are inextricably linked, and in particular rely on seamless flows of information; and decisions are taken by separate policy committees, with overlapping membership but each with a majority of dedicated members.

With the exception of the emergency-powers precept, I shall not defend those principles for delegation here.[3] They might seem innocuous. But, in fact, they pack a punch. For example, few—too few—independent agencies have clear objectives, so that high policy (decisions on values) is effectively delegated. My immediate purpose, however, is to draw out some of the implications for multiple-mission central banks.

For monetary regimes, some of the package is, of course, familiar. Most obviously, the principles for delegation support instrument-independence rather than goal-independence (a test not met

3. A preliminary explanation was given in Tucker, "Independent Agencies in Democracies: Legitimacy and Boundaries for the New Central Banks," the 2014 Gordon Lecture, Harvard Kennedy School, May 1, 2014. A fuller explication is forthcoming. Various of the principles draw on the work of Alberto Alesina and Guido Tabellini on whether to delegate to technocrats, of Paul Milgrom and Bengt Holmstrom on the incentive problems of multiple-mission agents, and of Philip Pettit on forging the people's purposes and on contestability. Among other things, the multiple-policy committee structure is incorporated in the Bank of England's post-crisis architecture.

everywhere), and also the importance of not making monetary policy decisions in order to pursue some distributional goal (as opposed to policy having distributional effects broadly foreseen by legislators). The apparent incommensurability between majoritarian control and commitment technologies turns out to be no more than a specter. Democracy comes first, and can choose commitment technologies for improving aggregate welfare if it wishes. Democratic legitimacy requires that the people's representatives determine whether the country should be tied to the mast of stability, what that mast looks like (the standards in the money-credit constitution), and that distributional *choices* are not handed over since the winners and, more important, the losers would not have representatives at the central bankers' policy table. The outlines of some constraints on central banks are starting to emerge.

Going further, three of the requirements for legitimate delegation help to open up, and perhaps dissolve, the distinctions and potential tensions between the monetary policy regime and the LOLR function that seemed, at first sight, so problematic.

They are the first, third, and fifth design precepts requiring, respectively, the central bank's powers and objectives to be set by legislators; the central bank to state the operating principles that guide its exercise of discretion; and the need for *ex ante* clarity around what happens when a central bank reaches the boundaries of a domain it has been delegated.

The need for regimes

At root, the principles for delegation require delegated responsibilities and powers to be framed as *regimes*. While that is familiar in the field of monetary policy, it is not so obvious that LOLR (or other central bank) functions have been laid down so carefully and clearly over the past century or more.

Operating principles for monetary
policy: the Taylor rule debate

Even within monetary policy (narrowly understood), there remain outstanding design questions. One of them preoccupies this country's legislature right now: whether to mandate *in legislation* a benchmark rule for the central bank's routine policy instrument, the short-term interest rate.

Rather than offering a firm view on whether or not the Taylor rule should be adopted by the Fed, I shall limit myself to observing that the debate can be thought of as being about how to implement the design precept that an independent agency should enunciate operating principles. For myself, that that be done by the agency is more important than that any particular set of principles or any particular instrument-rule be entrenched in a law that is justiciable via the courts.

In other words, the principles for delegation require that more be said than has, perhaps, been said about the constraints in "constrained discretion." Whether that should be pursued by moving to a lexicographic objective or by ex post facto publication of research on the "rule" best approximating past policy or by also publishing explanations of deviations from past patterns raises a rich set of issues that is being debated afresh. I will not go into it here, other than to say that, in order to avoid undue concentrations of power, we should prefer solutions that strengthen the role of individual committee members to those that would embed a single view. In that sense, there might be a trade-off between the clarity with which the reaction function is articulated and the degree to which power is dispersed.

Defining the LOLR regime

If debates about monetary regimes continue, rather more is needed in many jurisdictions to articulate and explain a regime for the LOLR liquidity reinsurance function.[4] Prerequisites for any such regime are that its terms should mitigate the inherent problems of adverse selection and moral hazard; be time-consistent; and provide clarity about the amount and nature of "fiscal risk" that the central bank is permitted to take on the state's behalf.

Compared with things prior to the 2007 phase of the crisis, some questions seem to be settled; for example, nearly all central banks now accept and have announced publicly, without legislative override, that they stand ready to lend against a wide range of collateral, including portfolios of illiquid loans to households and firms. I think it is also now conventional wisdom, as it should be, that excess collateral should be taken to leave the central bank's expected loss no greater than if it had bought Treasury bills, as under the minimal conception.

Other questions remain outstanding in many jurisdictions: for example, whether there are any circumstances in which the central bank should be permitted and, if so authorized, would be prepared to lend to non-banks or to act as a market-maker of last resort. Any reflection on those issues reveals the difficulty of making credible claims that the authorities will *never* undertake such operations. If that is correct, it would be as well to concentrate on designing a regime for them to do so under appropriate constraints.

Of those, surely the most important is that the central bank, a body of unelected officials, should not knowingly lend to a firm that is irretrievably and fundamentally insolvent. If "no monetary financing" is the golden rule for a credible nominal anchor, so "no

---

4. What follows is expanded upon in Paul Tucker, "The Lender of Last Resort and Modern Central Banking: Principles and Reconstruction," *Re-thinking the Lender of Last Resort*, BIS Paper No. 79, Bank for International Settlements, September 2014.

lending to irretrievably insolvent borrowers" should be the golden rule for the *liquidity* reinsurer. That "liquidity support" has become, for many people, synonymous with "solvency bailout" is a tragedy of the first order that saps away the legitimacy of central banks.

How a central bank lender makes those assessments of solvency, and how it values collateral, should be publicly understood in broad terms *ex ante* and, with appropriate lags, be capable of being assessed *ex post*.

This is not simply about estimating the solvency position of a potential borrower at the moment before any liquidity is provided. If the market is in the grip of a liquidity panic affecting an individual firm(s) or the system as a whole, the provision of liquidity might dispel the panic and restore the firm's solvency position. Faced with a problem of multiple equilibria, LOLR interventions might be able to get the economy and the distressed firm(s) back onto a healthy path. If, however, the firm is fundamentally bust (has a net assets deficiency) whatever the (realistic) economic outlook, then no amount of central bank lending can provide a cure.

None of that is to say that decisions that are decent *ex ante* would always generate good or satisfactory outturns *ex post*. This is essentially about forecasting: forecasting the effect of unusual liquidity provision on the path of the economy and asset prices and its effects on confidence in the firms in question. Making those forecasts is hard. As with any forecasts, there would be errors, although they should be broadly symmetric over the long run. Since this is, unavoidably, what is going on, it would be better to be clear about it, and for central banks to explain how they make such forecast judgments.

That is part of what would need to be covered in a central bank's LOLR operating principles. Then the nature and potential effects of LOLR liquidity reinsurance would be better understood in general, and particular decisions to lend (or not to lend) could be evaluated *ex post*.

The legislators' role, meanwhile, would be to set or bless the level of confidence on solvency necessary for liquidity support to be permitted; and to provide a statutory resolution regime for handling irretrievably bankrupt banks so as to make "no" from the LOLR credible.[5]

It is not obvious to me that many, or perhaps any, of those issues featured in the debates that led to the reform of the Fed's liquidity reinsurance functions. In particular, while appeals are made to the importance of central banks not lending to fundamentally insolvent firms, what that means is rarely spelt out and might not be widely understood.

Regimes have boundaries

What I hope that brief discussion makes clear is that, like monetary policy, the LOLR liquidity-reinsurance function could, and should, be framed as a regime. And as with any regime, it would need to have reasonably well-defined boundaries.

That being so, we have dissolved part of the dichotomy I set up at the outset between systematic monetary-policy regimes and an inherently flexible LOLR function. Like monetary policy, LOLR liquidity reinsurance is capable of being systematic. Admittedly, compared to monetary policy where policy is reset roughly monthly in most jurisdictions, it is much harder for observers to tell whether the central bank is sticking to a systematic LOLR policy because it gets activated relatively rarely. But that does not negate the point that the regime should have edges—that the central bank's discretion should not be unlimited or absolute.

Which, of course, poses the big question of what happens—or, normatively, what *should* happen—when the edges of any of these

5. See Paul Tucker, "The Resolution of Financial Institutions without Taxpayer Solvency Support: Seven Retrospective Clarifications and Elaborations," European Summer Symposium in Economic Theory, Gerzensee, Switzerland, July 3, 2014.

regimes (monetary, LOLR or, indeed, a field I am not covering here, macroprudential) are reached but there is more that the central bank could, in principle, do to shift the shape and size of the state's consolidated balance sheet in ways that would avert or contain a crisis.

What, in other words, is the proper role of unelected central bankers in the exercise of "emergency powers" and is it realistic that central banks can credibly commit to staying within their "proper role," however it is framed? The issues are real: what role should central banks play in decisions about whether to bail out, for example, Lehman, AIG, etc., without specific congressional sanction? They are, moreover, deep. I have encountered a wide range of views on them in the US.

Beyond the boundaries: emergency powers and "emergency institutions"

Outside the normal purview of economic researchers and policymakers, there is an active and contested debate among political theorists and constitutional scholars about the nature, acceptability, and even inevitability of "emergency powers" exercised by the executive branch of government when a nation is faced with an existential crisis. At one end of the spectrum are followers of the early-twentieth-century German writer Carl Schmitt, who maintained that "exceptions" from normal governance are both inevitable and acceptable. On this view, in a crisis constitutional conventions and democratic norms give way to what the executive feels it must do, revealing the true but usually hidden nature of the polity. If economists wonder what this has to do with us—that surely it's to do with national security, war, and terrorism, but not our field— think again. In the years immediately following the 2007–09 stage of the global financial crisis, Chicago and Harvard constitutional scholars Eric Posner and Adrian Vermeule argued that many of the measures taken by the US Treasury and the Fed fell fair and square within a conception of exceptional executive power.[6]

One elegant response to this line of thinking, articulated by political theorist Nomi Lazar, is that the posited distinction between the "exceptional" and the "normal" is an illusion.[7] First, some crises persist for years, becoming a more or less normal state of affairs. And small crises occur regularly but, nevertheless, sometimes require extraordinary measures: within finance, think of the savings and loan crisis in the United States, the HIH insurance crisis in Australia, or the 1970s secondary banking crisis and the early-1990s small-banks crisis in the United Kingdom.

Further, and profoundly, whether or not one accepts the category of "exceptional" circumstances in which constitutional conventions and rights get more or less junked, democratic accountability does not get thrown out of the window so long as the executive faces the prospect of future elections.

That seems to me to be correct and, more practically, to give us some pointers toward the construction of robust regimes.

First, contingency planning should be embedded in central-banking regimes as far as possible. We should not deny that crises can occur and that they will meet with, among other things, extraordinary liquidity-reinsurance actions, unless tightly binding our hands truly would crush, and I mean crush, the probability of their occurring. Given the ubiquity of regulatory arbitrage in a shape-shifting financial industry, that is hard.

Second, since it is inevitable that any state-contingent contract given to the central bank will eventually prove incomplete, it is

6. Eric A. Posner and Adrian Vermeule, *The Executive Unbound: After the Madisonian Republic* (Oxford, UK: Oxford University Press, 2010).
7. Nomi Claire Lazar, *States of Emergency in Liberal Democracies* (Cambridge, UK: Cambridge University Press, 2009).

necessary to state clearly upfront what happens then. For example, if the basic LOLR regime does not include liquidity reinsurance to shadow banks, should there be provision for that effective ban to be lifted in an emergency? If so, who should decide? The need to answer questions like that is precisely the message of the fifth design precept set out earlier.

But what does it mean? The most important point is that, as a body led by unelected policymakers, the central bank should not *itself* determine where it could reasonably venture beyond previous understandings of its boundaries. That should be sanctioned (or not) by elected representatives of the people, because they will be directly accountable.

Thus, I object less than some to the provision of the Dodd-Frank reforms that requires the Fed to get the permission of the treasury secretary (after consulting the president) to conduct certain liquidity-support operations.[8] In broad equivalence, where the Bank of England wishes to go beyond its published framework for providing liquidity support, it must obtain the permission of the chancellor of the exchequer. (That provides a healthy incentive for the published framework to be as complete as possible, while recognizing that at best it will only ever cater for the kinds of crises that have been experienced, witnessed, or imagined.)

Emergencies in macroeconomic demand management: credit policy

We have seen that the LOLR function can be framed as a regime but that, since its very purpose is to contain crises, it should be

8. The oddity is that the formal consent comes from the treasury secretary, who is no more elected than the Fed's governors. The democratic benediction comes from the mandatory consultation of the president. I assume that this cumbersome construction is adopted because of the convention that the president cannot be made accountable to Congress other than via impeachment.

clear what happens in "emergencies," defined as what lies beyond the regime's normal perimeter. Although, by contrast, monetary-policy regimes are framed mainly for routine use, it is no less true that their boundaries can be reached, too.

Thus, questions confronted by central bankers during recent years included: Can we and should we conduct quantitative easing (QE) against government bonds? Can we and should we buy private-sector instruments to stimulate demand by acting directly on credit premia?

Those questions received different answers in different jurisdictions, in most cases due to constraints in pre-existing laws that had not received much prior "compare and contrast" analysis among central bankers themselves, researchers, or political commentators. In Japan, the answer was: yes, yes. In the UK: yes, broadly no.[9] In the United States: yes, and sort of no. In the euro area: yes (after extensive debate), and we don't yet know.

Why did I say "sort of no" to whether the Fed could or should buy private sector paper? Legally, the answer was and remains unambiguous: it may not. But *economically* the population of instruments eligible for purchase included the government-backed Fannie Mae– and Freddie Mac–guaranteed mortgage-backed securities, so that the Fed was effectively making allocative decisions, directly subsidizing the supply of credit to households but not to firms. It is arguable that the venture would have sat more comfortably within standard tenets of central banking, and been more compliant with our "no big distributional choices" precept, if the Fed had been able to buy either neither or both of household and business loan portfolios. My point is to illustrate the need for more thinking on the construction of these parts of the regime.

9. The UK position was (and, I believe, is) that de jure the Bank of England was not legally constrained from buying private sector bonds, but that de facto it chose not to do so. Some Monetary Policy Committee members, notably Adam Posen, thought that a mistake.

Broad principles that could guide debates on such regimes might include the following:[10]

- Central bank balance-sheet operations should at all times be as parsimonious as possible consistent with achieving their objectives, in order to aid comprehensibility and accountability.
- Central banks should minimize risk of loss consistent with achieving their statutory objectives.
- In particular, if they are permitted to operate in private-sector paper in order to stimulate aggregate demand, they should operate in as wide a class of paper as possible and the selection of individual instruments should be as formulaic as possible, in order to avoid the central bank making detailed choices about the allocation of credit to borrowers in the real economy.

Where, broadly, the line is drawn should be the subject of political choice after public debate. As with emergency LOLR operations, if the line is moved during a crisis, that too should be determined or blessed by elected politicians.

In a US-type system, that power needs to be either openly delegated to the administration or consciously withheld. Where it is withheld, the legislature itself would have to make any in-crisis decisions on whether to authorize innovative operations, along with whether they were to be conducted by the central bank on its balance sheet under its (newly provided) discretion, or by the central bank as agent for the fiscal authority, or by the Treasury under delegated fiscal authority.

That line of argument seems to be grounded in the deepest principles of representative democracy, but it meets with one very serious, practical objection, an objection that applies to both the

10. An earlier, fuller version was set out in Paul Tucker, "The Only Game in Town? A New Constitution for Money (*and* Credit) Policy," Myron Scholes lecture, Chicago Booth School of Business, May 22, 2014.

LOLR and monetary policy examples. One could think of it as the Hamiltonian objection, as it amounts to those in power doing everything they can to protect the people.

The objection

Say the legislature is sclerotic, and simply cannot bring itself either to delegate authority to the executive branch in advance or to make real-time decisions itself in a crisis. And say the public, the American people, are desperately threatened by the crisis, which might even shatter the stability of society. Should not the agencies that can save the people act? Should not the US cavalry ride to the rescue?

Or say that members of the legislature publicly oppose the contemplated action while privately signaling their agreement? Does that license the central bank to act, on the grounds that the legislature has itself vacated the moral high ground vested in it constitutionally?

Or what if the legislature is likely to retaliate, once the dust has settled, by removing some of the central bank's powers, leaving it less equipped to respond to future crises? Should the central bank weigh the net present value of its acting today against the prospective costs of its being less able to act tomorrow? Or should it go ahead irrespective of the prospect of tighter future constraints, on the basis that if future crises are sufficiently grave, it should simply step around them (just as, in our thought experiment, it has stepped around "today's" constraints)?

These difficult questions, which are not utterly fanciful given political currents in the United States, turn on more than "narrow" welfare judgments. They involve weighing the intrinsic merits of democracy, and the risks of eroding support for democracy by violating its deepest principles.

My answer, as set out above, remains unchanged: that the unelected leaders of independent agencies cannot rightly take that burden onto themselves. If the legislature cannot or will not respond in the face of dire emergency or if it is Janus-faced or if reprisals are in the air, the moral and political burden of choosing must fall on the elected executive. If the question of emergency powers challenges some constitutional conventions but, against Schmitt and with Lazar, it does not undermine our most basic conceptions of democracy, the big choices should be in the hands of the elected executive, not unelected technocrats (just as, in a different sphere, the big decisions do not lie with the military).

So let me twist the knife.

What if it would be counterproductive for the president *openly* to approve an emergency course of action by the central bank? In contrast to the military sphere, it is not so easy to claim that the president has constitutionally ordained duties and powers in the economic sphere of the kind he has as the commander in chief. In that case, have our "welfarist" objectors got a point? Indeed, is their argument overwhelming if not acting might lead to a crisis that would prospectively lead to civil conflict threatening democracy itself? Should the central bank just do what it thinks to be right, regardless, possibly supported *privately* by the president?

I cannot see any clear *deontological* duties here. But nor can I see how a *welfare* assessment will suffice. One almost wants to fall back on old-fashioned Aristotelian ideas of *virtue*: i.e., if they find themselves there, we hope to have virtuous central bank leaders who will weigh the short term against the long term, welfare against majoritarian decision-taking, and so on. One or two truly great men among central bankers from the past fifty years might spring to mind. That feels precious, but also, it must be said, precarious. We seem to be stuck.

But we don't need to resolve our deepest moral dilemmas in order to shape principles for the design of regimes. And, fortunately, a practical prescription does emerge. We must strive to shrink as far as we possibly can the troublesome space in which there is neither a within-regime contingency plan nor an *ex ante* process with majoritarian credentials for determining in-crisis arrangements. Better to recognize that imperative up front when designing the central banking regime, in line with my fifth design precept for delegating to independent agencies.

Cooperation and coordination with the executive branch need not negate independence

To recap, then, the big questions for central banking regimes are (a) what powers should the central bank have during "peacetime" to alter the shape of the consolidated state balance sheet; (b) what extra powers, if any, should it be granted *ex ante* to help handle crises, and what should be the trigger for activating them; and (c) should the elected executive branch be empowered, by the legislature or under the constitution, to increase those central bank powers during crises.

More effort has typically gone into (a) than (b) and, in most jurisdictions, almost none has gone into (c).

We find an example of how (b) and, especially, (c) cause confusion in a quirk in the different approaches to the political economy of QE in the US and UK. In the US, there was no coordination between the Fed and the Treasury, on the grounds that that could compromise the Fed's independence.

In the UK, we took exactly the opposite view. Since we were changing the state's consolidated balance sheet in ways that carried risk for taxpayers but could also be offset by the Treasury, the Bank of England sought and received from government an up-front indemnity against the financial risk entailed and a public undertaking that it would not change its debt-management strategy. In the US, government debt maturities were lengthened, cutting across the Fed's stimulus. In the UK, that did not happen. But independence was not compromised as *we* decided, in the Bank's Monetary Policy Committee, how much QE to do and when.

One moral of the story is that independence does not preclude coordination, on the right terms. Another is that obtaining a sanction to innovate need not threaten independence. The challenge is for the central bank to remain the initiator of ideas for the use of its balance sheet.

Joined-up regimes under the money-credit constitution

Summing up so far, three points have run through this analysis. First, for democratic legitimacy delegated powers need to be constructed as regimes based on clear general principles. That applies no less to central banks than to other independent agencies, and applies no less to LOLR and to stability functions more generally than it does to monetary policy.

Second, the components of an economy's money-credit constitution (MCC) should cohere. That is to say, the regimes for the nominal anchor, for the regulation and supervision of fractional-reserve banking, for the state's provision of liquidity reinsurance, and for the constraints on how central banks pursue their functions must be joined up. At a conceptual level, they should be guided by some simple benchmarks, even if the reality cannot be as simple as would be feasible in a world that placed a lower value on freedom.

Third, emergencies should not be fenced off for on-the-spot in-crisis improvisation, but should be catered for, substantively and procedurally, within the overall MCC.

In terms of analogies with the state's most basic functions, the central bank emerges looking like a hybrid of the high judiciary and the military. Like the judiciary, the central bank's insulation must be secure when it comes to deciding the stance of monetary policy. But subject to that constraint, there are circumstances where, like the military, its crisis-management repertoire can be, and sometimes should be, determined by elected political leaders. How much such coordination is needed turns on the extent to which contingency plans have been coded-in up front. Not easy, but within reach.

There is, however, one important complicating factor that I have kept bracketed away. In terms of the results for society, the effects of any money-credit constitution depend on how fiscal policymakers conduct themselves. In saying that, I mean more than the elemental point that unsustainable public finances cannot coexist with monetary stability. There can be a particular problem of strategic interaction even where the public finances are sound—in fact, perhaps particularly then.

The only game in town: strategic interaction with the fiscal authority

Over the past eight years, it has become a common refrain that central banks have been the *only game in town*. Quite apart from the discomfort this causes the central bankers themselves as they fret about unwarranted expectations and possibly also about their legitimacy, there are other voices raising the possibility that over-reliance on central banks has led to inferior economic results or has entailed risks of impaired performance down the road.

Those sentiments can be detected in a wide variety of arguments. Of course, some suggest openly that it would have been better to support recovery through public-infrastructure investment, or with tax incentives for private investment, or through debt forgiveness.[11] Others focus more on the costs and risks of monetary stimulus. They suggest that the scale and nature of monetary easing have created risks to stability through fueling a search

11. Those arguments have been advanced by, for example, Larry Summers, Martin Feldstein, and Ken Rogoff.

for yield in domestic financial markets, or through spillovers into foreign, especially emerging-market, economies that could in time "spill back," or by withdrawing "safe assets" during a period when demand for such assets is unusually strong.[12] Although the point is rarely drawn out, the implication is that those risks would have been smaller if, in countries with fiscal capacity, less of the stimulus had come from monetary policy and more of it via debt-financed fiscal policy, since that would have resulted in an upward-sloping yield curve, a higher exchange rate, and more truly safe assets being in private-sector hands.

To be clear, I am not inviting agreement with any or all of those arguments. My purpose is to illustrate a deeper point about strategic interaction between different arms of macroeconomic policy. In the short run, at least, in countries with undoubted fiscal capacity, reliance on monetary policy looks to have been an attractive option for fiscal authorities as it lets them side-step the awkward party and national politics entailed by *overt* fiscal actions requiring a legislative vote.

The Bank for International Settlements has made the broadly similar point that aggressive monetary easing might have let legislators off the hook of making needed structural economic reforms directed at improving the efficiency of the real economy and raising permanent incomes. That is a concern that not a few commentators would feel is apt in the euro area and in Japan.

But what are central bankers meant to do: set their mandates to one side, sit on their hands, and undertake to resume business only if the politicians fulfill their side of a bargain designed by the monetary technocrats themselves? That would be for our unelected central bankers to elevate themselves to the position of Plato's guardians—precisely the fear that raises the legitimacy question.

---

12. Those arguments, although advanced by others too, are often associated with, respectively, Jeremy Stein, Raghuram Rajan, and Ricardo Caballero.

So here we have it: given their mandates, central banks have little or no choice—under democratic principles and under the rule of law—to do what they can to restore economic recovery consistent with keeping medium-term inflation expectations anchored. Elected policymakers know that and, further, are under no obligations to act themselves. In other words, the priority of democratic legitimacy for independent central banks can produce a strategic interaction with elected fiscal authorities that leads to what might sometimes (not always) be a flawed monetary/fiscal/reform mix.

In terms of the design of an economy's money-credit constitution, the big point is that in deciding what central banks should be able to do, it matters what incentives fiscal authorities have to use the instruments that they control, and how strategic interactions between different policymakers are framed. In other words, questions about the boundaries to central banking have to be taken together with what lies on the other side.

That should hardly be surprising given our description of the essence of what central banks do. They change the size and shape of the state's consolidated balance sheet in the pursuit of monetary-system stability. It obviously matters, therefore, how the fiscal authority is empowered and chooses to affect the state's balance sheet. The boundary between monetary policy and fiscal policy unavoidably becomes blurred once we move beyond the minimal conception, a setup in which the fiscal authority would take on many tasks typically associated with central banking.

The central bank operates therefore, at least implicitly, within a fiscal carve-out. Better that that be made explicit, with a *fiscal carve-out* being among the terms of the regimes delegated to a central bank under the economy's money-credit constitution. In other words, the MCC is not only about central banking and fractional-reserve banking, but also lies in the shadow of an economy's fiscal regime. Where to draw the lines depends partly on what the people want their elected representatives in the fiscal authority to decide and control.

What is missing, therefore, is a clearer, well-thought-through fiscal constitution. A cost of central bank independence seems to have been under-investment in thinking about and building fiscal institutions over the past quarter century—just as, more obviously, banking regulation and supervision were neglected.

We need, for example, to be clearer about how the state can commit to debt levels that reflect its role as catastrophe-insurer of last resort; how the public finances should factor in imbalances in productive capacity and the tax base; the role and power of automatic stabilizers; how schemes to subsidize the supply of credit to particular sectors or borrowers fit with the central bank–led money-credit constitution; how a government can commit not to provide solvency bailouts; and more.

Central bankers are hardly alone in having an interest in stimulating debate on those issues. For those who favor the minimal conception of central banking, the work is vital and, surely, urgent. But it is no less important for those who believe in a somewhat more expansive conception of central banking.

Meanwhile, none of that provides a reason for putting off updating and refining central bank regimes in a joined-up way. That must be done if we are to be served by monetary institutions that can combine credible commitment with effective crisis management on terms and in a manner consistent with democratic legitimacy.

Conclusion

I have been describing principles that can help resolve the apparent tension between systematic policy in normal times and flexibility in crises. My initial statement of the apparent dilemma proved badly flawed. LOLR liquidity reinsurance policy *can* be systematic, and *should* be framed within a regime. Further, just like the LOLR, monetary policy can reach the edges of its regime in circumstances where it could continue to be useful.

I have wanted to expose the risks of segmenting debates about monetary policy, the LOLR, and other responsibilities such as, increasingly, macroprudential policy; and I have wanted to underline that the question of what happens at a regime's boundaries—*any* regime's boundaries—simply cannot be ducked.

In their core function of money creation, so long as their instrument-independence is not suspended or repealed by the legislature, a central bank's control over its policy must be absolute, constrained only by the goal set for it. But in a crisis, it must cooperate and coordinate with the executive branch, which might (not must) be empowered to authorize emergency extensions of the central bank's powers to achieve stability, *provided* that first-order distributional choices are not delegated. On that basis, coherent central bank regimes can be constructed. These powerful, independent, unelected institutions end up looking like a hybrid of the high judiciary and the military.

Credible commitment or emergency institutions? Both. The solution lies, perhaps unsurprisingly, in the design of regimes: for monetary policy, for LOLR policy, for balance-sheet policy more generally, and also for macroprudential policy. In short, for anything delegated to central banks we need: clear objectives or standards to be set for monetary-system stability; an explicit fiscal carve-out; the central banks themselves to articulate the operating principles that will guide their exercise of discretion; and our elected legislators to determine whether regime boundaries are fixed or whether in a crisis they could be publicly flexed by politicians to give their central bank more degrees of freedom to restore stability. Together with constraints on private banking, those individual regimes must be joined-up, providing a coherent overall money-credit constitution for our economies, in peacetime and crises.

That is in some ways an optimistic note on which to end. Admittedly, it leaves a lot of choices to be made, a lot of work to be done, a lot of public debate for our elected representatives to foster and resolve. But not more than that . . . other, that is, than to stimulate renewed debate on the design of fiscal constitutions, so that next time our central banks are not the only game in town.

COMMENTS BY JOHN COCHRANE

Let me start by summarizing, and cheering, Paul's important points. The standard view says that perhaps monetary policy should follow a rule, but financial-crisis firefighting needs discretion: a big mop to clean up big messes; flexibility to "do what it takes"; "emergency" powers to fight emergencies.

I think Paul is telling us, politely, that this is rubbish. Crisis-response and lender-of-last-resort actions need rules, or "regimes," even more than monetary policy actions need rules.

Any decision is a mapping from states of the world to decisions. Rules constrain this mapping. Rules pre-commit one *ex ante* against actions that one will choose *ex post*, and regret. Monetary policy rules guard against "just this once" inflations. Lender-of-last-resort rules guard against "just this once" bailouts and loans.

But you need rules even more when the system responds to its expectations of your actions. And preventing crises is all about controlling this moral hazard.

To stop runs, our governments guarantee deposits and other loans; they bail out institutions and their creditors; they buy up assets to raise prices; and they lend like crazy. But knowing this, financial institutions take more risk than they would otherwise take and investors lend without monitoring, making crises worse. Institutions that can borrow at last resort don't set up backup lines of credit, don't watch the quality of their collateral, and don't buy expensive put options and other insurance, making crises worse. Investors who know that the Fed will stop "fire sales" don't keep some cash around for "buying opportunities," making fire sales worse. "Big banks are too complex to go through bankruptcy," the mantra repeats. But why do people lend to them, without the protections of bankruptcy? Because they know creditors, if not management and equity, will be protected.

"The world is ending. A crisis is no time to worry about moral hazard," bankers and government officials told us last time, and will tell us again. But the world does not end, and actions taken in this crisis are exactly the cause of moral hazard for the next one.

This isn't theory. When the Fed and Treasury bailed out Bear Stearns, and especially its creditors, markets learned, "Oh, Fed and Treasury won't let an investment bank broker-dealer go under." Lehman turned down capital offers, and the reserve fund put 40 percent of its assets in Lehman paper.

The severe crisis and recession coincident with Lehman's failure, together with the massive and improvised response—many flavors of TARP (Troubled Asset Relief Program), auto company bailouts, and so on—have arguably created the "rule" in participants' minds about what will happen next time.

Plans, self-imposed rules, promises, guidance, and tradition are not enough. Given the power, every one of us will bail out. We won't risk being the captain of the *Titanic*, and we'll let the next guy or gal deal with moral hazard. A central banker facing a crisis is like a father holding an ice cream cone, facing a hungry three-year-old. Sure, Mom's rule says dinner always before dessert. We know what's happening to that ice cream cone.

The central bank and Treasury must not be able to bail out what they should not bail out, to lend where they should not lend, to protect creditors who should lose money. That's the only way to stop it. More importantly, it's the only way to persuade the moral-hazarders that all the fine words in the boom will not melt quickly in the emergency.

Two central quotes summarize the Tucker view, and I entirely agree.

> Prerequisites for any such regime are that its terms should mitigate the inherent problems of adverse selection and moral hazard; be time-consistent; and provide clarity about the amount and nature

of "fiscal risk" that the central bank is permitted to take on the state's behalf.

At a schematic level, a money-credit constitution for today might have five components: inflation targeting plus a reserves requirement that increased with a bank's leverage plus a liquidity-reinsurance regime plus a resolution regime for bankrupt banks plus constraints on how the central bank is free to pursue its mandate.

Now, let me offer a gentle critique.

How are we doing toward the Tucker regime? Not well.

The Dodd-Frank and Basel "regime" has no serious limits at all. Ask yourself, what institutions are not "systemic" and cannot become so designated? What institutions or creditors won't be bailed out—can't be bailed out? What are the securities the Fed or Treasury won't and can't buy or lend against? What are the asset prices that they won't and can't prop up?

Paul points out the difficulties. Yes, "constraints" are good. But just what constraints? We can channel Bagehot, "against good collateral," to "illiquid but not insolvent" institutions. Except, as Paul reminds us, what's good collateral, when no one will take anything but treasuries? How do you tell illiquid from insolvent when prices have tanked and markets are frozen? It's not so easy.

More deeply, the Bagehot rules are flawed. If it were clear who is illiquid and who is insolvent, there wouldn't be a crisis. Private lenders would happily support the clearly solvent. And runs happen at institutions that investors fear are insolvent. If you want to stop runs you have to prop up at least the creditors of potentially insolvent institutions. Bagehot's rules may constrain the central bank; they may be good rules for a prudent investor; they may address moral hazard. But they are not obviously optimal rules to stop crises or to prevent them from occurring in the first place.

Worse, when we figure all this out, how do we write binding laws or regulations that will effectively constrain bailout-hungry officials? For example, Paul Volcker proposed a fine, clear rule: "Thou shalt not finance proprietary trading with deposits." Which, six hundred pages and counting later, is utter mush.

So here we are, six years after our crisis—or eighty-two years after 1932, or one-hundred-thirteen years after 1907, or, heck, three hundred years after 1720—and as eminent a thinker and practitioner as Paul still needs to invite future thought on what these rules ought to be, let alone just what legal restrictions will actually enforce them and communicate that expectation.

I fear that the next crisis will be upon us long before Paul has figured it out, and a century before he gets the Basel committee, the Fed, European Central Bank, Financial Stability Oversight Council, Congress, Parliament, Securities and Exchange Commission, and so on to go along.

So, I agree with pretty much all Paul has to say. But I infer the opposite message. If this is what it takes to rescue the house of cards, then we need a different house, one not made of cards. We need to stop crises from happening in the first place.

To its credit, that is the other half of our contemporary policy response. This time, finally, the army of regulators and stress-testers will see the crisis coming; with their Talmudic rules and interpretations, and their great discretion, they will stop any "systemically important" financial institution from losing money, despite the moral hazard sirens, and without turning that financial system into something resembling the Italian state telephone company circa 1965. Good luck with that.

Consider an alternative: Suppose banks had to fund risky lending by issuing equity and long-term debt. Suppose mortgage-backed securities were funded by long-only, floating net-asset-value mutual funds, not overnight repurchase agreements. Suppose all fixed-value demandable assets had to be backed 100 percent by our abundant supply of short-term treasuries. Then we really would not have runs in the first place . . . and a lot of unemployed regulators.

Why do we not have such a world? Originally, because you can't do it with the financial, computational, and communications technology of the 1930s or 1960s. But now we can. More recently, I think, because moral hazard so subsidizes the current fragile system. But now we can change that.

Paul mentioned this possibility, but gave up quickly, conditioning his remarks on a view that society has decided it wants fractional-reserve banking. Well, maybe society needs to rethink that decision.

Really, just why is it so vital to save a financial system soaked in run-prone overnight debt? Even if borrowers might have to pay 50 basis points more (which I doubt), is that worth a continual series of crises, 10 percent or more down-steps in GDP, 10 million losing their jobs in the United States alone, a 40 percent rise in debt to GDP, and the strangling cost of our financial regulations?

A last point: Paul unites financial with monetary and fiscal policy. That's crucial. The last crisis raised US national debt from 60 percent to over 100 percent of GDP. The next one will require more. At some point we can't borrow that much.

But take this thought one step further. The next crisis could well be a sovereign debt crisis, not a repetition of a real estate-induced run. Crises are by definition somewhat unexpected, and come from unexpected sources.

To be concrete, suppose Chinese financial markets blow up— surprise, surprise—discovering a lot of insolvent debt. The stress is too much for the International Monetary Fund and Europe, so Greece goes, followed by Italy, Spain, and Portugal, half of Latin America, and a few American states. Pair that with war in the Middle East—ISIS explodes a dirty bomb, say—requiring several trillion dollars.

Now governments are the ones in trouble. They won't be able to borrow trillions more, bail out banks, or lend of last resort. In a global sovereign debt crisis, even Paul's regime would turn out to be a superb Maginot line. The current regime wouldn't be that strong.

A financial system deeply dependent on the government put would be finished. This is the lesson of Europe. A southern government default would have little consequences if its banks were not so embroiled in government finances.

But a financial system uncoupled from government finances would survive.

In sum, I cheer pretty much everything Paul said. But it's an outline for a plan that will take decades to fill in. And all in the service of keeping the house of overnight debt cards going.

So the lesson I take is that instead, we should finally take seriously the other, centuries-old, simple alternative: equity-funded banking, government-provided interest-paying money, mirroring that great nineteenth-century innovation—government-provided banknotes—and a purge of run-prone assets.

GENERAL DISCUSSION

MICHAEL BORDO: OK, I had a couple of thoughts while you were talking, Paul. One was about Milton Friedman and Henry Simons's plan for 100 percent reserve banking, which I guess John was getting to. That's what Friedman thought would solve the problem. From his perspective, or Simons's perspective in the 1930s, had the United States had 100 percent reserve banking, the banking panics that caused the Great Depression could have been avoided. And the second one, if Allan Meltzer were here, I'm sure he would have asked, would be about Bagehot's rule. "Isn't that enough? If we have an effective lender of last resort, why do we have to come up with something else?"

PAUL TUCKER: I will start with your question about Bagehot and then come to the Chicago plan on narrow banking.

The Bagehot rule is sometimes misunderstood or, alternatively, needs enriching. I think the former, but that's about history, not the substance. What Bagehot is often thought to have said, and some central banks seem to say, is that provided a central bank lends against good collateral, the operation is OK. In other words, provided the central bank is confident of getting its money back, it's OK. But that is absolutely wrong. Indeed, it can involve what in my country is called fraudulent preference. Imagine an institution that is net-balance-sheet insolvent, indeed irretrievably so. In other words, it does not have enough assets to repay all creditors in full, but imagine it also has some Treasury bonds. This bank suffers a liquidity problem, and the central bank lends to it against the Treasury bonds. Well, the central bank gets its money back because its exposure is covered by Treasury bonds. But the operation fails to revive the institution—inevitably so—because it is truly net-balance-sheet insolvent; liquidity assistance cannot remedy that. So the firm goes into liquidation, and some people lose money. And here is the rub. Those short-term creditors who ran get away whole, because of the liquidity assistance. But the term unsecured creditors get less money back than they would have done if the firm had gone into liquidation right at the beginning. That is because the central bank took the best assets, the Treasury bonds; the term creditors lose their share of the claim on those assets. Something wrong has happened here. Preconditions for central bank lending are not only the availability of good collateral, but also that the firm is not irretrievably insolvent (taking account of any expected effect of the lending operation on the path of the economy, asset prices, etc.).[13]

Now, so far as I know, Bagehot deals with this only briefly, but he does deal with it. He uses the word "sound" when he describes whom a central bank might lend to. As you will definitely know, Michael, Bagehot was writing in the wake of the Overend and Gurney Crisis in 1866. And the key thing about Overend and Gurney, a massive bill market dealer, was that the Bank of England let it go bust and then provided liquidity assistance to the rest of the system in order to contain the panic and restore stability. As I recall, the bank put in one of its deputy governors or a former governor, and two people from other banks, to have a look at the firm. And they came back and said, "This institution is unsound."

Meaning: it was bust. And so this comes back to the need to ensure that for central bank LOLR lending, there is a test: Is this firm fundamentally, irretrievably insolvent or not?

Your second point was about the Simons, at one point Friedman, recently Larry Kotlikoff, and now Cochrane plan for narrow banking. The first thing I'd say is that John's version is coherent and serious because it goes beyond saying, "Let's con-

---

13. Tucker, "The Lender of Last Resort."

fine the assets of de jure banks to treasuries or central bank reserves." That formulation, which is the usual one, isn't coherent or, in my view, serious, because it does not address what happens when somebody reinvents the economic substance of banking somewhere else, in a different legal form. Thus, the aim of the policy as typically framed inevitably gets subverted. John's version makes it clear that it has to be a policy with universal application, which gets close to saying that all short-term debt should be outlawed. In the same spirit, Larry Kotlikoff advocates all financial intermediation being via mutual funds of various kinds.

The risk with that policy is that you do it, and society says, "Oh, the supply of credit is being constrained, and that's a really bad thing." In other words, a debate that starts off being about the riskiness of monetary institutions morphs into a debate about the supply of credit. And here is a strange but striking thing: some of the strongest political advocates of the Chicago plan in the 1930s were focused on credit, not money. As Senator Bronson Cutting put it during the debates on the floor of the Senate about this, "Private financiers are not entitled to any profit on credit."[14] In other words, some political proponents didn't say, "Oh, it's tremendously important to have the creation of money taken out of private hands." Rather, they said, "We have no business allowing credit to be allocated by profit-making institutions. That needs to be in the hands of the state." I think, therefore, the political-economy robustness test that Friedman, Simons, Fisher, Cochrane, Kotlikoff need to pass is whether that would be the outcome of their plan; that faced with problems in the supply of credit, the state would be expected to—and would—step in; a world of Fannie and Freddie for everything. I come from a country which, among its other problems, does

14. Ronnie J. Phillips, "The Chicago Plan & New Deal Banking Reform," Jerome Levy Economics Institute, Working Paper No. 76, 1992.

not have Fannie and Freddie. That would be my challenge to Milton Friedman, Henry Simons, and my friend John, who I doubt believes in the socialization of credit supply.

MICHAEL BORDO: My comment or question is related to what Paul just said. Based on Steve Haber and Charles Calomiris's *Fragile by Design*, it seems that a lot of the things that are wrong with the financial system is that people use the political system to make some gains and to do some things through the financial system that would be harder to directly do. And so you give us hope, and we see that there's variation across countries where some financial systems are more robust than others. But underlying this is that a lot of what went wrong in this crisis was facilitated by the political system.

ROBERT HODRICK: Paul mentioned that there are multiple equilibria in these situations where there is potentially insolvency versus illiquidity. It seems that there is a real need to effectively mark the assets of the bank to market, and I conjecture that is incredibly difficult to do in the financial crisis. So, if we're going to go down that route, we need some way to value the assets. If they're not trading, we have to figure out what they would be worth if they traded, and it seems like a pretty difficult thing to do.

TUCKER: You're absolutely right. But the key thing is that, at least implicitly, those judgments are already made by central bankers in their monetary policy role. I don't know whether Kevin would want to speak to what I am going to describe as it relates to the Fed, but let me describe things at the Bank of England after autumn 2008. Putting lender of last resort on one side, we are sitting in a monetary policy committee that decides its own forecasts for the economy, and from early on in the crisis that meant asking: What's going to happen to credit conditions? So we have staff presenting to us on the capital adequacy of the banking system, and whether the various policy interventions, including liquidity provision, would affect the path of the economy, asset prices, the soundness/weakness of the banks and thus their supply of credit. So what I'm saying amounts in practice to, "Hold on. In one room, the monetary policy room, we're doing all that in a fairly systematic way, recognizing massive error bands but having to form a view on the path of bank soundness in order to forecast the economy. So why in another room cannot we more explicitly assess the effect of policy measures on bank soundness when doing lender-of-last-resort policy?" When you lend to these firms, you simply cannot avoid having to decide whether you think it's going to be sound, what you think the collateral is going to be worth, conditional upon the proposed operation. How long do we think we're going to hold it for? Thus, I am arguing that the central banks ought to be much more transparent about how they go about that evaluation. Further, incentives would be changed if they were more transparent about how they go about that kind of evaluation; they would be incentivized to make those assessments more systematically than perhaps they are around the world at the moment. I do not see why a strong, intensive process exists for inputs to monetary policymaking but not for inputs into LOLR decisions. There is massive uncertainty in both, so that cannot be a justification for not having a more systematic approach based on forecasts.

JOHN COCHRANE: I disagree with what you [Hodrick] said about the wonders of mark-to-market. Forcing companies to fail the minute they don't pass the mark-to-market test assumes asset prices are random walks, which they're not. Price declines do revert, so a company that is underwater on a mark-to-market basis may well be able to pay its debts in the future. Marking to market is fine to produce information, but you shouldn't fail companies the minute they don't pass the test. When prices aren't random walks, that rule doesn't work.

That's the other problem with Bagehot's rule. Why only lend against safe collateral? Why is that the optimum that will stop a run? Our government lent against bad collateral because it wanted to stop a run of the depositors. Bagehot's rule is a good one for running a hedge fund, but central banks aren't supposed to only do that.

TUCKER: May I just add to that very quickly, please? My way, another way to make what I think is the same point, is to imagine that the fall in asset values is entirely (100 percent) to do with a liquidity crunch in the asset markets, so there's going to be a massive spike in liquidity premia. Should that be a sufficient condition to put the whole of the banking system into liquidation? Well, if the authorities do nothing, it might end up coming to that because the fall in asset prices will push the economy onto a lower path. But that would be perverse on the assumption that it is a pure liquidity shock. But of course if the shock were not one of liquidity but to a shift in fundamentals or a realization that fundamentals had been misperceived, then the policy options and conclusions are quite different. My point is simply that the authorities unavoidably have to make judgments about whether there is a shift in fundamentals or purely in liquidity premia. If they were more transparent about how those judgments affect policy and about how they make those judgments, e.g., whether they are assuming a random walk or not, then the oversight by Parliament or Congress would be a lot cleaner than it is at the moment.

PETER FISHER: Paul, terrific effort, and I've got all the sympathies in the world for both your and John Cochrane's comments. But I'm haunted that it's not just politics that prevents us from getting rid of fractional-reserve banking. It's that money is the exchangeable claim we accept. And it's not just political leaders who might want to have a money-credit nexus. We all might. The politics is us. Once we start accepting a form of money that's backed by someone's exchangeable claims, we're off to the races. And so liquidity illusion is not just in the banking system. It's a fundamental feature of the velocity of finance we've come to accept. I have all the sympathy for your objective, but I don't think we get there, given we all can start accepting exchangeable claims backed by credit. Structured investment vehicles and conduits are just a microcosm of that. I think the challenge isn't just that the politicians get it wrong. I think we can get it wrong collectively.

COCHRANE: We accept claims to short-term treasuries happily. The question is, why do investments backed by other assets have to be fixed-value, immediately demandable claims? There is a good parallel in the nineteenth century. Banks issued notes backed by real estate investments. And there were runs because occasionally the investments were worth less than the notes. But the banks said, "Heavens, you can't get rid of bank notes! We won't be able to provide credit anymore if we can't issue notes." Well, we finally got tired of that and said, "You know what? No more bank notes. The Treasury is going to issue all of the currency." And, the world didn't end. Banks were still able to borrow and lend.

FISHER: Did that solve the liquidity illusion problem? We moved it on to a series of others, and that's my challenge. How do you stop moving it on? I grant you, you can specify state bank notes from the state of Alabama from 1872.

COCHRANE: Money and credit don't have to be linked anymore, because we have instant communications technology. You could pay for coffee by bumping an iPhone and selling stocks.

FISHER: I think you have to write a rule that prohibits that; that's persuasive to me. And I'm sympathetic to the endeavor.

COCHRANE: Well, we're here to talk about Paul's paper, not mine.

KEVIN WARSH: Let me just lob into the discussion, with a thought which is a little more responsive to Paul's point. I think Paul rightly describes the committee dynamics of the Bank of England, where there are duly constituted committees of mixed membership, which have these differing responsibilities. Paul's right, of course; in the US, the power is really all vested in the same committee. It's really the same people at the Fed making the decisions. It's not nineteen people convening around a table. It's the same decision-makers (though not written in the statute) that are having an overwhelming influence at critical moments in time. So at least at the Bank of England, responsibilities are duly designated to subject-matter specific committees, each with its own operating principles. Here, especially in crises, because of the culture of the Federal Reserve, the role of the chairman, we seem to have a much more personality-driven and individual-driven set of decisions based on more of an ad hoc nature of a discussion.

On the question that Paul asked about how the decision is made: in the Federal Reserve's statute, the Board of Governors approves its lender-of-last-resort facilities. The statute is reasonably clear. But, it approves them on the recommendation of the Reserve Bank in which the crisis is manifesting itself. So it's not quite that the board has to come to a judgment. The Reserve Bank has to make its own judgment—no probabilities, no certainties, no confidence intervals—and the board isn't compelled to do anything more than to audit how the Reserve Bank had done its analysis. So the following tends to happen: the Reserve Bank closest to the failing institutions comes to its judgment on the proper response. The Board of Governors would then have to overrule that judgment if the members thought that the process was afoul. So it's an interesting nuance in how the Fed's system works.

On Paul's earlier question about the decision at the time of crisis and the subsequent bailout under the lender of last resort: I'd just make a bit of a distinction. One, is this the failure of an institution, where the failure is sui generis? Or is the problem seemingly endemic to the system? And the crisis that we just experienced was recognized far too late to be a crisis that could be managed at the level of an individual bank. The weaknesses were manifesting themselves across institutions. Hence, the judgment of lender of last resort to which Paul refers is largely about whether the institutions would be solvent absent central bank support. And again, because you're relying in the first instance on the judgment of a Reserve Bank's recommendation, not the Board's recommendation, people put in office by the president and confirmed by the Senate, you can see why the incentives [tend] toward a greater inclination to bending rules to support the firms. So just to put a fine point on that, there have been many books written about Lehman Brothers and whether the Federal Reserve had the authority or whether it had decided this was a moment for showing that moral hazard means something. My experience with the relevant decision-makers suggests that they were prepared to bail out all firms that they could. It was only in that case where the Reserve Bank couldn't plausibly find the story they could tell, they would recommend not coming to the rescue. If they could have found a credible story in which Lehman Brothers had sufficient assets, they would have told the story. But the Reserve Bank was far from being able to find sufficient unencumbered assets, that even the Reserve Bank, whose inclinations were all but perfectly clear to the board and to the general public, found itself incapable of supporting a bailout.

CHARLES PLOSSER: I just want to make one clarification. The ultimate authority to lend to Lehman Brothers did not rest with the Reserve Banks but with the Board of Governors (BOG) under Section 13(3) of the Federal Reserve Act. Reserve Banks could lend against sound collateral to depository institutions through the discount window, but Lehman did not qualify. Indeed,

Reserve Banks were not supposed to lend to failing institutions. The FDIC oftentimes would put pressure on the banks to lend to a failing institution for other reasons, such as during a transition to resolution. Even though the FDIC had the authority to lend to them, they wanted the Fed to do it.

So lending under Section 13(3) to Lehman Brothers, Bear Stearns, or AIG was ultimately a BOG decision, not a Reserve Bank decision, at the end of the day. Granted that a Reserve Bank had to execute the action, which New York did in all those cases. But the decision rights actually rested with the Board of Governors.

Reserve Banks typically have a pretty good idea about the banks in their districts and what conditions they're in. It is with the non-banks and non-depository institutions, which didn't have access to the discount window, where the problem actually made itself much more complicated and difficult, and both Bear Stearns and Lehman Brothers were examples. But Bear Stearns in particular was difficult because the Fed had little knowledge of its financial details.

So I think that part of this question of providing a lender-of-last-resort facility is the challenges of the so-called shadow banking system and who has the knowledge and authority to lend to them when they don't have access to the traditional discount window.

GEORGE SHULTZ: The question of history here, as I understood it from reading, is that there was a very active bailout of Lehman Brothers under way. At the last minute, some British regulatory authorities pulled the rug out from under the process, so it failed. It was a surprise to the market and it was a disappointment to the Fed. Is that incorrect? What you said is a little different from that.

WARSH: Paul and I were in an interesting conversation at the moment that George references. But my recollection of events— Paul, weigh in on this—by the time we found ourselves on that

Sunday morning, my recollection differs in some respects from what I read in various books. By my recollection, the bank regulators in the United Kingdom had given their authority for a large British bank to buy at least some substantial portion of the Lehman assets. The US government was thrilled, quite looking forward to that, and was willing to take back certain enumerated assets that would be "over-collateralized" which would be subject to some form of a Bagehot rule. But, if I recall, the British government, sometime between that Saturday night and that Sunday morning, said something to the effect of: "We will not take the risks associated with this."

TUCKER: It's not *quite* right, but it's got much of the substance. Mervyn [King] and I were in—I'm not sure this has been said publicly before—were in his office that Saturday morning finalizing a paper we'd been working on for six months to complete an overhaul of the Bank of England's liquidity insurance regime: the biggest changes for a century as we were formalizing and making public a series of facilities. Well, we heard about Lehman's acute difficulties for the first time that Saturday morning. The technical block on the deal, as I recall, was that the regulators, the FSA (Financial Services Authority), a separate institution, did not give Barclays a waiver on the need for them to get shareholder approval. (Peter would have been a director of the FSA at the time.) What motivated that? Well, it was a decision by the FSA, but a decision that both the government and the Bank of England were completely comfortable with. And it actually goes back to the substance of our conversation. So, do these people to whom UK officials are now talking in the US know whether Lehman is solvent or not, fundamentally insolvent or not, know the limits of the problem? No, they seem not to. Are they prepared to provide liquidity to sustain it? No, it appears not. Do they seem to have had a very generous liquidity policy up to now? Yes. Therefore, is it likely that they think

Lehman is insolvent? It seemed like it. If Lehman is insolvent and Barclays buys Lehman, is the British government likely to face the prospect of buying Barclays plus Lehman over the next fortnight or month or so—or week or days? Yeah, that seems like a reasonable prospect. Do we think in those circumstances that the US government would share in the risk-taking? That seems unlikely, given the circumstances. Is this, therefore, a set of circumstances where the UK should contingently provide "capital of last resort" to the US broker-dealer system? No. I think it was one of the easier judgments that the so-called tripartite authorities faced during the whole crisis.

WARSH: And my recollection is consistent with that, in that those decisions were not asked until it got to the level of the chancellor and the leadership of the central bank.

TUCKER: It was very late.

JOHN TAYLOR: Because the logic is: It was obvious what the answer would be. Right?

WARSH: At the level of the regulators below the Bank of England, below the chancellor, those questions were not asked. And the US government's perspective seemed modeled on the Bear Stearns–JP Morgan deal, where the Federal Reserve would inherit some Maiden Lane–type assets with appropriate collateral. But, in the case of Lehman, there were greater risks—as Paul says—unbounded risks.

TUCKER: Unbounded risks that might realistically end up essentially amounting to a sovereign risk transfer. Can I just pick up on another point, John, if I may, between what Kevin said and what Charlie said? If, as you describe, the decision about firm fundamentals—solvency, insolvency—is made by the Reserve Banks, the Federal Reserve Board effectively has an option whether to make its approval based on the integrity of the Reserve Bank's procedure or its own view of the substance. I would guess, given what you say, that the statute is consistent with either. Even if the Board takes the former approach—i.e., "We're going to check the integrity of the procedure"—I would guess it would be tremendously helpful if the Federal Reserve Board laid out the standard that they wanted the Reserve Banks to follow, so that different Reserve Banks all followed the same standard. Maybe it has.

But the more important point is this very strange thing in this country, where typically accountability to Congress goes only via members of the Board. And I can't understand, whether or not they're nominated by the president and confirmed by the Senate, why regional bank presidents can't be called to testify in front of a congressional committee on their policy decisions.

But my impression is that it doesn't happen very much. If you're taking massive decisions, then you have to explain them to the elected representatives of the people. My point is that the current (and recurring) debate about the process for appointing Reserve Bank presidents can be separated from their need to be accountable, as public officials.

SHULTZ: Let me present a less charitable view of what happened. First of all, let me come back to Mike's comment, which I interpreted as meaning that when the government encouraged what you have to call "stupid lending," a lot of it occurred, and it managed to suck the private sector in handily so they could then blame the private sector. That's broadly what happened. Now at the same time that the private sector saw this, the head of Citicorp gets up and says, "As long as the music is playing, you've got to get up and dance." If you were a regulator, wouldn't your light go on? It didn't. Nobody did anything. Why? Because the New York financial community owns the New York Fed. They appoint the head of it. Talk about regulatory capture. George Stigler would blush at this.

Then comes Bear Stearns with a big intervention by the Treasury and the Fed, which are glued together in this whole process.

The Fed winds up holding all the toxic assets. As the *Wall Street Journal* put it, Jamie Dimon took them to school and JP Morgan walked off like a bandit. But the authorities transmitted the message that they didn't think the system could be maintained if they let even a little outfit like Bear Stearns go down. What was the head of Bear Stearns, or the former head, doing while all this was going on? He was playing bridge in Chicago. You have to ask yourself what kind of people these are who don't even pay attention to their own business when it's blowing up. Something's seriously wrong.

Then came Lehman Brothers. The expectation was transmitted very strongly that Lehman Brothers would not be allowed to fail. And for reasons you were discussing, in the market's view it suddenly was allowed to fail. When it happened that way, the orderly processes of bankruptcy that were in place didn't hold, so this whole process worked itself into a comedy of errors. There was bad news all around. Then what happened? The secretary of the treasury and the chairman of the Fed went before Congress on bended knee and said, "The sky is falling! We have to have a huge amount of money." To do what? To buy all those toxic assets, which was transparently impossible. It's almost as though they decided to do everything they could to upset the apple cart, to get everybody convinced that everything was unmanageable and out of control. How else could you say, "The sky is falling, we need all this money, and we don't know what to do with it"?

Then what did they do? They decided to give the money to the big banks. They called in a number of them—six, I think—and some of them were in good shape, some were not. So the powers that be thought they knew who was weak and who was strong, but the market wasn't strong enough to figure that out so everybody had to take the money. When one of the bankers said he didn't want to take the money, they said, "We will regulate the hell out of you unless you take this money." That is a completely improper use of power and it raises this question: Can you trust these organizations with that much power? The answer is obviously no. On the other hand, the regulatory process has unfolded to give you more power. I'm giving a non-monetary guy's look at this.

I had the following experience. I had been secretary of labor. Then I became the new director of the Office of Management and Budget, and I found out that a financial organization called Penn Central had mismanaged its affairs badly and was about to go bankrupt.

Arthur Burns, who was chairman of the Fed, was chairman of the Council of Economic Advisers when I was on the staff and he probably had something to do with me becoming secretary of labor. In any case, Arthur was formidable. It wasn't just that he was a smart economist and all that; he was a giant. Helmut Schmidt, the chancellor of Germany, called him the pope of economics. When he spoke, that was it.

So Arthur thought that if Penn Central went down, it would cause a crisis of the financial system, and he worked out a bailout via the Pentagon somehow. I never could figure out how that was done but when I found out about it, I argued against it. Half of me was saying, "What am I doing here, arguing with Arthur Burns about financial markets?" But I had my views, so I was arguing. At a critical moment, in walks the savviest political counselor in the world, a man named Bryce Harlow. He said, "Mr. President, in its infinite wisdom, the Penn Central has just hired your old law firm to represent them in this matter. Under the circumstances, you can't touch this with a ten-foot pole." So there was no bailout. Arthur did a masterful job of flooding the system with liquidity. And guess what? The failure of Penn Central strengthened the financial system because it caused everybody to stop and say, "Wait a minute. We'd better be careful here." So instead of a problem, there was a positive result. It wasn't that anybody had the courage to let it go; it just happened, but it was instructive.

I had the same experience in a different way as secretary of labor. I made lots of speeches when I was a professor at the University of Chicago saying that the Kennedy and Johnson administrations were intervening too much in big labor disputes on the grounds that intervening would avert a national emergency. The result was that the whole process of private bargaining was eroding. That's moral hazard, and it happens everywhere. I said to a group of lawyers once that if the president hangs out his shingle, he'll get all the business; you don't make your best offer until you get to the White House. I thought this was a bad thing. So in October of '68, the longshoremen on the Gulf and East Coasts went on strike. President Johnson thought this would create a national emergency. Under Taft-Hartley, he enjoined the strike and there was fast-track authority to the Supreme Court. The Supreme Court agreed with the president, so the injunction held. Then it expired around January 18, 1969, and I was sworn in as secretary of labor on January 21. The press said, "OK, Mr. Professor, now you're secretary of labor. What are you going to do?"

So I went to the president and discussed this with him. I said, "Mr. President, your predecessor was wrong and the Supreme Court was wrong. This dispute will cause a lot of kerfuffle in New York City, and they think that will be a national emergency, but it won't. You can hang tough for three or four weeks and I'll get some good mediators going. Once they're convinced it's not going to the White House, we can get this settled and then we'll send a big message." It worked out that way and we had practically no more Taft-Hartleys. It changed people's expectations.

I think what you all have to keep in mind is that it isn't just money supply and numbers. It's the way that what you do profoundly affects people's attitudes. In the labor case, it had a profound impact on the way people worked together with each other. And moral hazard happens everywhere. Intervention changes the situation. Many people say, "Hooray, the Fed saved the system," but I'm not so sure. I think a lot of serious mistakes were made.

CHAPTER TWO

Policy Rule Legislation in Practice

Alex Nikolsko-Rzhevskyy, David H. Papell,
and Ruxandra Prodan

The Federal Reserve Accountability and Transparency Act of 2014, introduced into the House of Representatives Financial Services Committee in July 2014, engendered both positive and negative reactions. On the positive side, Allan Meltzer testified before the Senate Banking Committee, "So you need a rule which says, look, you said you were going to do this, and you have not done it. That requires an answer, and that I think is one of the most important reasons why we need some kind of a rule." On the negative side, in a hearing before the House Financial Services Committee, Federal Reserve Chair Janet Yellen called the proposal a "grave mistake" which would "essentially undermine central bank independence." Alan Blinder wrote, "In a town like Washington, the message to the Fed would be clear: depart from the original Taylor rule at your peril." In later testimony before the Senate Banking Committee, Yellen said, "I'm not a proponent of chaining the Federal Open Market Committee in its decision-making to any rule whatsoever."[1]

The proposed legislation specifies two rules. The Directive Policy Rule would be chosen by the Fed, and describes how the Fed's policy instrument, such as the federal funds rate, would respond

We thank Michael Bordo, Michael Dotsey, and John Taylor for helpful comments and discussions.
1. See Appelbaum (2014), Blinder (2014), and Taylor (2015a, b, c).

to a change in the intermediate policy inputs, presumably inflation and one or more measures of real economic activity such as
the output gap, the unemployment rate, and real GDP growth.
If the Fed deviated from its rule, the chair of the Fed would be
required to testify before the appropriate congressional committees as to why it is not in compliance. In addition, the report must
include a statement as to whether the legislated policy rule substantially conforms to the Reference Policy Rule, with an explanation or justification if it does not. The Reference Policy Rule is
specified as the sum of (a) the rate of inflation over the previous
four quarters, (b) one-half of the percentage deviation of real GDP
from an estimate of potential GDP, (c) one-half of the difference
between the rate of inflation over the previous four quarters and
two, and (d) two. The Reference Policy Rule is the original Taylor
(1993) rule.

The Financial Regulatory Improvement Act of 2015 was introduced into the Senate Banking Committee in May. It replaces the
current semi-annual monetary policy report to Congress by the
Fed with a quarterly report by the Federal Open Market Committee (FOMC) explaining the policy decisions of the FOMC over the
prior quarter and the basis for those decisions. The report would
include a description of any rule or rules that provide the basis for
monetary policy decisions, including short-term interest rate targets set by the FOMC, and a mathematical formula for each rule
that models how monetary policy instruments will be adjusted
based on changes in quantitative inputs. The FOMC would also be
required to explain any changes of the rule(s) in the current report
from the rule(s) in the most recent quarterly report. The FOMC is
not required to follow any rule or rules, but is required to denote
which rule(s) it has used or considered. There is no equivalent of
the Reference Policy Rule in the Senate bill.[2]

---

2. Taylor (2011) advocates the adoption of legislated monetary policy rules and Taylor
(2015d) discusses the Senate draft bill.

The House and Senate bills have more commonalities than differences. Both bills would increase transparency by tying the Fed's congressional reporting and testimony to policy rules. While the House bill explicitly mentions deviations from the rule, the requirement in the Senate bill that the FOMC explain policy decisions over the prior quarter and the basis for those decisions implicitly requires explanation of deviations. While the Senate bill explicitly requires explanation of changes of the rule(s) in the current report from the rule(s) in the most recent quarterly report, the requirement in the House bill that the Fed describe the Directive Policy Rule implicitly requires explanation of changes.[3]

Nikolsko-Rzhevskyy, Papell, and Prodan (2014) provide evidence that economic performance is better under rules-based than under discretionary eras. Using real-time data on inflation and the output gap from 1965 to 2013, we calculate policy rule deviations, the absolute value of the difference between the actual federal funds rate and the rate prescribed by (1) the "original" Taylor rule described above, (2) a "modified" Taylor rule with a coefficient of one, instead of one-half, on the output gap, and (3) an "estimated" Taylor rule from a regression of the federal funds rate on a constant, the inflation rate, and the output gap. We identify monetary policy eras by allowing for changes in the mean of the policy rule deviations with tests for multiple structural breaks, with discretionary eras defined by large deviations and rules-based eras defined by small deviations. Using six loss functions involving inflation and unemployment, we show that economic performance is uniformly better in rules-based than in discretionary eras, with the ratio of the loss during discretionary eras to the loss during rules-based eras largest for the original Taylor rule, next largest for the modified Taylor rule, and smallest for the estimated Taylor rule.

---

3. The Senate bill uses the word "deviation" of the rules in the current and prior reports. In order to avoid confusion, we use the terms "deviation" from the rule and "changes" in the rule.

In this paper, we analyze the implications of legislated rules. Consider the following counterfactual. Suppose that the policy rule legislation had been in effect from 1954, when federal funds rate data are first available, through 2015. When would deviations from the rule have been large enough to trigger congressional testimony under the House bill or require explanation under the Senate bill? We first assume that the existence of the legislation would not have altered the Fed's policy rate and consider whether or not the Fed would have been in compliance with the legislation. Since the rule is chosen by the Fed, this leads us to then consider how the Fed might have changed the rule in order to have avoided large deviations during various periods and to speculate how, looking forward, the proposed legislation might change Fed behavior.

While both of the bills have passed out of committee, neither has been taken up by the full chamber and we do not know (1) whether the proposed legislation will ultimately become law and (2) what the specifics of the legislation would be if it is enacted. We therefore need to make several choices in order to define the scope of our inquiry. First, we use only real-time data which was publicly available. In particular, we do not use Greenbook output gap and inflation forecast data because it was not publicly available except after a long lag, currently seven years. Even if it were to be publicly available, using Fed-generated output gaps and inflation forecasts would create a (perceived or actual) moral hazard problem that seems undesirable. Second, the legislation does not define what constitutes a deviation. Based on the results in Nikolsko-Rzhevskyy, Papell, and Prodan (2014), where rules-based (discretionary) eras closely correspond to departures of the federal funds rate of less than (greater than) 2 percent from the rate implied by the original Taylor (1993) rule, we define a deviation as a greater than 2 percent departure of the federal funds rate from the rate implied by whatever rule is being used. Third, the Senate bill requires quarterly reporting while the House bill requires semi-annual reporting in

conjunction with the monetary policy report. We define a deviation of greater than 2 percent during any quarter as the criteria for
not being in compliance, while recognizing that extended deviations are different than short-term deviations. Fourth, since the
Senate bill does not include a Reference Policy Rule, we will use
"legislated policy rule" to denote the Directive Policy Rule in the
House bill and the policy rule in the Senate bill.

We consider two candidates for the legislated policy rule. The
first is the original Taylor (1993) rule. The second is a modified
Taylor rule with a coefficient of one, instead of one-half, on the
output gap. Between 1954 and 1990, there are no official real-time
measures of potential output, so we use real-time data on the GDP
deflator and real GDP from the Philadelphia Fed to construct measures of inflation and the output gap. Because no single method
of detrending produces output gaps for the full sixty-year period
that are consistent with real-time approximations using Okun's
Law during recessions, we use linear detrending until 1973 and
quadratic detrending thereafter. Starting in 1991, real-time output
gaps can be calculated from the Philadelphia Fed real-time GDP
data and Congressional Budget Office (CBO) estimates of potential GDP, and a wider range of real-time inflation rates are available. The policy rate is the federal funds rate through 2008 and the
shadow federal funds rate in Wu and Xia (forthcoming) during the
zero lower bound period from 2009 to 2015.

We first consider the full period from 1954 through 2015 using
real-time GDP inflation and detrended output gaps. Suppose that
the original Taylor rule was the legislated policy rule. Fed policy
generally adhered to the rule from 1954 to 1974, with short deviations associated with the recessions of 1957–1958, 1960–1961, and
1969–1970, and one longer deviation in 1967 and 1968. Policy was
back on track during the early 1970s, with only one short deviation
in 1971. Starting in 1974, however, there was an extended period
of negative deviations during the Great Inflation followed by an

extended period of positive deviations during the Volcker disinflation. Fed policy consistently adhered to the rule during the Great
Moderation, with no deviations from late 1985 through 2000. Starting in 2001, however, deviations again became the norm rather
than the exception, with extended periods of negative deviations
from 2001 to 2006 and 2011 to 2015.

Now suppose that the modified Taylor rule was the legislated
policy rule. There are many more deviations during the 1950s and
1960s, with the federal funds rate consistently more than 2 percent
above the prescribed rate from 1958 to 1961 and consistently more
than 2 percent below the prescribed rate from 1965 to 1969. The
subsequent low deviations period lasts from 1969 to 1977, with the
period of negative deviations during the Great Inflation from 1977
to 1979. The results for the Volcker Disinflation, Great Moderation,
and early-to-mid-2000s are similar to those with the original Taylor rule. The similarity does not extend to the more recent period,
as there are positive deviations in 2009 and 2010 and no deviations
in 2011 to 2015.

While considering the implications of policy rule legislation
over a long historical period provides a broad overview, calculat-
ing real-time output gaps over this period involves making arguable choices about the appropriate method of detrending. We
repeat the same thought experiment starting in 1991, when real-
time output gaps calculated using CBO potential GDP estimates
are first available, through 2015. Since the Fed paid more attention
to the Consumer Price Index (CPI) in the 1990s and the Personal
Consumption Expenditure index (PCE) in the 2000s, we consider
headline and core versions of the CPI and PCE which are available
for all or most of the period.

We organize our analysis around several well-known examples
of monetary policy evaluation using Taylor rules. Poole (2007)
and Taylor (2007) report large deviations from the original Tay-

lor rule for 2003–2005 with CBO output gaps and CPI inflation. We follow Poole by using real-time data, and find that the deviations were greater than 2 percent in 2001, 2003–2004, 2008–2009, and 2011–2015. If the original Taylor rule were the legislated policy rule, most of the 2000s would have triggered congressional testimony. The general pattern of deviations is not affected if the CPI is replaced by the PCE.

Taylor's findings were disputed by several senior Fed officials. Kohn (2007) argued that the large deviations reported by Taylor became much smaller if core, rather than headline, CPI were used to calculate inflation. If the legislated policy rule was the original Taylor rule with core CPI inflation, there would not have been deviations greater than 2 percent during 2003–2005. There would, however, have been greater than 2 percent deviations during 2001–2002 and 2011–2015.

Bernanke (2010) criticized Taylor's analysis on the grounds that inflation forecasts, rather than inflation rates, should be the basis for prescribed Taylor rule policy rates and discussed how core PCE inflation was used by the FOMC as an indicator of the underlying trend of inflation. We compute deviations if the original Taylor rule with CBO output gaps and core PCE inflation were used for the legislated policy rule. While there were no deviations larger than 2 percent before 2012, including the 2003–2005 period highlighted by Taylor (2007), the deviations were greater than 2 percent for most quarters between 2012 and 2015.

Yellen (2012) argued that the modified Taylor rule with a higher output gap coefficient was both a better description of Fed policy and closer to optimal policy than the original Taylor rule. In order to analyze the impact of the legislation under this rule, we compute deviations if the modified Taylor rule with CBO output gaps and PCE inflation were used for the legislated policy rule. Recent Fed policy under this rule is generally in accord with the legislation, as there were no deviations greater than 2 percent from 2011 through early 2014. There were, however, deviations greater than 2 percent in 1992, 2000–2004, 2008–2010, late 2014, and early 2015.

Most recently, Yellen (2015) argued that the fixed equilibrium real interest rate of two in the original Taylor rule should be replaced by a time-varying rate. We compute deviations using the original Taylor rule with the Laubach and Williams (2003) time-varying equilibrium real interest rate, CBO output gaps, and PCE inflation as the legislated policy rule. Under this specification, Fed policy since the end of the Great Recession is even more in accord with the proposed legislation than the Yellen (2012) specification, with no deviations greater than 2 percent from 2010 through early 2014. There were, however, deviations greater than 2 percent in 2003–2005, 2008–2009, and late 2014.

The central result of the paper is that, among the class of rules we consider, there is no single legislated policy rule that would have avoided large deviations over extended periods of time. While this is not surprising for the entire period, with the Great Inflation followed by the Volcker disinflation, it is perhaps surprising that the same result holds for the 2000s and the 2010s. Passage of policy rule legislation would potentially place the Fed in a quandary. While the Fed can both choose and change the rule, too frequent changes would leave it open to criticism that it is actually following a purely discretionary policy. A legislated policy rule would encourage the Fed to follow more predictable policies, as in 1954 to 1974 and 1985 to 2000, than less predictable policies, as in 1975 to 1984 and 2001 to 2015. Based on the historical evidence in Meltzer (2009) and Taylor (2012) and the statistical evidence in Nikolsko-Rzhevskyy, Papell, and Prodan (2014) that economic performance is better in rules-based than in discretionary eras, we believe that this would be a positive development.

Legislated policy rule deviations

The centerpiece of the House and Senate bills is the legislated policy rule. This rule is chosen by the Fed, and describes how the federal funds rate would respond to a change in inflation and one or more measures of real economic activity. There are several important aspects of the legislation that are designed to ensure transparency. Under the House bill, if the Fed deviated from its rule, the chair of the Fed would be required to testify before the appropriate congressional committees as to why it is not in compliance. Under the Senate bill, the FOMC would make quarterly reports to Congress that describe any rules that provide the basis for monetary policy decisions. Since the original and modified Taylor rules use the output gap, we restrict our attention to rules where the output gap is the only measure of real economic activity.[4]

Taylor (1993) proposed the following monetary policy rule:

$$i_t = \pi_t + \phi(\pi_t - \pi^*) + \gamma y_t + R^* \tag{1}$$

where i_t is the target level of the short-term nominal interest rate, π_t is the inflation rate, π^* is the target level of inflation, y_t is the output gap, the percent deviation of actual real GDP from an estimate of its potential level, $\pi_t - \pi^*$ is the inflation gap, the percentage deviation of inflation from the target level of inflation, and R^* is the equilibrium level of the real interest rate. Combining terms,

$$i_t = \mu + \alpha\pi_t + \gamma y_t, \tag{2}$$

where $\alpha = 1 + \phi$ and $\mu = R^* + \phi\pi^*$.

---

4. Legislated policy rules could also incorporate measures of real economic activity such as the unemployment gap, output growth, and/or output gap growth. We don't consider such specifications in the paper.

Taylor postulated that the output and inflation gaps enter the central bank's reaction function with equal weights of 0.5 and that the equilibrium level of the real interest rate and the inflation target were both equal to 2 percent, producing the following equation,

$$i_t = 1.0 + 1.5\pi_t + 0.5y_t \tag{3}$$

The most widely used alternative to the original Taylor rule increases the size of the coefficient on the output gap from 0.5 to 1.0, producing the following specification,

$$i_t = 1.0 + 1.5\pi_t + 1.0y_t. \tag{4}$$

We call this rule the modified Taylor rule. Rudebusch (2010) and Yellen (2012) use variants of this rule to justify unconventional policies after the federal funds rate hit the zero lower bound.[5] Policy rule deviations are defined as the difference between the actual federal funds rate and the interest rate target implied by either the original or the modified Taylor rule with the above coefficients.

In order for our analysis to be operational, we need to make several assumptions. The proposed legislation does not specify how large a deviation would need to be in order to trigger congressional testimony. In Nikolsko-Rzhevskyy, Papell, and Prodan (2014), we use Bai and Perron (1998) and Perron and Qu (2006) tests for multiple structural changes to define rules-based (low) and discretionary (high) deviation eras for various policy rules. For the original Taylor (1993) rule, the rules-based (discretionary) eras closely correspond to departures of the federal funds rate of less than (greater than) 2 percent from the rate implied by the rule, with a correlation of 0.80 between the metrics. We therefore define a deviation as a greater-than-2 percent departure of the federal

---

5. Yellen (2012) called this rule the "balanced-approach" rule. We use the term "modified" in order to utilize more neutral language.

funds rate from the rate implied by whatever legislated policy rule is being used.

While the House bill states that, if the Fed deviated from its rule, the chair of the Fed would be required to testify before the appropriate congressional committees as to why it is not in compliance, it does not specify exactly how this would occur. The Fed currently submits the Monetary Policy Report semi-annually to the Senate Committee on Banking, Housing, and Urban Affairs and to the House Committee on Financial Services, along with testimony from the Fed chair. One possibility for implementing the policy rule legislation would be for a statement declaring whether or not the Fed is in compliance with the legislated policy rule to be included in the Monetary Policy Report and, if not, for the Fed chair to testify as to why it is not in compliance. If implemented in this manner, the Fed would certify each February and July whether it is in compliance based on currently available data. The Senate bill would replace the current semi-annual monetary policy reports to Congress by the Fed with a quarterly report published by the FOMC, while still requiring the Fed chair to testify semi-annually. In this case, the difference between the actual and legislated rules-based federal funds rate would presumably be part of the quarterly FOMC report. Since we do not know whether either of these bills will ultimately become law, we simply report the quarterly deviations of the federal funds rate from the rate prescribed by various rules.

When estimating Taylor rules, it is common practice to include one or more lagged values of the federal funds rate on the right-hand side. This is problematic for constructing legislated policy rules for several reasons. First, while interest-rate-smoothing rules derived from optimizing models with a coefficient of one on the lagged interest rate, as in Levin, Wieland, and Williams (1999), can, in principle, be used for legislated policy rules, deviations from these rules cannot distinguish between rules-based and discretionary eras using the methods of Nikolsko-Rzhevskyy, Papell, and Prodan (2014). Second, legislated rules based on estimated Fed reaction functions assume that past Fed behavior is optimal which, if true, would obviate the need for rules. This problem is exacerbated with rules that incorporate large coefficients on lagged interest rates, which risk locking the Fed into past mistakes in an attempt to smooth the rates.

Real-time data

The prescribed Taylor rule interest rate is calculated from data on inflation and the output gap. Following Orphanides (2001), the vast majority of research on the Taylor rule uses real-time data that was available to policymakers at the time that interest rate-setting decisions were made. In order to implement the policy rule legislation, the data also need to be publicly available. This rules out Greenbook data unless the Fed changes its release policy, as it is currently only available with about a seven-year lag.

The Real-Time Data Set for Macroeconomists (RTDSM), originated by Croushore and Stark (2001) and maintained by the Philadelphia Fed, contains vintages of nominal GDP, real GDP, and the GDP deflator (GNP before December 1991) data starting in 1965:Q4, with the data in each vintage extending back to 1947:Q1. Data for the federal funds rate is available starting in 1954:Q3. Since we want to use the longest available span of data, we construct semi-real-time vintages between 1954:Q3 and 1965:Q4 using the earliest available 1965:Q4 vintage.

We construct inflation rates as the year-over-year change in the GDP deflator, the ratio of nominal to real GDP. While the Fed has emphasized different inflation rates at different points in time, real-time GDP inflation is by far the longest available real-time inflation series. This is the inflation rate that Taylor (1993) calculated with revised data.

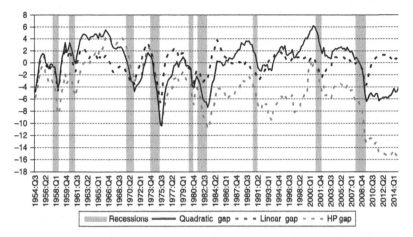

FIGURE 2.1. Real-time output gaps using linear, quadratic, and Hodrick-Prescott detrending

Source: Authors' calculations

In order to construct the output gap—the percentage deviation of real GDP around potential GDP—the real GDP data need to be detrended. We use real-time detrending, where the trend is calculated from 1947:Q1 through the vintage date. For example, the output gap for 1965:Q4 is the most recent deviation from the trend calculated from 1947:Q1 to 1965:Q3, the output gap for 1966:Q1 is the most recent deviation from the trend calculated from 1947:Q1 to 1965:Q4, and so on, replicating the information available to policymakers. The lag reflects the fact that GDP data for a given quarter are not known until after the end of the quarter.

The three leading methods of detrending are linear, quadratic, and Hodrick-Prescott (HP). Real-time output gaps using these methods are depicted in figure 2.1. In contrast with output gaps constructed using revised data, where the trends are estimated for the entire sample, there is no necessity for the positive output gaps to equal the negative output gaps. While there are considerable differences among the gaps, the negative output gaps correspond closely with National Bureau of Economic Research (NBER) recession dates for all three methods.

None of the three real-time output gaps provide a good approximation of the perceptions of policymakers over the entire period. Nikolsko-Rzhevskyy and Papell (2012) and Nikolsko-Rzhevskyy, Papell, and Prodan (2014) use Okun's Law, which states that the output gap equals a (negative) coefficient times the difference between current unemployment and the natural rate of unemployment, to construct rule-of-thumb output gaps based on real-time unemployment rates, perceptions of the natural rate of unemployment, and perceptions of the Okun's Law coefficient. Focusing on the quarters of peak unemployment associated with the recessions in the 1970s and 1980s, the congruence between real-time Okun's Law output gaps and real-time linear and quadratic detrended output gaps is fairly close, while the real-time HP detrended output gaps are always too small. We performed similar calculations for the recessions of the late 1950s and early 1960s. During that period, the congruence between real-time Okun's Law output gaps and real-time linear detrended output gaps is fairly close, while the real-time quadratic and HP detrended output gaps are always too small.

Real-time linear detrending, however, is not the solution, as the output gap becomes negative in 1974 and stays consistently negative, reflecting the long-term flattening of growth rates following the productivity growth slowdown starting in 1973. More recently, HP detrended output gaps depict a V-shaped recovery from the Great Recession, with the output gap positive since 2011. With quadratic detrended output gaps, the recovery from the Great Recession has been flat, with the output gap slowly closing since 2011. For these reasons, we use real-time linear detrending until 1973 and real-time quadratic detrending thereafter to construct output gaps for the policy rule calculations.[6]

6. The results are robust to switching from linear to quadratic detrending anytime between 1971:Q2 and 1976:Q1.

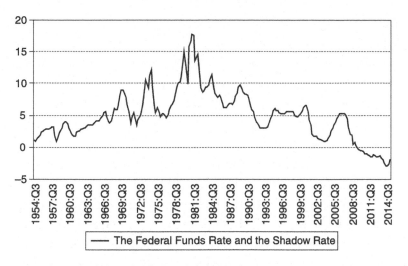

FIGURE 2.2. The federal funds rate and the shadow rate

Source: Federal Reserve Bank; Cynthia Jing Wu and Fan Dora Xia, "Measuring the Macroeconomic Impact of Monetary Policy at the Zero Lower Bound," *Journal of Money, Credit, & Banking* (forthcoming).

The policy rate is the effective (average of daily) federal funds rate for the quarter. The federal funds rate is constrained by the zero lower bound starting in 2009:Q1 and is therefore not a good measure of Fed policy. Between 2009:Q1 and 2015:Q1 we use the shadow federal funds rate of Wu and Xia (forthcoming). The shadow rate is calculated using a nonlinear term structure model that incorporates the effect of quantitative easing and forward guidance. The actual and shadow rates are depicted in figure 2.2. The shadow rate is consistently negative between 2009:Q3 and 2015:Q1, with the most negative value in 2014:Q2. It stayed negative through 2015:Q1 even though the FOMC suspended its asset purchase program in October because, as discussed by Yellen (2015), the stimulus provided by unconventional monetary policy depends on the stock, not the flow, of longer-term assets held by the Fed.

The time span for our more recent analysis is determined by CBO data availability. To calculate real-time CBO output gaps, we use quarterly estimates of potential GDP from "The Budget and Economic Outlook" published in January/February of every year since 1991. Starting in 2007, due to CBO's frequent and substantial potential GDP revisions, we also use data from the August updates. This data is combined with real-time actual GDP from the Philadelphia Fed RTDSM to obtain the output gap as the log-difference between the two values. Because GDP is updated quarterly and potential GDP is updated annually or semi-annually, we use forecasts of potential GDP between the CBO updates.[7]

The data for all of the inflation measures is from the Philadelphia Fed RTDSM, which contains quarterly vintages of the Consumer Price Index starting in 1994:Q3, monthly vintages of the core Consumer Price Index starting in 1999:M1, quarterly vintages of the Price Index for Personal Consumption Expenditures starting in 1965:Q4, and quarterly vintages of the core Price Index for Personal Consumption Expenditures starting in 1996:Q1.[8] Real-time inflation is calculated as the year-over-year log-change in the index. Following Koenig (2004), who argued that the Fed paid more attention to CPI inflation in the 1990s and PCE inflation in the 2000s, we use both measures.

Policy rule legislation from 1954 to 2015

We construct the following counterfactual. Suppose the policy rule legislation had been in place from 1954, when federal funds rate data are first available, through 2015. When would the devia-

---

7. The CBO did not issue an update for August 2013. This creates a problem because, in July 2013, the Bureau of Economic Analysis substantially changed how GDP was calculated. Since we do not have an August 2013 update, output gaps for 2013:Q3 and 2013:Q4 based on potential GDP forecasts from the February 2013 update reflect changes in actual, but not potential, GDP. We therefore use potential GDP from the February 2014 update to construct output gaps for 2013:Q3 and 2013:Q4.

8. For the core Consumer Price Index, we treat mid-quarter (second month) releases as quarterly releases.

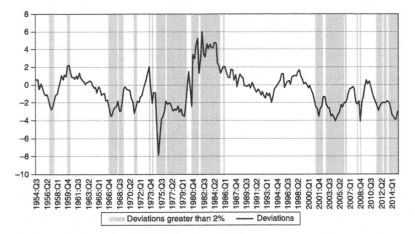

FIGURE 2.3. Original Taylor Rule: 1954–2015
Source: Authors' calculations.

tions from the legislated policy rule have been large enough for the Fed to not be in compliance and trigger congressional testimony under the House bill or require explanation under the Senate bill? As discussed above, we use the federal funds rate as the policy rate (with the shadow rate after 2008), the GDP deflator to calculate real-time inflation, and linear and quadratic detrended real GDP to calculate real-time output gaps. The criterion for a deviation is if the policy rate is greater than 2 percent above or below the rate prescribed by the rule.

The results if the legislated policy rule were the original Taylor rule are illustrated in figure 2.3. Fed policy was in compliance with the legislation during the Eisenhower, Kennedy, and the early part of the Johnson administration. There were short deviations in 1956:Q4 to 1957:Q2 and 1959:Q4 to 1960:Q1 just prior to the recessions starting in 1957:Q3 and 1960:Q2. The policy rate was below the prescribed rate in 1956–1957 and above the prescribed rate in 1959–1960. The first sustained deviations occurred during the latter part of the Johnson administration from 1966:Q4 to 1969:Q1, with the policy rate consistently below the prescribed rate. There were two short deviations during the Nixon administration, in 1971:Q1 to 1971:Q2 following the recession of 1969 to 1970 and in 1974:Q1 during the recession from 1973 to 1975.

Large deviations became the norm starting in late 1974. The federal funds rate was consistently more than 2 percent below the rate prescribed by the original Taylor rule during the Great Inflation from 1974:Q4 to 1979:Q3 and consistently more than 2 percent above the rate prescribed by the original Taylor rule during the Volcker disinflation from 1980:Q4 to 1985:Q1.[9] Fed policy was again in compliance with the legislation during the Great Moderation, as there were no deviations greater than 2 percent from 1985:Q3 to 2001:Q1. The periods when the Fed would not have been in compliance with the legislation if the legislated policy rule were the original Taylor rule are in accord with the results in Taylor (1999), who describes the federal funds rate as "too high in the early 1960s, too low in the late 1960s, too low in the 1970s, on track in 1979–1981, too high in 1982–1984, and on track in the late 1980s and 1990s."

It is often argued that, because Fed policy is forward-looking, policy evaluation should be conducted using inflation forecasts rather than realized inflation rates. While it would be problematic for the Fed to define compliance with a legislated policy rule on the basis of its own forecasts, it would not be precluded from using these forecasts to justify deviations. We calculated, but do not report, deviations using four-quarter-ahead Greenbook inflation forecasts starting when they became available in 1973:Q3. The only difference between using realized inflation and inflation forecasts is that the start of the period where the federal funds rate was consistently more than 2 percent below the rate prescribed by the original Taylor rule is pushed back from 1974:Q4 to 1976:Q1. Dur-

9. There is also a negative deviation in 1980:Q3 associated with the imposition of credit controls.

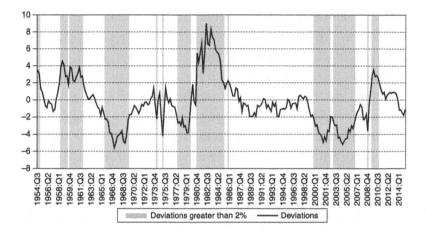

FIGURE 2.4. Modified Taylor rule: 1954–2015

Source: Authors' calculations

ing this period, the Fed consistently overestimated how quickly high rates of unemployment would bring down inflation.

Large deviations again became the norm in the 2000s and 2010s. The federal funds rate was consistently more than 2 percent below the rate prescribed by the original Taylor rule from 2001:Q2 to 2002:Q2, 2003:Q1 to 2006:Q2, and 2011:Q3 to 2015:Q1. One issue with the results for the 2000s is that the quadratic detrended output gap did not become negative during or following the recession of 2001 even though the unemployment rate rose from 4 percent in 2000 to 6 percent in 2003. We calculated, but do not report, deviations with HP detrended output gaps, which turn negative starting in 2001:Q1. In this case, there are deviations greater than 2 percent from 2003:Q4 to 2005:Q2, which is close to the results in Taylor (2007).

We now consider how the results would change if the legislated policy rule were the modified Taylor rule. As illustrated in figure 2.4, there were many more occasions when policy would not have been in compliance with the legislation in the 1950s and early 1960s, with deviations greater than 2 percent in 1954:Q3 and

1958:Q4, almost consistently between 1958:Q2 and 1961:Q4, and consistently from 1965:Q3 to 1969:Q2. Aside from 1974:Q1 and 1975:Q1, Fed policy was in compliance until 1977 when, starting in 1977:Q3, there was an extended period of consistently negative deviations at the peak of the Great Inflation until 1979:Q3 and an extended period of consistently positive deviations during the Volcker disinflation from 1980:Q1 to 1985:Q1. Fed policy was again in compliance with the legislation during the Great Moderation, as there were almost no deviations that were greater than 2 percent from 1985:Q2 to 1999:Q3. Starting in 1999:Q4, however, the deviations were consistently greater than 2 percent through 2006:Q3 and from 2009:Q3 to 2010:Q3. There are no deviations greater than 2 percent from 2010:Q4 through 2015:Q1.

There are strong elements of commonality whether the original or the modified Taylor rule is used as the legislated policy rule. The latter part of the Johnson administration, the Great Inflation, the Volcker Disinflation, and the early-to-mid-2000s all contain extended periods when the federal funds rate was more than 2 percent above or below the prescribed rate under both rules. Neither version of the rule produces a consistent pattern of adherence. While the original Taylor rule produced low deviations during most of the 1950s and the early 1960s, it produced high deviations during the late 1960s and between 1975 and 1985. With the modified Taylor rule, the high deviations during the Great Inflation did not start until late 1977, but there were many more periods in the 1950s and 1960s when the deviations were greater than 2 percent.[10] While only the original Taylor rule produces deviations greater than 2 percent from 2011 to 2015, the modified Taylor rule produces more deviations greater than 2 percent from 2000 to 2010.

---

10. We find more differences between the original and modified Taylor rules than Taylor (1999) because we use real-time data with linear and quadratic detrending and he uses revised data with HP detrending. The differences are described in Nikolsko-Rzhevskyy and Papell (2015).

Policy rule legislation from 1991 to 2015

We proceed to construct the same counterfactual as above using data from 1991:Q1, when real-time CBO output gaps are available, through 2015:Q1. The question that we pose is, again, when would the deviations from the legislated policy rule have been large enough for the Fed to not be in compliance and trigger congressional testimony? For the more recent period, the legislated policy rule will also depend on how inflation is measured because we are able to use headline and core real-time CPI and PCE inflation in order to correspond more closely with the measures that were followed by the Fed. Starting in 2009, the combination of quantitative easing and forward guidance made the federal funds rate, set at between 0 and 0.25 percent, an incomplete measure of Fed policy, and we therefore use the shadow federal funds rate calculated by Wu and Xia (forthcoming) between 2009 and 2015. All of the subsequent analysis uses real-time CBO output gaps.

We first consider deviations if the legislated policy rule were the original Taylor rule with inflation measured by the CPI. This analysis is in the spirit of Poole (2007) and Taylor (2007), and the results are depicted in figure 2.5.[11] The first deviation greater than 2 percent is in 2001:Q2 to 2001:Q4, followed by extended periods of deviations from 2003:Q1 to 2005:Q1, 2008:Q1 to 2009:Q4, and 2011:Q2 to 2015:Q1. The results are very similar if inflation is measured by the PCE. As shown in figure 2.6, there are deviations from 2003:Q1 to 2004:Q3, 2008:Q1 to 2008:Q4, 2009:Q3 to 2009:Q4, 2011:Q3 to 2012:Q2, and 2013:Q4 to 2015:Q1. Whether inflation is measured by the CPI or the PCE, the Fed would not have been in compliance with the legislated policy rule for most of the period since 2003.[12]

---

11. The real-time CPI data start in 1994.
12. The deviations in response to the financial crisis in 2008 are common to all specifications.

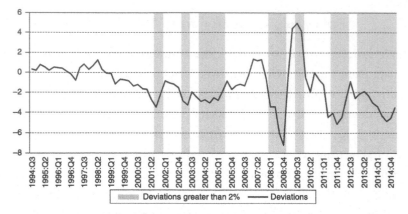

FIGURE 2.5. Original Taylor rule with real-time CBO output gaps and CPI inflation: 1994–2015

Source: Authors' calculations

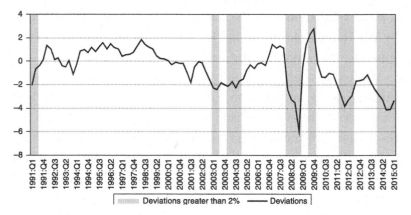

FIGURE 2.6. Original Taylor rule with real-time CBO output gaps and PCE inflation: 1991–2015

Source: Authors' calculations

If the policy rule legislation had been enacted by 1990, it is quite possible that the Fed would have adopted the original Taylor rule with headline CPI inflation as the legislated policy rule. It is doubtful, however, that this choice would have been continued through the 2000s and 2010s. We proceed to consider alternatives that have

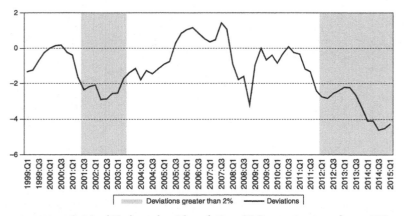

FIGURE 2.7. Original Taylor rule with real-time CBO output gaps and core CPI inflation: 1999–2015

Source: Authors' calculations

been proposed by prominent Fed officials. Kohn (2007) argued that Fed policy between 2003 and 2005 was much closer to the prescriptions of the original Taylor rule with core instead of headline CPI inflation. The implications of making this specification the legislated policy rule are illustrated in figure 2.7. This change eliminates the sustained deviations from 2003 to 2005 and 2008 to 2009 but doesn't eliminate the deviations from 2012 to 2015. It also adds an additional period, 2001:Q3 to 2003:Q1, when the Fed would not have been in compliance with the legislated policy rule.

Another argument was made by Bernanke (2010), who criticized Taylor's analysis on the grounds that inflation forecasts, rather than inflation rates, should be the basis for prescribed Taylor rule policy rates. In the context of policy rule legislation, we have argued that Greenbook or other Fed forecasts create a moral hazard problem which makes them inappropriate for the legislated policy rule. Bernanke, however, discusses how core inflation was used by the FOMC as an indicator of the underlying trend of inflation.[13] In the

13. Dokko et al. (2009), the Fed staff paper released as background to Bernanke's speech, contrasts the Taylor rule prescriptions with headline CPI and core PCE inflation.

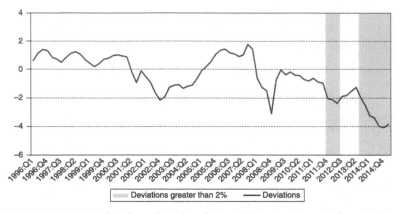

FIGURE 2.8. Original Taylor rule with real-time CBO output gaps and core PCE inflation: 1996–2015

Source: Authors' calculations

spirit of Bernanke's analysis, the deviations if the original Taylor rule with CBO output gaps and core PCE inflation were used for the legislated policy rule are depicted in figure 2.8. While there were no deviations larger than 2 percent before 2012, including the 2003–2005 period highlighted by Taylor (2007), there were deviations in 2012:Q1 to 2012:Q2 and consistent deviations between 2013:Q3 and 2015:Q1.

Yellen (2012) argued that the modified Taylor rule with a higher output gap coefficient was both a better description of Fed policy and closer to optimal policy than the original Taylor rule. The deviations if the modified Taylor rule with CBO output gaps and PCE inflation were used for the legislated policy rule are shown in figure 2.9. While there were no deviations greater than 2 percent from 2011:Q1 through 2014:Q2, there were deviations greater than 2 percent in 1992, the early 2000s, 2007:Q3 to 2010:Q1, and 2014:Q3 to 2015:Q1.

A different argument was recently made by Yellen (2015), who argued that, because the equilibrium real interest rate is low by historical standards, the fixed rate of two in the original Taylor rule

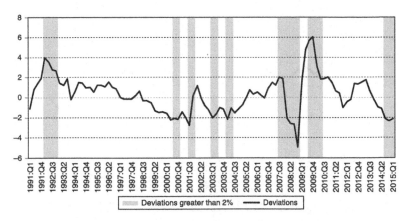

FIGURE 2.9. Modified Taylor rule with real-time CBO output gaps and PCE
inflation: 1991–2015
Source: Authors' calculations

should be replaced by a time-varying equilibrium real interest rate.
Since she did not advocate that the original Taylor rule be replaced
by the modified Taylor rule, we compute deviations using the original Taylor rule with the Laubach and Williams (2003) time-varying
equilibrium real interest rate, CBO output gaps, and PCE inflation
as the legislated policy rule. The results are depicted in figure 2.10.
While there were no deviations that would have triggered congressional testimony from 2010:Q1 through 2014:Q2, there were deviations greater than 2 percent in 2001:Q3 and 2001:Q4, 2002:Q1 to
2005:Q1, 2008:Q1 to 2009:Q4, and 2014:Q3.[14]

Laubach and Williams have recently posted real-time estimates
of the equilibrium real interest rate from 2005:Q1 to 2014:Q4,
which are discussed in Williams (2015). The results for the real-
time equilibrium real interest rate are exactly the same as for the
revised equilibrium real interest rate. There are no deviations
greater than 2 percent from 2005 to 2007, consistent deviations in

14. The most recent estimate is for 2014:Q4, so we cannot investigate whether there was a
deviation in 2015:Q1. The updated estimates can be found at http://www.frbsf.org/economic
-research/economists/john-williams/Laubach_Williams_updated_estimates.xlsx.

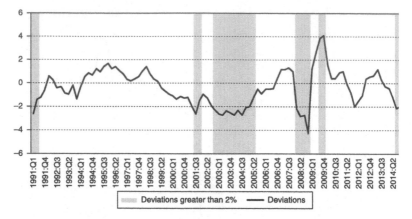

FIGURE 2.10. Original Taylor rule with real-time CBO output gaps, PCE infla-tion and time-varying equilibrium real interest rates: 1991–2015

Source: Authors' calculations

2008 and 2009, and only one deviation (2014:Q3) between 2010 and 2014.[15]

There is less commonality among potential legislated policy rules between 2001 and 2015 than between 1954 and 2000. The original Taylor rule with CPI inflation produces large deviations in the early-to-mid-2000s and 2010s. Replacing headline CPI infla-tion with core CPI inflation decreases the large deviations in the mid-2000s but increases the large deviations in the early 2000s, while incorporating core PCE inflation only produces deviations in the 2010s. The modified Taylor rule with PCE inflation and the original Taylor rule with PCE inflation and a time-varying equi-librium real interest rate produce the fewest large deviations in the 2010s but add more large deviations in the 2000s. The overall result is that rules which produce deviations less than 2 percent in the first half of the 2000s produce deviations greater than 2 per-cent in the first half of the 2010s, and vice versa.

15. The real-time model estimates can be found at http://www.frbsf.org/economic-research/economists/john-williams/Laubach_Williams_real_time_estimates_2005_2014.xlsx.

Conclusions

The legislated policy rules proposed by the Federal Reserve Accountability and Transparency Act of 2014 and the Financial Regulatory Improvement Act of 2015 have the potential to transform the conduct of monetary policy. For the first time, the Fed would have the obligation to explicitly state a benchmark for how the federal funds rate would respond to variables such as inflation and the output gap. While the Fed would choose its own legislated policy rule, it would be required to explain deviations from the rule and changes in the rule.

This paper poses a counterfactual. Suppose that the policy rule legislation had been in place for the past sixty years. When would the Fed have been in compliance, and when would deviations from or changes to the rule have triggered congressional testimony under the House bill or required explanation under the Senate bill? We consider two candidates for the legislated policy rule: the original Taylor rule and a modified Taylor rule with a larger output gap coefficient. Based on data availability, we use linear/quadratic detrending and CBO estimates of potential output to calculate real-time output gaps and several measures of headline and core inflation.

The major issue with compliance between 1954 and 1985 would have been extended deviations from the legislated policy rule. While the deviations with the original Taylor rule were less than 2 percent during most of the 1950s and early 1960s, they were typically greater than 2 percent during the late 1960s and between 1975 and 1985. While the modified Taylor rule mitigated some of the deviations in the 1970s, it increased the number of deviations in the 1950s. Either version of the rule would have produced extended periods in which the Fed would not have been in compliance with the legislation. In contrast, there are no periods of extended deviations with either rule during the Great Moderation from 1985 to 2000.

The major issue with compliance between 2001 and 2015 would have been changes in the legislated policy rule. The more recent debate started with Poole (2007) and Taylor (2007), who documented large deviations from the original Taylor rule between 2003 and 2005. In response to these results, Kohn (2007), Bernanke (2010), and Yellen (2012, 2015) proposed different specifications which, if used as the legislated policy rule, would not have produced deviations greater than 2 percent during the period studied by the authors, but would have produced deviations greater than 2 percent earlier and/or later. In contrast with the pre–Great Moderation period, the Fed could have been in compliance with the legislation, but only by changing the policy rule during the period.

We conclude by considering the implications of the proposed legislation going forward. If the legislated policy rule did not alter Fed behavior, our results for the 2000s and 2010s lead us to believe that a rule which is designed to produce small current deviations may very well produce large future deviations which, in turn, would require changes in the rule for the Fed to remain in compliance. In that case, the legislation would increase transparency, but not affect policy. Alternatively, the desire to avoid too frequent changes in the rule may very well influence the Fed in the direction of sticking with its chosen rule. In this scenario, the policy rule legislation would, while neither specifying nor requiring adherence to a particular rule, increase the predictability of monetary policy. Based on historical and statistical research showing that economic performance is better in rules-based than in discretionary eras, we believe this would be a desirable outcome.

COMMENTS BY MICHAEL DOTSEY

It is a pleasure to participate in this conference as a discussant of "Policy Rule Legislation in Practice" by Alex Nikolsko-Rzhevskyy, David H. Papell, and Ruxandra Prodan. The paper investigates how often a monitoring procedure such as the one suggested in the Federal Reserve Accountability and Transparency Act (H.R. 5018), the so-called Audit the Fed legislation, would indicate noncompliance. In the act, two rules are used to judge compliance. One is a reference policy rule that stipulates that the funds rate should be set according to the original Taylor rule, and the other is a directive policy rule chosen by the Fed. The Fed must also justify its choice of this rule if it does not substantially conform to the original Taylor rule. To gauge noncompliance, the paper examines the funds rate setting suggested by various Taylor rules and judges funds rate deviations of greater than two hundred basis points as indicating noncompliance of monetary policy with rule-like behavior. An important message of the paper is that whether the Fed is in compliance or not depends on the particular rule chosen to gauge Fed behavior, how one measures the output gap, and which inflation rate is used in the rule. Thus, accountability measures may not be very robust and could result in excessive and needless meddling with the policy process.

The legislation also opens up a host of issues regarding central bank independence. By directly overseeing particular settings of the funds rate rather than evaluating the FOMC's performance with regard to the end goals of policy, the act may be ill-conceived because the original Taylor rule might not be consistent with optimal policy. Indeed, the analysis of Giannoni and Woodford (2002)

Any views expressed herein are those of the author and not necessarily those of the Federal Reserve Bank of Philadelphia or the Federal Reserve System.

indicates that optimal rules would likely involve significant inertia and depend on lags and forecasts of output gaps and inflation, and could depend on wage inflation as well. Serious evaluation of the desirability of the legislation involves determining what is a good rule, what constitutes a deviation, the role of model uncertainty, and the effect of political pressures on monetary policy that would certainly arise under such.

To analyze these issues in more detail, I will look at what is referred to as an "outcome-based rule," which includes inertial terms and more lags of output gaps. This rule also appears to describe monetary policy more accurately than a simple Taylor rule. Employing an outcome-based rule indicates that over the period 2001–2009, monetary policy was actually in compliance with the rule. Also, I will look at two loss functions and examine whether deviations from the rule are associated with welfare losses. I find that they do not appear to be. I will then turn to a more detailed discussion of the role of monitoring based on recent work by Walsh (2015) and Ilbas, Roisland, and Sveen (2012). I will conclude by discussing the usefulness of monetary policy reports as a better alternative to the elaborate monitoring mechanism envisioned in H.R. 5018.

Analyzing an outcome-based rule

Examining the implications of simple Taylor rules may be viewed as a somewhat limited exploration of whether the Fed has behaved well or badly. The form of those rules would be optimal only in a very stylistic model of the economy, and the initial Taylor rule was not proposed to describe optimal policy, but to indicate that the Fed behaved systematically. The analysis of Giannoni and Woodford (2003) indicates that monetary policy has not been too far off from an optimal targeting rule, at least in their estimated economy. With that observation as background, I will use what is referred to as an outcome-based rule (see the cited Monetary Policy Alternatives

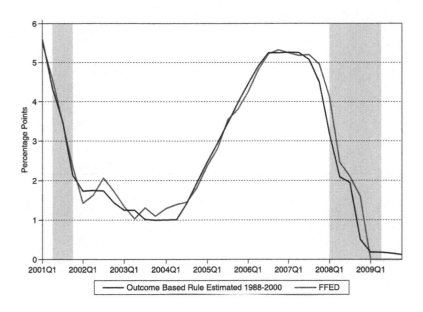

FIGURE 2.11. Outcome-based rule estimate and actual Fed funds rate

Source: Author's calculations

(Staff of the Federal Reserve Board of Governors 2006)), which describes Fed behavior rather well. This rule is given by

$$f_t = 1.16 + 1.13 f_{t-1} - 0.34 f_{t-2} + .21(0.56 + 1.68\, n_t^{avg} + 3.08\, Gap_t - 2.17\, Gap_{t-1})$$

where n_t^{avg} is a four-quarter average of core PCE inflation and Gap is an output gap measure constructed by staff at the Board of Governors. Both measures are "nowcasts" of the current quarter and are subject to revision. The coefficients in the rule are obtained by estimating the rule over the period 1988–2000 using real-time data. Figure 2.11 indicates the actual funds rate and the out-of-sample predicted funds rate that would have been prescribed by the rule over the period 2001–2009.[16]

16. I stop the exercise in 2009, because the output gap measures are classified after that date.

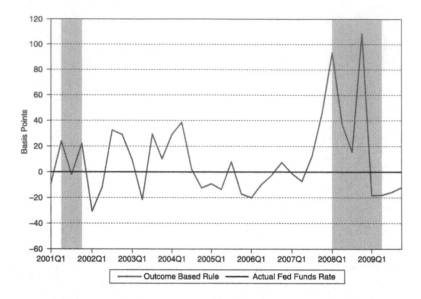

FIGURE 2.12. Difference of outcome-based rule and actual Fed funds rate
Source: Author's calculations

Thus, past Fed behavior is a good guide to current behavior and, with the exception of 2008 and 2009, when the inertial characteristics of the rule implied a slightly delayed reduction in the funds rate by about a quarter, there are no significant discrepancies between what the Fed did and what the rule prescribed. Indeed, figure 2.12 indicates that it is rare to find discrepancies greater than twenty basis points, and I doubt it would have been difficult for the Fed to defend its somewhat more aggressive response to the recession than was implied by the rule.

It is also important to ascertain whether actual policy resulted in significant welfare losses. I do so by looking at two loss functions. The first is the typical equally weighted quadratic loss function over inflation deviations from target and the output gap, $L_t = (n_t-2)^2 + (Gap_t)^2$. It is doubtful that this loss function corresponds to any actual welfare-based measure, but it is often used when analyzing the effects of policy. The other is a loss function derived from the basic New Keynesian model in Walsh (2005) and is given by $L_t = [(n_t-2) - .5(n_{t-1}-2)] + .048(Gap_t)^2$. From the evidence displayed in figure 2.13, there do not appear to be severe welfare consequences attached to the conduct of monetary policy. Also, the correlation between the absolute difference of policy from the reference rule and welfare losses is quite small, indicating that small deviations from the rule do not have any appreciable systematic effects on welfare.

An important caveat is that loss functions are model-specific, so that the exercise fails to confront issues dealing with robustness. However, the analysis presented in this section indicates that the proposed legislation is trying to fix a nonexistent problem. The unprecedented oversight embodied in the legislation would likely

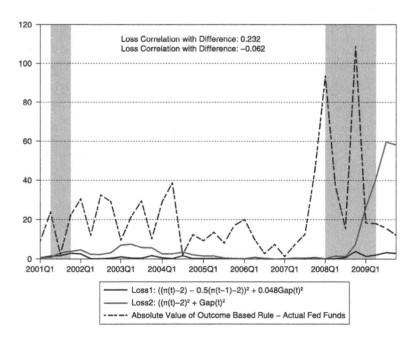

FIGURE 2.13. Loss functions and difference of outcome-based rule and actual Fed funds rate

Source: Author's calculations

have unintended consequences of significantly politicizing monetary policy, indicating that this bill is probably a bad idea.

Why monitor?

Monitoring independent agencies is, however, not in general a bad idea. The potential benefits with respect to monetary policy are discussed in Walsh (2015) and Ilbas, Roisland, and Sveen (2012). Monitoring can actually reduce political pressure when the policy goal is clearly articulated, such as a specific inflation target. Having the target monitored gives it more substance and makes it less likely to be temporarily abandoned. It also reduces the pressure to attempt economically infeasible things such as lowering the unemployment rate persistently below its natural rate, which would result in target misses. Both of these monitoring issues, however, deal with ultimate goals rather than instrument monitoring. Instrument monitoring, though, can potentially help alleviate the time inconsistency problem policymakers face and thus make economic stabilization more efficient. Walsh shows that if one knows the exact economic model and there are no measurement issues concerning the data, then both goal- and instrument-based monitoring can be useful. An important assumption is that the model-based output gap is used in the rule. If, instead, one replaces the model-based gap with a purely statistical gap, then generally it is not beneficial to employ instrument monitoring. Also, once it is the model-based gap that is appropriate, robustness issues certainly come to the fore. In practice, we have little idea of what the correct model is and hence what the optimal rule looks like. Further, the analysis of Giannoni and Woodford (2002) indicates that it is likely to be quite complex. The optimal rule is model-dependent and the profession is far from having a representative model.

The robustness issue is taken up in Ilbas, Roisland, and Sveen (2012), who abstract from political pressure effects that are dealt with in Walsh (2015). They use three models in their analysis: Smets and Wouters (2003) is the benchmark model, and the models of Fuhrer and Moore (1995) and Rudebusch and Svensson (1999) are the alternative models. The intuition behind looking at instrument monitoring using a simple rule is that although the simple rule may not be optimal in any particular model, it may have good properties across models. Rule-based guidance may then be helpful, and they implement this guidance by attaching deviations from the rule to the loss function. Their analysis points to benefits of benchmarking policy with simple rules, but does not imply a mechanistic adherence to the rule.

The role of monetary policy reports

That last conclusion points to the usefulness of monetary policy reports, many of which do exactly what Ilbas et al. prescribe. The benchmarking of policy to simple rules can provide a platform by which to judge policy. It forces the policymaker to communicate reasons for deviating and helps clarify the concerns that are influencing policy. Such exercises improve transparency and help align the public's expectations with those of the policymaker. Doing so has been widely shown to improve the efficiency of policy as well as economic welfare. Further, talk is not cheap, and the guidance provided by such reports helps alleviate concerns associated with time inconsistency problems. Requiring regular, detailed reports would represent a more beneficial approach to congressional oversight than a bill that overemphasizes the interest rate outcomes derived from any particular rule. Requiring such reports would also be consistent with practices followed by many of the world's central banks.

Conclusion

To briefly conclude, the monitoring called for in the Federal Reserve Accountability and Transparency Act is ill-conceived, bringing additional political pressure to a nonexistent problem. Past FOMC behavior has been quite systematic, and it has largely achieved the goals set forth in the Federal Reserve's dual mandate. While monitoring per se is potentially beneficial, the conditions for this type of monitoring to be desirable are simply not in evidence. A better idea might be to require a more detailed monetary policy report or to perhaps do nothing at all.

GENERAL DISCUSSION

JOHN TAYLOR: This is a point of clarification for David and Mike. Could one of you explain why Mike gets such different results from David in terms of compliance?

DAVID PAPELL: It's the difference between inertial rules and non-inertial rules.

TAYLOR: That is what I thought. If you put in a lagged dependent variable, as for an inertial rule, you're basically saying: We're going to continue what we are doing even if it's a mistake. You can't distinguish between lagged dependent variables and serially correlated errors. We know that from years and years of experience. So by putting a lagged dependent variable in, you're effectively saying where we are now is good, and so if we move a little bit away from that, it's still pretty good even though it may be very bad based on the rule without inertia. I'm not saying which is right or wrong, but that's the reason for the difference.

MICHAEL DOTSEY: I think that in a lot of these models, the optimal rule that would come out would have inertia in it. That's not something that's unusual to find. Because like in Woodford and Giannoni where they sort of find out what is the optimal rule which depends on state variables, and then say: How do we translate that rule and decentralize it into a rule based on inflation and output gaps? They get a fairly complicated rule that depends on lags of the interest rate and other variables—

TAYLOR: The estimated ones?

DOTSEY: No, no. Out of the model-based rules it said the Fed should be doing something quite inertial, looking at more than just contemporaneous variables.

ANDREW LEVIN: The big issue is to control for the size of the deviations when you are using the different approaches. As long as the process is stationary, you're never going to get a 2 percent deviation with a lagged coefficient, because the Fed never does a surprise move of 2 percentage points.

PAPELL: There are two big issues. One issue is the size of the deviations. We know inertial rules fit better than non-inertial rules. We know if you stick in two lagged interest rates you can fit in better than one lagged interest rate. A year ago, when we gave our paper here, the first idea that we had was to look at deviations from a wide variety of policy rules. We looked at the five rules that John looked at in the 1999 book. Three of them were inertial rules and two were non-inertial rules. If you try to look at deviations from the inertial rules with these postulated coefficients and try to statistically relate this to rules-based or discretionary periods, you got absolutely nothing. There was no relation in the sense that, when we tried to use that and look at periods of good and bad performance, we found nothing. So I don't think it's just the size of the coefficient. If it was just the size of the coefficient, then we could do fifty basis points instead of two hundred basis points, and it would be no problem. It's that the inertial rules don't give you the kind of differentiation that the non-inertial rules do.

LEVIN: I'd like to clarify a couple things about outcome-based rules, partly because I worked with Alejandro Justiniano on the estimation of the Fed's outcome-based rule. All of the relevant information about that rule is publicly available, because the rule was developed in 2004 and updated in 2005 and 2006, and those FOMC documents have been in the public domain for the past few years. I will say simply that this rule was obtained via data-fitting rather than out-of-sample forecast analysis. In developing the rule, Alejandro spent a lot of time analyzing model selection criteria like AIC and BIC to determine how many lags should be included and how much extra parameters should be penalized. But the basic purpose of the exercise was to find an outcome-based rule that fit the actual federal funds rate reasonably well over the period from 1987 to about 2005 or 2006. It's worth noting, by the way, that the fitted rule has two lags of the federal funds rate as well as current and lagged values of the output gap. And I'm sure that Alejandro will be glad to hear that you think he did a good job. [Laughter.]

DOTSEY: I would say that would be the reference that you would sort of use.

LEVIN: My guess is the spirit of what the people in Congress are thinking of, and what John Taylor has proposed in some of his op-eds, isn't about what sorts of fancy econometrics can be done to provide the best *ex post* fit to the data. Rather, the intent would be to identify specific policy rules that seem to work reasonably well, and then economists can assess those rules using out-of-sample forecasts and model evaluations. That's a little bit closer, I think, to what David Papell is trying to do. I wouldn't say that you should rule out the possibility of including an inertial component, as John Williams and Athanasios Orphanides studied in their work and that also showed up in some of our joint papers. Interest rate smoothing has an element of replicating commitment-type solutions, and so that should certainly be considered in designing benchmark rules.

Now leaving all of that aside, the fundamental issue here is transparency. The Federal Reserve itself has already been using policy rules for many, many years in its internal deliberations. So I frankly don't see any reason why those rules can't be included in quarterly monetary policy reports or other types of Fed communications to help the public and elected officials get a better understanding of how the FOMC is reaching its decisions. And if policymakers have been using a particular rule for a while, and decide that its coefficients should be adjusted or that the rule simply isn't useful anymore, then they can just explain that.

Furthermore, as John Taylor and I have discussed on various occasions, there doesn't necessarily have to be just one single rule. It might well be a reasonable approach to have two or three different reference rules. And that could be a key part of the solution for addressing some of the perennial questions about how to formulate and utilize simple benchmark rules. For example, it seems pointless to debate whether a given rule should utilize CPI or core CPI or PCE or core PCE. After all, in assessing the appropriate policy stance, the Fed is trying to determine what's the underlying trend of inflation. And at certain points in time a movement in the CPI that is obviously transitory may be absent from other inflation measures such as core PCE. On the other hand, there are times when the overall CPI is starting to move and it's evident that other measures such as core PCE are going to catch up. Thus, it's simply not the case that any single inflation measure is always best while all of the other measures are deficient. Consequently, there's no reason why policymakers can't refer to several alternative benchmark rules with different measures of inflation in explaining the rationale for their policy decision. For example, they might say, "We're putting a little bit more weight on this particular rule right now, because we think that the movement of food and energy prices is an important part of the inflation pressures that we're seeing and hence merits a policy response." And isn't that essentially in the spirit of what John Taylor has been advocating?

TAYLOR: Yes.

JOHN WILLIAMS: I think I'm going to pick up on some of what Mike and what Andy have already said. This could sound like a technical point, but I actually think it is a deeper point for thinking about rule-based accountability, and that is that a lot of models that we use, I would say the vast majority of models we use for monetary policy analysis, do have this implication that you want to have inertia in your policy, that you do want to have the lagged interest rate in the rule, basically, as Andy said, a link to basically achieving more of a commitment-like equilibrium. This has implications for when you think about the issue of how you hold the central bank accountable. Are you following the rule? Are you acting in a systematic basis? In assuming the rule were designed to be something close to welfare-maximizing, you would have this problem that Mike and this discussion were highlighting, that you would basically be saying, "I've got a lagged interest rate here, it looks like it's great." And it would be very hard in practice if you were following the optimal policy rule to distinguish between sins and saint-like behavior. I mean it could be the fact that the lagged interest rate is a very powerful state variable for good theoretical reasons. Or it could be that you're just carrying the mistakes from the past. So I just think that even if I'm describing it in a rather technical way, I think that when you think about what we know from optimal monetary policy, we would face this problem in actually trying to hold the central bank accountable, because it's really hard to distinguish between optimal monetary policy by looking at the action and something that would really just be carrying the past mistakes forward.

One thing I just want to say in David's paper, which I did find interesting and educational, is it kind of makes me nervous about this whole Taylor rule-ology. This is like Kremlinology, where we're looking at pictures and trying to figure out the patterns, and what were people really thinking. And what does this mean? And since I'm on the panel, I'll hold my comments to later about some of the issues around trying to use compliance to a policy rule as the best way to measure your thinking, your analysis, your decision-making, and come back to something I'm sure Paul will have a view on and maybe many others about the difference between that and having a goal as really basically what you're being held accountable to. And basically, trying to make the best policies to reach that.

But going back to that issue, the issue that Mike and Andy and really everyone was talking about is a problem you're going to face if you try to hold a central bank accountable to an interest rate rule, and that interest rate rule has a lot of inertia in it. Thanks.

CHARLES PLOSSER: I just want to follow up on some of Andy's comments. At this conference last year, I proposed, and have continued to advocate, exactly what Andy's been talking about. It is a way for the Fed and the FOMC to usefully proceed. The staff regularly prepares estimates of various rules and their implications for the path of economic activity. From my perspective, the actual conversation around those is not as useful or as helpful as it could be, even within the meetings. But they could usefully be part of publicly available information that is reported in a monetary policy report. The FOMC would be expected to talk about its policy choices in the context of perhaps several reference rules that are widely discussed in the academic literature and thought to be robust. I think that that would change the tone of the conversation and improve the communication of a monetary policy strategy. It would also force the committee to explain itself in the context of benchmarks or guidelines, whether the rules have a lot of inertia or not. Being more transparent through the publication of such an analysis, the committee would enhance its communication through a coherent and systematic discussion of why it chooses its policy at any point in time. Mike Dotsey and I, along with the research staff at the Federal Reserve Bank of Philadelphia, have worked on examples of how one might write a monetary policy report, or at least this section of a monetary policy report that tries to do exactly such an exercise.

So I think at the end of the day this is about communication and accountability, and not necessarily toward the specification of a specific rule, but accountability and a commitment to a framework that forces the committee to talk in a particular way about monetary policy strategy.

Economists almost always model monetary policy as rule-like or systematic. Most forecasting models assume such behavior as well. Yet policymaking remains highly discretionary and, as a result, it is difficult to communicate and highly unpredictable. The approach I've advocated forces the committee to be less discretionary, or at least justify its discretion in the context of a much more coherent and systematic framework. I think that's the power and value of this, and this is exactly what I talked about at the conference last year.

CARL WALSH: I think there are at least three different interpretations or rules at play in policy discussions that have come up here. One is what Charlie just articulated; that it is useful for internal discussions at the policymaking decision stage. And because forecasts are necessary for policy actions, we can't do forecasts unless we forecast what the central bank is going to do. So we can't construct forecasts without implicitly using some sort of rule, and using a variety of rules and seeing what their implications are for outcomes seems very important for the policy discussion.

Rules can also be important for helping the public predict what monetary policy is going to do. And so some central banks provide forecasts of their policy rate as part of the process of being transparent and helping the public understand where policy is going. Here, it seems like the presence of multiple policy rules makes that more difficult. In some sense you have to reach a consensus on what rule is going to be used to describe future policy.

And then the third role, which is probably more closely tied to the accountability aspect, is the role of a rule to potentially restrict policy discretion, that is, to restrict the flexibility of the central bank. And here I think there's a potential problem with having aspects of the rule determined by the central bank itself. We have the experience of monetary targeting in the US, where

Congress mandated that the Federal Reserve establish targets for monetary aggregates, and the Fed produced multiple targets for multiple monetary aggregates. The criticism was that there was always at least one monetary aggregate that came in on target. And so it really didn't serve much of a role for promoting accountability. And then on top of that, there was lots of criticism of the Fed for employing base drift in which it just re-benched the level of the money supply to incorporate any past target misses. So in some sense the accountability aspect is served more strongly if the reference rule, in some sense, is specified outside the central bank.

Now the parallel with inflation targeting is we have many inflation-targeting countries where the government sets the inflation target, which always seemed to me more consistent with the issues of democracy, the role of elected officials, and then the role of the central bank in implementing the policy. In some countries, the central bank defines the inflation target, and that seems more problematic on many dimensions. I think you may have some of the same aspects with respect to a rule if the rule is to serve as a measure of accountability, versus whether it's something to help guide policy and used to help explain policy to the public.

PETER FISHER: Yes, just some observations to provoke people. I was responsible for seven years for what was, in effect, an experiment in rules versus discretion. As head of fixed income at BlackRock, where we managed a trillion dollars of other people's money, we had quantitative investment teams who tended to follow rules, and we had traditional fund managers who had few rules and more discretion. So we had rule-based teams and discretionary teams, and I was responsible for all of their performance. My conclusion on rules versus discretion is that there are two types of errors. There's the type one error of too much change, of time inconsistency, whatever you want to call it. And the type two error is of too little change, of overconfidence, of too much time consistency. Discretionary fund management teams are capable of both types of errors. The quantitative, rule-based teams tend not to commit the type one error of too much change, of time inconsistency but they are prone to the type two error of overconfidence, of too much time consistency. Reducing type one errors is essentially the gain you get from having rules over discretion. I think that's consistent with what John was saying a moment ago.

The other thing now I want to put on the table in this context, just as a challenge, is the challenge of what transparency of decision-making does to the role of expectations in monetary policy. I find this actually the most problematic aspect of the last decade, that if we never change the market's expectations, that if we so thoroughly have embedded in the market a view of where the forward curve is headed, that when the committee meets and opines, expectations never change, so what's monetary policy doing? And I state that as a dilemma, not as an end in itself, but as a point of departure. And my own view is that the episode of '04–'06 was significantly one in which the committee congratulated itself for never changing the forward curve when it announced decisions. That's another challenge to this question of how much disclosure to give to decision rules. I'm a fan of transparency but I also think that transmission mechanism is about changing expectations. And if we denude ourselves of too much influence over expectations, I'm not sure where we've left monetary policy.

PAUL TUCKER: There are two things I want to bring into the discussion that haven't been present so far. I do not favor at all goal independence. I think it's wrong in a democracy where we expect our elected representatives to make decisions about objectives and values, after public debate. And secondly I think it's absolutely imperative that what I call *operating principles* disclose how an unelected agent is operating a systematic policy. Those two points are in the background to what I want to add to the discussion.

The first thing that I think hasn't been brought to the table is that there is a big, deep question about putting a precise rule— and this isn't just about John's rule, but any old rule—in legislation, because it makes it justiciable. And the one thing that I will assert is that to the extent that there's a democratic deficit inherent in an unelected central bank, it cannot be repaired by unelected Supreme Court justices. Often, legal scholars in the United States will talk about agencies being *accountable* or *overseen* by the courts. But a thought experiment about central banks absolutely blows that out of the water. The idea that the part of the educated elite who studied law can heal the democratic deficit inherent in the policymaking by the part of the educated elite who studied economics misses the point of democracy. So I think while we certainly need something that makes the Fed, the Bank of England, the European Central Bank, and their peers disclose how their policy is systematic and binds them to a systematic policy, I wouldn't want to do that in a way where it gets played out in the Supreme Court. That doesn't mean that nothing should be under the law. It's a question about *what* should go into the law.

The second consideration that hasn't been picked up yet is about the role of committees, and we will of course come back to that later on with Kevin's paper. If the purpose of delegation is to insulate policy, with a clear goal, from day-to-day politics, then we should be against delegating these powers to one person, either de jure or, just as importantly, de facto. There is no way the Bank of England would have got monetary independence in 1997 had there not been a requirement for decisions being taken on a truly one person-one vote basis. Eddie George's greatest gift to UK monetary policy was and remains that. Even though he was a tremendously dominant man, he ensured as chair that it really was one person-one vote. And Mervyn King sustained that, and indeed allowed himself to go into the minority on many occasions, including Charlie Bean and I voting on more than one occasion to leave him in the minority. And that did not diminish Mervyn's authority. What I am describing was what really strengthened the monetary policy debate in the UK in a way that Kevin will talk about this afternoon.

That is background to the question or dilemma I want to pose. If a regime truly involves one person-one vote, rather than mechanisms for trimming the chair, how can the committee commit itself to a particular systematic policy? Reconciling those two desiderata is not easy. This amounts to asking whether a systematic policy determined by just one person is better or worse than a true one person-one vote system. I think the solution has to involve a democratic committee having processes that harness centripetal and well as centrifugal forces. As I saw it, the Bank of England has since 1997 aimed to do that through its process for producing a collective forecast of the outlook for inflation.

JOHN COCHRANE: There are two important points we haven't talked about. First: what is the nature of the rules, once we start putting in lags and other variables? Suppose that we get a regression that fits with 100 percent R squared, with lots of lags and extra variables. We don't want to put that rule into legislation going forward, though. Doing so would enshrine that the Fed's rule from the last fifty years was optimal. The whole point of this exercise it that maybe the Fed didn't do everything perfectly. So regression fit is not at all a good measure of a desirable rule.

That point holds especially for the lags. It is natural to summarize a rule by saying, "Here's where we think interest rates should be, as a function of inflation and unemployment. We'll get there slowly." Almost all policy consists of a target and then gradual adjustment. The point here is to find the target, and much less to prescribe the adjustment process.

Second, a key aspect of a rule is what variables are excluded, not just what variables are included. A rule that directs the Fed to respond to inflation and unemployment by implication tells the Fed to ignore exchange rates, house prices, stock prices, bond prices, credit spreads, "credit availability," and the cries of a long string of interest groups that would like the Fed to intervene in one market or another. A key aspect of an independent bank is a restriction on its responsibilities and tools. No, you can't drop money from helicopters, you can only lend, to banks, and on good collateral. We should pay more attention not just to the Fed's unemployment and inflation responses, but call it to task for its increasing willingness to try to manage and respond to all sorts of other variables.

TAYLOR: Let me just say that what David and also Carl Walsh have done in the papers for this conference is very constructive. They've taken actual legislative proposals and analyzed them rigorously. I agree that the idea that you can justify anything you want is worrisome. But with accountability, one remedy to that—as David shows—is that even if you can justify what you're doing today with some argument, that same approach is not likely to work next time. And so you can look like you're slipping from one argument to another all the time, which raises a lot of credibility issues.

Regarding the issue that it is hard for a large number of policymakers on the FOMC or any other monetary policy committee to be involved in a decision about a strategy for the policy instruments, history shows that the Fed figured that out with the money growth targeting when they were required to do so. They decided on a range for several different aggregates. As you know, Congress took those requirements out of the law in 2000, and didn't replace them with anything. So I think that such reporting requirements can work. It's not impossible. You might want to have a range of rules.

And more generally—this is something I picked up from George Shultz—it's really a strategy we're talking about. What's the Fed's strategy? There are many organizations that benefit from having a strategy. And sometimes they do it better, and sometimes they do it worse. But having a strategy is what we're trying to get at here. And mathematical formulas are perhaps not always the best way to describe a strategy. The legislation doesn't have to have a specific reference rule. The Senate version of the policy rules bill doesn't have that, and some people prefer that.

REFERENCES

Appelbaum, Binyamin. 2014. "Yellen Says Restraining the Fed's Oversight Would be a 'Grave Mistake.'" *New York Times,* July 16.

Bai, Jushan, and Pierre Perron. 1998. "Estimating and Testing Linear Models with Multiple Structural Changes." *Econometrica* 66: 47–78.

Bernanke, Ben. 2010. "Monetary Policy and the Housing Bubble." Speech delivered at the American Economic Association meeting, Atlanta, Georgia, January 3.

Blinder, Alan. 2014. "An Unnecessary Fix for the Fed." *Wall Street Journal,* July 17.

Croushore, Dean, and Tom Stark. 2001. "A Real-Time Data Set for Macroeconomists." *Journal of Econometrics* 105 (November): 111–130.

Dokko, Jane, Brian Doyle, Michael Kiley, Jinill Kim, Shane Sherlund, Jae Sim, and Skander Van den Heuvel. 2009. "Monetary Policy and the Housing Bubble." Unpublished. Federal Reserve Board.

Fuhrer, Jeff C., and George Moore. 1995. "Inflation Persistence." *Quarterly Journal of Economics* 110, no. 1: 127–159.

Giannoni, Marc P., and Michael Woodford. 2003. "Optimal Inflation Targeting Rules." NBER working paper no. 9939, August.

Giannoni, Marc P., and Michael Woodford. 2002. "Optimal Interest Rate Rules: II. Applications." NBER working paper no. 9420, December.

Ilbas, Pelin, Oistein Roisland, and Tommy Sveen. 2012. "Robustifying Optimal Monetary Policy Using Simple Rules as Cross-Checks." Norges Bank research working paper no. 2012–22, December 17.

Koenig, Evan. 2004. "Monetary Policy Prospects." *Economic and Financial Policy Review* 3, no. 2, Federal Reserve Bank of Dallas: 1–16.

Kohn, Donald L. 2007. "John Taylor Rules." *BIS Review* 116:1–7.

Laubach, Thomas, and John Williams. 2003. "Measuring the Natural Rate of Interest." *Review of Economics and Statistics* 85, no. 4 (November): 1063–1070.

Levin, Andrew, Volker Wieland, and John Williams. 1999. "Robustness of Simple Monetary Policy Rules under Model Uncertainty." In *Monetary Policy Rules*. Edited by John Taylor. Chicago: University of Chicago Press: 263–299.

Meltzer, Allan. 2009. *A History of the Federal Reserve, Vol. 2*. Chicago: University of Chicago Press.

Monetary Policy. 2012. Proceedings of FRB of Kansas City Symposium. Jackson Hole, Wyoming, September: 463–76.

Nikolsko-Rzhevskyy, Alex, and David Papell. 2012. "Taylor Rules and the Great Inflation." *Journal of Macroeconomics* 34, no. 4: 903–918.

Nikolsko-Rzhevskyy, Alex, and David Papell. 2015. "Real-Time Historical Analysis of Monetary Policy Rules." Unpublished. University of Houston.

Nikolsko-Rzhevskyy, Alex, David Papell, and Ruxandra Prodan. 2014. "Deviations from Rules-Based Policy and Their Effects." *Journal of Economic Dynamics and Control* 49: 4–18.

Nikolsko-Rzhevskyy, Alex, David H. Papell, and Ruxandra Prodan. 2015. "Policy Rule Legislation in Practice." Manuscript.

Orphanides, Athanasios. 2001. "Monetary Policy Rules Based on Real-Time Data." *American Economic Review* 91, no. 4 (September): 964–985.

Perron, Pierre, and Zhongjun Qu. 2006. "Estimating restricted structural change models." *Journal of Econometrics* 134, no. 2: 373–399.

Poole, William. 2007. "Understanding the Fed." Federal Reserve Bank of St. Louis *Review*, 89, no. 1 (January/February): 3–4.

Rudebusch, Glenn. 2010. "The Fed's Exit Strategy for Monetary Policy." Federal Reserve Bank of San Francisco *Economic Letter*, June 14.

Rudebusch, Glenn D., and Lars E.O. Svensson. 1999. "Policy Rules for Inflation Targeting." In *Monetary Policy Rules*. Edited by John Taylor. Chicago: University of Chicago Press: 203–253.

Smets, Frank, and Raf Wouters. 2003. "An Estimated Dynamic Stochastic General Equilibrium Model of the Euro Area." *Journal of the European Economic Association* 1, no. 5: 1123–1175.

Staff of the Federal Reserve Board of Governors. 2006. "Monetary Policy Alternatives." January.

Taylor, John B. 1993. "Discretion versus Policy Rules in Practice." *Carnegie Rochester Conference Series on Public Policy* 39: 195–214.

Taylor, John B. 1999. "A Historical Analysis of Monetary Policy Rules." In *Monetary Policy Rules*. Edited by John Taylor. Chicago: University of Chicago Press: 319–348.

Taylor, John B. 2007. "Housing and Monetary Policy." In *Housing, Housing Finance, and Monetary Policy*. Proceedings of FRB of Kansas City Symposium. Jackson Hole, Wyoming, September: 463–76.

Taylor, John B. 2011. "Legislating a Rule for Monetary Policy." *Cato Journal* 31, no. 3: 407–415.

Taylor, John B. 2012. "Monetary Policy Rules Work and Discretion Doesn't: A Tale of Two Eras." *Journal of Money, Credit, & Banking* 44, no. 6: 1017–1032.

Taylor, John B. 2015a. "A Feature Not a Bug in the Policy Rules Bill." *Economics One* (blog), February 24.

Taylor, John B. 2015b. "Requirements for the Fed to Describe Its Strategy." Testimony before the Senate Banking Committee. March 3.

Taylor, John B. 2015c. "Witness Allan Meltzer and the Ouija Board Analogy." *Economics One* (blog), March 10.

Taylor, John B. 2015d. "The Senate Moves Ahead on a Policy Rules Bill." *Economics One* (blog), May 12.

Walsh, Carl E. 2005. "Endogenous Objectives and the Evaluation of Targeting Rules for Monetary Policy." *Journal of Monetary Economics* 52: 880–911.

Walsh, Carl E. 2015. "Goals and Rules in Central Bank Design." CESifo working paper no. 5293, April.

Williams, John. 2015. "The Decline in the Natural Rate of Interest." Federal Reserve Bank of San Francisco, March 2.

Wu, Jing Cynthia, and Fan Dora Xia. Forthcoming. "Measuring the Macroeconomic Impact of Monetary Policy at the Zero Lower Bound." *Journal of Money, Credit, & Banking*.

Yellen, Janet. 2012. "Perspectives on Monetary Policy." Speech at the Boston Economic Club Dinner, June 6.

Yellen, Janet. 2015. "Normalizing Monetary Policy: Prospects and Perspectives." Remarks at the Federal Reserve Bank of San Francisco, March 27.

CHAPTER THREE

Goals versus Rules as Central Bank Performance Measures

Carl E. Walsh

On December 20, 1989, the New Zealand Parliament gave unanimous approval to the Reserve Bank of New Zealand Act of 1989, thereby formally inaugurating the world's first inflation-targeting regime. The Act also launched a global wave of central bank reforms that have clarified the policy responsibilities of central banks, increased their independence, and provided clear measures of accountability against which their performance could be judged. These reforms have also promoted a greater level of transparency, transforming the way many central banks communicate their policy decisions and signal their future policy intentions. In general, accountability in inflation-targeting regimes is strengthened by the public nature of the announced target and by the requirement that the central bank produce inflation reports or otherwise explain policy actions and their consistency with the announced target. Achieving the target becomes a measure of the central bank's performance.

A central bank's performance measure—the observable variable (or variables) by which the public and elected officials can judge

This chapter is based on C. E. Walsh, "Goals and Rules in Central Bank Design," *International Journal of Central Banking*, September 2015, from which three sections are reprinted. I would like to thank participants at the Reserve Bank of New Zealand and International Journal of Central Banking Conference, "Reflections on 25 Years of Inflation Targeting," Wellington, New Zealand, December 1–2, 2014, and the Central Bank Governance and Oversight Reform Policy Conference at the Hoover Institution, May 15, 2015, as well as seminar participants at the Norges Bank, for their comments and suggestions.

whether the central bank has acted in a manner consistent with its charter—does not need to be based on an ultimate goal of monetary policy such as inflation. A central bank could be assigned and held accountable for achieving targets that are not themselves among the final goals of monetary policy. For example, in the 1970s, the US Congress required the Federal Reserve to establish target growth rates for the money supply. Money growth rates are intermediate targets, neither an ultimate goal of policy nor something directly controlled as an instrument.

Another alternative would be to judge the central bank's performance by comparing the central bank's instrument to the value prescribed by a legislated instrument rule. In fact, the US House of Representatives and Senate have recently held hearings on bills that would establish an interest rate rule, with the Fed required to justify deviations of the federal funds rate from the rule.[1] The rule plays the role of the central bank's performance measure. Taylor (2012) illustrates how an instrument rule can be used to assess *ex post* the Federal Reserve's policy.

Performance measures can differ, therefore, in terms of whether they focus on ultimate goals of macroeconomic policy while allowing for instrument independence, as is the case with inflation targeting, or whether they limit the instrument independence of the central bank, as would be the case with a legislated instrument rule. Both inflation targeting and other goal-based regimes such as price-level targeting, speed limit policies, and nominal income targeting frameworks have been extensively analyzed in the litera-

---

1. Hearings were held in July 2014. According to the *Financial Times* report on Janet Yellen's February 25, 2015, testimony before the US House Banking Committee, "the Fed chair swatted down calls from Republicans for the institution to be subject to mechanical rate-setting rules, saying she did not want its discretion to be 'chained.'" See Sam Fleming, "Janet Yellen defends US central bank independence," *Financial Times*, Feb. 15, 2015. See also John Taylor's recent testimony before the House Subcommittee on Financial Services (July 22, 2015) in support of a rule-based strategy.

ture.[2] However, a similar analysis of regimes that base account-ability on adherence to an instrument rule is absent from the lit-erature, a gap the present paper seeks to fill.

Of course, there is a huge literature that studies the role of Tay-lor rules, and variants of Taylor's original rule have become a stan-dard method of specifying monetary policy in both theoretical and empirical models. Simple rules have played a large role in the literature on policy robustness (e.g., Levin and Williams 2003 and Taylor and Williams 2010). Ilbas, Røisland, and Sveen (2012) con-sider model uncertainty and show that including deviations of the policy rate from a simple rule can improve macroeconomic out-comes, allowing the central bank to cross-check its policy against a rule that is potentially robust across a variety of different models. However, they ignore any distortions to the central bank's objec-tives over inflation and the output gap that might arise from politi-cal pressures on monetary policy. These distortions play a central role in my analysis, while I ignore model uncertainty.

Tillmann (2012) is closest to the present paper in that he consid-ers outcomes under discretion when the central bank minimizes a loss function that differs from social loss by the addition of a term reflecting deviations of the policy rate from the rate implied by a simple Taylor-type rule.[3] He finds that some weight should be placed on this new term when inflation shocks are serially cor-related, a result similar to that of Clarida, Galí, and Gertler (1999),

2. To cite just three examples, Vestin (2006) provides an early analysis of price-level target-ing; Walsh (2003b) compares price level targeting, output gap growth rate (speed-limit) policies, and nominal income policies; and Billi (2013) studies nominal income policies in the face of the zero lower bound on nominal interest rates.

3. The monetary policy loss function incorporated into the Norges Bank's DSGE model (N.E.M.O.) actually includes a term of the form $(i_t - i_t^*)^2$ that penalizes deviations of i_t from a reference interest rate i_t^*. Previous versions of N.E.M.O. set i_t^* equal to the value given by a simple instrument rule. Currently i_t^* is equal to the "normal" nominal interest rate, defined as the rate consistent with inflation equal to target and a zero output gap. This term is intended to add an implicit weight on financial imbalances in policy determination. See Lund and Robstad (2012) and Evjen and Kloster (2012).

who found a role for a Rogoff conservative central banker in a new Keynesian model only when inflation shocks were serially correlated. Walsh (2003a) shows that it can be optimal to place additional weight on inflation even when shocks are serially uncorrelated in the face of political distortions that cause the central bank's objectives to differ from those of society. These distortions generate a rationale for performance measures that is absent from the work of Tillmann (2012).

The rest of the paper is organized as follows. The section on Goals, Rules, Independence, and Accountability discusses the distinction between goal-based and rule-based performance measures. An important distinction that arises is whether central bank reform is designed to constrain the central bank or to constrain the government. In the section on The Performance of Goal-Based and Rule-Based Regimes, I employ a simple model to compare two forms of reform. The first (and standard) approach emphasizes the assignment of an inflation goal; the second approach uses an instrument rule to assess the central bank's performance. The simple model allows analytic results to be derived. To evaluate the alternatives in a more realistic setting, an estimated model incorporating sticky wages and sticky prices is used in the section on Goals and Rules in an Estimated Model with Sticky Prices and Wages. The final section includes Extensions and Conclusions.

Goals, Rules, Independence, and Accountability

Central bank reforms over the past twenty-five years have been aimed at removing, or at least reducing, causes of poor monetary policy outcomes. Three causes of poor policy have been emphasized in the literature. First, short-term political pressures, often related to a country's election cycle, can distort policy decisions, resulting in an emphasis on near-term economic activity at the cost of longer-term objectives. Given that monetary policy operates with long lags, a central bank buffeted by short-term political pressures might have difficulty in achieving longer-term objectives, including low and stable inflation. And, if monetary policy has its primary effects on inflation through its influence on real economic activity, expansionary policies would first produce an economic boom, with inflation coming only later. This potentially creates an incentive for politicians to pressure central banks for expansionary policies timed to election cycles; a boom leading up to an election would benefit incumbents, while the inflationary costs would only be incurred later.[4] Such pressures would be incompatible with maintaining low and stable inflation.

Second, real economic distortions cause inefficiencies that can create a systematic bias toward expansionary policies. For example, in standard new Keynesian models, monopolistic competition in goods and/or labor markets means the economy's level of economic activity in a zero-inflation environment is too low relative to its efficient level. While monetary policy can attempt to close this gap in the short run by deviating from a policy of price stability, it cannot systematically and sustainably close it. Attempts to do so will ultimately fail, leaving the economy with excessively volatile inflation. Distortions arising from real economic inefficiencies and those due to political pressures on central banks may be related; the presence of real distortions may explain why politicians seek to pressure central banks to engage in expansionary policies.

Third, even in the absence of political pressures or attempts to use monetary policy to achieve unachievable objectives, policymakers may lack the ability to commit credibly to future policies, leading to inefficient intertemporal policy responses to distortionary shocks. Distortions resulting from discretionary policy played a large role in the academic literature seeking to explain why

4. An extensive coverage of political business-cycle models can be found in Drazen (2000).

political pressures or the pursuit of unachievable objectives would lead to undesirably high inflation.[5] In the Barro-Gordon framework used to investigate the inflation bias of discretion, removing short-term political pressures and assigning achievable goals to the central bank also succeeded in eliminating the distortion due to discretion. However, in new Keynesian models, with their emphasis on forward-looking expectations, discretion continues to produce inefficient outcomes even in the absence of political pressures or unsustainable goals.

Given these three potential sources of policy distortions, what central banking reforms might lead to improved monetary policy outcomes? I focus on two alternatives, both of which can be viewed as establishing a performance measure for the central bank that is used to assess policy outcomes. Performance measures provide metrics based on observable variables for evaluating the central bank's policy choices.[6] The definition of the performance measure is an important aspect of central bank reform; it affects the central bank's incentives and provides the basis for ensuring accountability in the conduct of policy.

Inflation targeting is the primary example of a reform that establishes a performance measure based on an ultimate goal of policy. The second type of reform emphasizes rules, with adherence to a rule the basis for assessing the central bank's performance. In either case, the power of the performance measure indicates how important the measure is in the overall assessment of policy. For example, a strict inflation-targeting regime in which the central bank is instructed to care only about achieving the target is an example of a high-powered regime.

---

5. See chapter 7 of Walsh (2010) for a survey of the literature on the inflation bias resulting from discretionary policies in models based on the time-inconsistency of optimal policy analysis of Kydland and Prescott (1977) as applied to monetary policy in the framework of Barro and Gordon (1983). See also Cukierman (1992).

6. For the theory of performance measures, see Baker (1992), Baker, Gibbons, and Murphy (1994), and Frankel (2014).

The model of reform provided by the 1989 Reserve Bank of New Zealand Act and the associated Policy Targets Agreement between the central bank and the government was one that focused on an ultimate goal, a goal achievable by monetary policy. It essentially created a contract between the elected government and the central bank designed to affect the policy choices of the Reserve Bank by altering the incentives of both the government and the central bank.[7] Incentives were affected by publicly establishing a clear policy goal, assigning responsibility for achieving it to the Reserve Bank, and establishing a system of accountability based on the goal. The elected government could alter the bank's goal by changing the Policy Targets Agreement, but this had to be done in a public manner, and the government could not interfere in the implementation of monetary policy. The Act, together with the Policy Targets Agreement, created a performance measure for the Reserve Bank; it was to be evaluated on the basis of the consistency between its policy actions and the achievement of its inflation target.

The public nature of the goal helped insulate the central bank from political pressures; by granting the Reserve Bank a high level of instrument independence to implement policy, the Act further limited the scope for short-term political factors to influence policy decisions. Thus, a key characteristic of the reform was to constrain elected governments from influencing the implementation of monetary policy.[8]

While greater independence may shield monetary policy from political influences, it cannot ensure policy is only directed toward

---

7. Walsh (1995b) and Walsh (1995a).

8. Important papers on this relationship include Bade and Parkin (1984), Cukierman, Web, and Neyapti (1992), and Alesina and Summers (1993). See also Cukierman (1992). Criticism of the view that central bank independence is a solution to high inflation is provided by Posen (1993). The negative relationship between indexes of central bank independence and inflation held only for developed economies. Carlstrom and Fuerst (2009) find increases in central bank independence can account for two-thirds of the better inflation performance among industrialized economies over the past twenty years.

achieving obtainable goals. An independent monetary authority may still face a temptation to pursue unsustainable objectives if, for example, real distortions imply steady-state output is inefficiently low.[9] Thus, the reforms instituted in New Zealand focused on an achievable goal of monetary policy—inflation—while allowing the central bank the independence to achieve this goal. In the terminology of Debelle and Fischer (1994), the Act established a central bank that lacked goal independence but enjoyed instrument independence.

This type of reform—clear specification of goals together with greater central bank independence—became common during the 1990s.[10] Making the goals public helps to promote accountability, particularly if the central bank is assigned a single policy goal such as price stability or a target for inflation. Independence also has the potential to make the central bank less accountable, so Debelle and Fischer (1994) argued that independence needed to be limited and that independence to set instruments but not to define goals offered the best blueprint for central bank reform.

Central bank reforms emphasizing goals, instrument independence, and accountability are not the only shape reforms could have taken. An alternative could define performance measures that, unlike price stability, are not among the ultimate objectives of macroeconomic policy. For example, during the 1970s and 1980s, the role of intermediate targets in monetary policy implementation was widely discussed, and proposals for establishing target growth rates for various monetary aggregates were common. In 1975, a

9. The academic literature based on the model of Barro and Gordon (1983) generally did not distinguish between politically generated pressures for economic expansions and socially efficient but unsustainable attempts by the central bank to generate expansions. Both were captured by assuming that, even with flexible prices and wages, the economy's output would be below the desired level.

10. The movement of many central banks toward greater independence and transparency is discussed by Crowe and Meade (2007) and Blinder, Ehrmann, Fratzscher, De Haan, and Jansen (2008). See Dincer and Eichengreen (2014) for an updated measure of transparency that illustrates this trend.

US House of Representatives concurrent resolution called on the Federal Reserve to publicly announce monetary growth targets. The Full Employment Act of 1978 mandated publicly announced, annual growth targets for the money supply, and the Federal Reserve was required to report to Congress on its success in achieving the targets.[11] The Federal Reserve was assigned an objective— monetary growth targets—and in principle was held accountable for achieving these objectives, but the resulting targets were not among the ultimate goals of macroeconomic policy. However, the Fed was allowed to define its growth rate targets, weakening the target's role in constraining the Fed and in promoting accountability. Any constraining effect of announced monetary growth targets was further weakened by the Fed's practice of rebasing the level of the target path for monetary aggregates annually, ensuring that past target growth rate misses were compounded into the level of the monetary aggregates.[12]

Intermediate targets generally served as poor performance measures for monetary policy as the correlation between the targets and the ultimate objectives of monetary policy was often weak. In the United States, rapid monetary growth combined with falling inflation in the early 1980s made the aggregate targets poor guides for policy; the practice of base drift, while allowing the Fed greater flexibility in setting policy, weakened the usefulness of monetary growth rate targets as a means of ensuring policy accountability.[13]

Rather than using a goal such as inflation as the central bank's performance measure, the central bank could be assessed by comparing the setting of its instrument to a benchmark rule for the policy

11. See Walsh (1987).

12. For an analysis of base drift and the conditions under which it can be appropriate, see Walsh (1986). Inflation targeting leads to a similar situation in that the price level is allowed to be non-stationary. For some evidence that this is the practice in Australia, New Zealand, Sweden, and the United Kingdom, but not Canada, see Ruge-Murcia (2014).

13. In a similar manner, inflation targeting weakens accountability if price stability is the actual goal, as it is in many central bank charters.

instrument. A strict, or high-powered, rule-based system would eliminate any instrument independence and completely remove discretion from the policy process, directly solving any problems that arise from allowing policymakers discretion in implementing policy. In fact, Barro and Gordon (1983) and Canzoneri (1985) long ago argued that, absent private central bank information about the state of the economy, the central bank should have no discretion but instead be required to follow a rule that delineates the actions it should take as a function of the state of the economy.[14]

But just as an inflation targeting regime does not need to be one of strict inflation targeting, a rule-based system does not need to be a strict (high-powered) regime. A flexible rule-based regime, much like flexible inflation targeting, would establish a rule but allow the central bank to deviate from the rule. Deviations would then need to be explained, or justified, by policymakers, just as a failure to meet an inflation target requires policymakers to explain why the target was missed. The power of the rule as a performance measure would depend on the weight given to such deviations in evaluating and holding the central bank accountable. The advantage of a rule-based system is that it increases the predictability of policy, is transparent, and simplifies the process of ensuring accountability.[15]

Legislating rules for the central bank reduces both goal and instrument independence. As Tirole (1994) notes, rules are imposed when agents cannot be trusted with discretion. In a series of recent papers, John Taylor has argued that a commitment to a rule for monetary policy produces better outcomes than occur in regimes that emphasize central bank independence (Taylor 2011,

---

14. Walsh (1995b) showed that aligning the central bank's incentives with observables such as inflation overcame the private information problem highlighted by Canzoneri (1985). Athey, Atkeson, and Kehoe (2005) revisit the rules-versus-discretion debate in the presence of private information.
15. Taylor (2012) provides an example of how the Taylor rule can be used to assess Federal Reserve performance.

2012, 2013). He suggests overall macroeconomic performance was superior during periods in which the Federal Reserve acted in a systematic, predictable manner, and that forcing the Fed to adhere more closely to a rule would improve economic outcomes. After reviewing rules versus central bank independence, he concludes, "The policy implication is that we need to focus on ways to 'legislate' a more rule-based policy" (Taylor 2011, 16).

Given the unprecedented actions by the Federal Reserve and other central banks during the financial crisis, it is not surprising that proposals have emerged for rule-based reforms designed to limit the Fed's discretion. In July 2014, hearings were held in the United States on H.R. 5018. which would impose several rule-based requirements on the Fed. First, the Federal Open Market Committee (FOMC) would be required to identify a Directive Policy Rule, which would identify the policy instrument and "describe the strategy or rule of the Federal Open Market Committee for the systematic quantitative adjustment of the Policy Instrument Target to respond to a change in the Intermediate Policy Inputs" (section 2C(c)(2)). Intermediate Policy Inputs, defined in section 2C(a)(4), include "any variable determined by the Federal Open Market Committee as a necessary input to guide open-market operations" but must include current inflation (together with its definition and method of calculation) and at least one of (i) an estimate of real, nominal or potential GDP, (ii) an estimate of a monetary aggregate, or (iii) an interactive variable involving the other listed variables. In addition, the Directive Policy Rule must "include a function that comprehensively models the interactive relationship between the Intermediate Policy Inputs (section 2C(c)(3))" and "the coefficients of the Directive Policy Rule (section 2C(c)(4))."

Perhaps more significantly in terms of constraining the Fed's flexibility, the proposed legislation also defines a Reference Policy Rule and section 2C(c)(6) requires that the FOMC must report "whether the Directive Policy Rule substantially conforms to the

Reference Policy Rule." If it doesn't, the FOMC will need to provide a "detailed justification" for any deviation of the Directive Policy Rule and the Reference Policy Rule.

The proposed bill is quite specific about the Reference Policy Rule. Section 2C(a)(9) defines the Reference Policy Rule as the federal funds rate given by

$$i_t^{RPR} = 4 + 1.5\left(\pi_{t-1} - 2\right) + 0.5\ln\left(\frac{GDP_t}{GDP_t^{potential}}\right), \tag{1}$$

where π_{t-1} is the inflation rate over the previous four quarters. This reference policy rule is the Taylor rule (Taylor 1993). If average inflation is equal to 2 percent and the gap between GDP and potential is zero, then the policy rate will equal 4 percent. Thus, the rule assumes an inflation target of 2 percent and an average real interest rate of 2 percent.

Federal Reserve Chairwoman Janet Yellen said July 16, 2014, in testimony before the House Financial Services Committee, "It would be a grave mistake for the Fed to commit to conduct monetary policy according to a mathematical rule." In contrast, John Taylor in a July 9, 2014, *Wall Street Journal* opinion piece argued in favor of the bill. Section 2C(e)(1) does allow that the Act is not meant to require the FOMC to implement the strategy set out in the legislation if the "Committee determines that such plans cannot or should not be achieved due to changing market conditions." If such a situation occurred, the FOMC would have forty-eight hours to provide the US comptroller general and Congress with an explanation and an updated Directive Policy Rule. In turn, the comptroller general would then have forty-eight hours to conduct an audit and issue a report to determine whether the FOMC's updated Directive Policy Rule is in compliance with the bill.

Rule-based performance measures suffer from at least three potential problems. First, determining the right rule is difficult.

Even in quite simple theoretical models, the optimal instrument rule can be extremely complex (for example, see Woodford 2010). A complex rule, even if known, might be hard to explain to the public, thereby reducing the ability of a rule-based performance measure to ensure policy transparency and accountability. Second, any optimal rule is optimal only with reference to a specific model, so changes in the economy's structure or our understanding of it will produce changes in the optimal rule. Third, it may not always be possible to characterize policy in terms of a single instrument rule. A rule for a short-term policy interest rate would no longer be meaningful if interest rates were at the zero lower bound, nor would it give guidance for balance-sheet policies. Thus, instrument rules are likely to be less robust to structural changes than goal-based systems.[16] However, early work such as Levin, Wieland, and Williams (1999) and Rudebusch (2002) suggested simple rules may be robust to model uncertainty. These considerations argue for adopting a simple but robust rule such as the Taylor rule but one that also includes escape clauses.[17] Choosing which rule, and how accountability is to be maintained when the rule might not apply, must involve balancing the gains from limiting discretion against the costs of potentially forcing monetary policy to implement a bad rule.

Table 3.1 summarizes the general characteristics of goal-based and rule-based reforms. I exclude examples of reforms based on intermediate targets such as money growth rates as they are inefficient systems both for achieving ultimate goals and for restricting the central bank's instrument setting. Goal-based and rule-based

16. But alterations in the economy's structure can also affect policy goals. For example, a change in price indexation would change the definition of inflation volatility that generates inefficiencies and that should appear in the measure of social welfare.
17. See also Taylor and Williams (2010). Svensson (2003) provides a general critique of relying on Taylor rules, while Benhabib, Schmitt-Grohé, and Uribe (2001) argue Taylor rules do not rule out ZLB equilibria.

TABLE 3.1: Types of Central Bank Reforms

	Goals Based	Rules Based
Examples	Inflation targeting	Exchange rate pegs
	Price level targeting	Gold standard
		Instrument rules (H.R. 5018)
CB independence		
Goal	Varied	Low
Instrument	High	Low
Constrains	Central Bank	Central Bank
	Government	
Flexibility	Varied	Varied
Transparency	Varied	High
Accountability	High	High
Robustness	High	Low

Source: Author's calculations

reforms have different implications for a central bank and for macroeconomic outcomes. They differ in terms of the type of independence the central bank enjoys and in terms of whom they are designed to constrain. Both can allow for flexibility and both provide the public with the ability to assess policy and, in principle, hold the central bank accountable.

Under rule-based accountability, the central bank is required to specify clearly its instrument and the rule it uses to determine the setting of that instrument. Deviations from the rule are allowed, but the central bank is required to explain the rationale for any such deviations. In contrast, under goal-based accountability, the objectives of the central bank are made clear—if these are set by the government, the central bank lacks goal independence—but in the pursuit of these goals the central bank enjoys instrument independence. In this case, the central bank is required to explain how its actions are consistent with achieving the goals.

The Performance of Goal-Based
and Rule-Based Regimes[18]

In this section, a simple model is used to highlight the tensions that arise between accountability and flexibility under different performance measures and to explore how these tensions are addressed by goal-based and rule-based accountability. While the model used is quite simple, it helps to illustrate the effects of different policy regimes, leaving to the following section the use of an estimated model to evaluate goal-based and rule-based systems.

Let π^* be the socially optimal steady-state inflation rate, taken as exogenous and constant for simplicity, and define $\hat{\pi}_t \equiv \pi_t - \pi^*$ as actual inflation relative to the optimal rate. Assume social loss is given by

$$L_t^s = \frac{1}{2} E_0 \sum \beta^i \left(\hat{\pi}_{t+i}^2 + \lambda x_{t+i}^2 \right), \tag{2}$$

where $x_t \equiv x_t - x^*$ is the (log) gap between output and the socially efficient output level. Policy is delegated to a central bank with instrument independence but subject to possible political pressures that affect the goals the central bank pursues. Specifically, assume that absent any assignment of a performance measure, the central bank acts to minimize

$$L_t^{cb} = \frac{1}{2} E_t^{cb} \sum \beta^i \left[\left(\hat{\pi}_{t+i} - \varphi_{t+i} \right)^2 + \lambda \left(x_{t+i} - u_{t+i} \right)^2 \right] \tag{3}$$

where φ and u are mean zero stochastic shocks that represent deviations of the central bank's objectives from their socially optimal values. These can be thought of as representing unmodeled political pressures affecting the policy choices of the central bank or

18. This and the following sections are reprinted from Walsh (2015), which is available at http://www.ijcb.org/journal/ijcb15q4a10.htm and which contains an appendix that provides details on the derivations of all results.

simply as distortions introduced by the preferences of the central
bank policy authorities. In keeping with the now common practice
in the analysis of monetary policy, I assume a fiscal tax/subsidy
policy is in place that eliminates any steady-state inefficiencies.
Thus, I ignore distortions arising from attempts to systematically
affect the level of steady-state output.

The economy is characterized very simply by a new Keynesian
Phillips curve given by

$$\hat{\pi}_t = \beta E_t \hat{\pi}_{t+1} + \kappa x_t + e_t, \tag{4}$$

and an expectational Euler equation given by

$$x_t = E_t x_{t+1} - \left(\frac{1}{\sigma}\right)\left(i_t - E_t \hat{\pi}_{t+1} - \phi_t\right), \tag{5}$$

where ϕ_t and e_t are taken to be exogenous stochastic processes.
Equation (4) is consistent with the standard Calvo model if firms
who do not optimally choose their price instead index their price
to π^*. Under optimal discretionary policy with i.i.d. shocks, the
unconditional expected social loss is

$$L_t^s = \frac{1}{2}\left(\frac{1}{1-\beta}\right)\left[\left(\frac{\lambda}{\lambda+\kappa^2}\right)\sigma_e^2 + \left(\lambda^3+\kappa^2\right)\left(\frac{1}{\lambda+\kappa^2}\right)^2\left(\lambda^2\sigma_u^2+\kappa^2\sigma_\varphi^2\right)\right] \tag{6}$$

In the absence of political distortions represented by u and ϕ
(and maintaining the assumption of i.i.d. shocks), social loss
would be

$$\frac{1}{2}\left(\frac{1}{1-\beta}\right)\left(\frac{\lambda}{\lambda+\kappa^2}\right)\sigma_e^2 \leq L_t^s.$$

I next investigate whether holding the central bank accountable
for achieving a goal such as the inflation rate or for adhering to a
rule for setting the instrument can help lower social loss.

Delegation

Government in a pre-game stage defines a performance measure for the central bank. A goal-based regime specifies the central bank's objectives in terms of π and/or x, the two ultimate objectives on which social welfare depends. A rule-based regime specifies that assessment of the central bank's performance is based on a comparison of the policy instrument and the value implied by a simple instrument rule. I represent each type of regime by assuming the central bank continues to have preferences over actual outcomes given by (3) but is also concerned with minimizing deviations of outcomes from the bank's assigned performance measures. The weights attached to these additional performance measures represent the power of the respective measure. Nesting both regimes, the central bank is assumed to set policy under discretion to minimize

$$L_t^{cb} = \frac{1}{2}E_t^{cb}\sum \beta^i \left[\left(\hat{\pi}_{t+i} - \varphi_{t+i}\right)^2 + \lambda\left(x_{t+i} - x_{t+i}^*\right)^2 + \tau\hat{\pi}_{t+i}^2 + \delta\left(i_{t+i} - i_{t+i}^r\right)^2 \right], \quad (7)$$

where τ is the implicit weight placed on achieving the inflation target (equivalently, the degree of central bank conservatism in the terminology of Rogoff 1985) and δ is the weight placed on setting the interest rate equal to i^r, the rate implied by the rule.[19] We can rewrite L_t^{cb} as

$$L_t^{cb} = \frac{1}{2}E_t^{cb}\sum \beta^i [(1+\tau)\hat{\pi}_{t+i}^2 - 2\varphi_{t+i}\hat{\pi}_{t+i}\lambda x_{t+i}^2 - 2\lambda u_{t+i}x_{t+i} + \delta(i_{t+i} - i_{t+i}^r)^2],$$

where terms independent of policy have been dropped.[20]

---

19. For simplicity, I only consider goal-based regimes defined in terms of inflation and not the output gap.

20. For evidence that the Fed has implicitly placed some weight on the Taylor rule, see Kahn (2012) and Ilbas, Røisland, and Sveen (2013).

Since private agents are forward-looking in making decisions, optimal policy under discretion will result in lower social welfare than would the fully optimal commitment policy. The distortionary shocks φ_{t+i} and u_{t+i} also reduce welfare. The question for central bank design is whether a goal-based system with $\tau > 0$ or a rule-based system with $\delta > 0$ can, in an environment of discretionary decision-making, improve welfare. In other words, in a pre-game stage, would the government choose non-zero values of τ and/or δ if it wished to minimize (2)?

I first consider the case of a goal-based regime in which $\delta = 0$ but τ is chosen optimally. Then the case of a rule-based regime with $\tau = 0$ and δ chosen optimally is analyzed. Finally, the case in which both τ and δ are jointly chosen is considered.

The Assignment of Goals

When the government assigns objectives to the central bank based on realized inflation, we have the case studied in Walsh (2003a). The analysis in that paper only considered distortionary shocks affecting the output objective of policy (i.e., $u \neq 0$ but $\varphi \equiv 0$) and also assumed the central bank had imperfect information about cost shocks, an extension I ignore here.

With $\delta = 0$, the central bank's problem under discretion can be written as

$$\min_{\hat{\pi}_t, x_t, i_t} \frac{1}{2}(1+\tau)\hat{\pi}_t^2 - \varphi_t\hat{\pi}_t + \frac{1}{2}\lambda x_t^2 - \lambda u_t x_t$$

subject to (4) and (5). The nominal interest rate i is the instrument of monetary policy. Shocks are assumed to be i.i.d.[21] It is straightforward to show that equilibrium inflation and the output gap are given by

---

21. The case of serially correlated shocks is dealt with in the numerical analysis of section 4 based on an estimated model.

$$\hat{\pi}_t = \left[\frac{\kappa\lambda u_t + \kappa^2\varphi_t + \lambda e_t}{\lambda + \kappa^2\left(1+\tau\right)} \right]$$

$$x_t = \left[\frac{\lambda u_t + \kappa\varphi_t - \kappa\left(1+\tau\right)e_t}{\lambda + \kappa^2\left(1+\tau\right)} \right].$$

The central-bank-design problem is to pick τ to minimize the unconditional expectation of social loss. The optimal value of τ is given by

$$\tau^* = \left(\frac{\lambda + \kappa^2}{\lambda^2}\right)\left(\frac{\lambda^2\sigma_u^2 + \kappa^2\sigma_\varphi^2}{\sigma_e^2}\right) \geq 0. \tag{8}$$

If $\varphi_t = 0$, (8) reduces to the case considered in Walsh (2003a). In this case, $\tau^* = (\lambda + \kappa^2)(\sigma_u^2/\sigma_e^2)$ increases linearly in λ and in the volatility of the distortionary shock to policymakers' goals (σ_u^2) relative to the volatility of cost shocks (σ_e^2). In the absence of both distortionary shocks u and φ, $\tau^* = 0$, consistent with the findings of Clarida, Galí, and Gertler (1999), who showed there is no gain from appointing a Rogoff conservative central banker when the cost shock is serially uncorrelated. When distortionary shocks are present, τ^* is positive even when shocks are serially uncorrelated. The greater the variability of the political distortions represented by u and φ, the larger is the optimal τ and the more the central bank needs to be made accountable based on $\hat{\pi}_t$. Equivalently expressed, the more variable the wedge between social objectives and goals pursued by the central bank, the more high-powered (or the stricter) the inflation-targeting regime needs to be.

A rise in the volatility of cost shocks increases the potential value of stabilization policy and so τ^* falls, as a more flexible inflation targeting regime is desirable. With more potential gain from flexibility, the optimal regime assigns less weight to achieving the inflation target. Importantly, τ^* is independent of aggregate demand shocks operating through the expectational IS relationship, as the central bank always has an incentive to neutralize the impact of such shocks on inflation and the output gap.

The Assignment of Rules

Now suppose a legislated instrument rule is used to assess the central bank's performance. In contrast to objectives based on an ultimate goal such as inflation, the central bank's objectives are distorted based on how it sets its actual policy instrument. In terms of (7), $\tau = 0$ but δ may be non-zero. The central bank's problem takes the form

$$\min_{\hat{\pi}, x, i} \left[\frac{1}{2}\hat{\pi}_t^2 - \varphi_t\hat{\pi}_t + \frac{1}{2}\lambda x_t^2 - \lambda u_t x_t + \frac{1}{2}\delta(i_t - i_t^r)^2 \right]$$

subject to (4) and (5). Because the central bank is judged in part on how it sets its instrument, the expectational IS equation becomes relevant for its policy choice. Assume that the reference rule is defined by

$$i_t^r = \psi_\pi \hat{\pi}_t + \psi_x x_t.$$

The first-order conditions for the central bank's problem imply

$$i_t = i_t^r + \frac{1}{a\delta}\left[\kappa(\hat{\pi}_t - \varphi_t) + \lambda(x_t - u_t) \right],$$

where

$$a \equiv \sigma + \psi_x + \kappa\psi_\pi.$$

In the absence of the rule-based performance measure, the central bank would set the term in brackets equal to zero. The greater the value of δ—that is, the more costly it becomes for the central bank to deviate from the reference policy rule—the smaller the role this unconstrained optimality condition plays in the setting of i_t and the closer i_t comes to equaling the benchmark rule value.

For the case of serially uncorrelated shocks, equilibrium inflation and the output gap are equal to

$$\hat{\pi}_t = \left[\frac{\kappa\alpha\delta\phi_t + \kappa\lambda u_t + \kappa^2\varphi_t}{\lambda + \kappa^2 + a^2\delta}\right] + \left[\frac{\lambda + a\delta(\sigma + \psi_x)}{\lambda + \kappa^2 + a^2\delta}\right]e_t$$

$$x_t = \frac{\alpha\delta\phi_t + \lambda u_t + \kappa\varphi_t - (\kappa + a\delta\psi_\pi)e_t}{\lambda + \kappa^2 + a^2\delta},$$

and social loss is

$$\mathcal{L} = \frac{1}{2}a^2(\lambda + \kappa^2)\left[\frac{\delta}{\lambda + \kappa^2 + a^2\delta}\right]^2\sigma_\phi^2 + \frac{1}{2}\lambda^2(\lambda + \kappa^2)\left[\frac{1}{\lambda + \kappa^2 + a^2\delta}\right]^2\sigma_u^2$$
$$+ \frac{1}{2}\kappa^2(\lambda + \kappa^2)\left[\frac{1}{\lambda + \kappa^2 + a^2\delta}\right]^2\sigma_\varphi^2 + \frac{1}{2}\left\{\frac{[\lambda + a\delta(\sigma + \psi_x)]^2 + \lambda[\kappa + a\delta\psi_x]^2}{[\lambda + \kappa^2 + a^2\delta]^2}\right\}\sigma_e^2.$$

Minimizing $\mathcal{L}$ with respect to δ implies the optimal weight on the rule-based objective is

$$\delta^* = \frac{(\lambda + \kappa^2)(\lambda^2\sigma_u^2 + \kappa^2\sigma_\varphi^2)}{(\lambda + \kappa^2)^2\sigma_\phi^2 + \Lambda\sigma_e^2}, \tag{9}$$

where

$$\Lambda \equiv [(\sigma + \psi_x)\kappa - \lambda\psi_\pi]^2. \tag{10}$$

To help interpret the expression for δ^*, assume initially that there are no aggregate demand shocks ($\phi \equiv 0$). In this special case,

$$\delta^* = \left(\frac{\lambda + \kappa^2}{\Lambda}\right)\left(\frac{\lambda^2\sigma_u^2 + \kappa^2\sigma_\varphi^2}{\sigma_e^2}\right). \tag{11}$$

Comparing (11) to (8) shows that both depend on $(\lambda + \kappa^2)$ $(\lambda^2\sigma_u^2 + \kappa^2\sigma_\varphi^2)/\sigma_e^2$; as the variability of distortionary shocks u and φ

increases relative to the variability of cost shocks e, the optimal τ^* and the optimal δ^* both increase. They do so for the same reason: allowing the central bank less flexibility becomes desirable when distortionary shifts in goals are more variable. The optimal τ^* and δ^* are both decreasing in the volatility of inflation shocks; as the scope for welfare-improving stabilization policy increases, the cost of distorting the central bank's objectives by requiring it either to place more weight on inflation variability or to match the benchmark instrument rule becomes more costly.

The expression for δ^* given in (11) was derived for arbitrary policy response coefficients ψ_x and ψ_π. Suppose instead that these were optimally chosen. For example, continuing with the special case of no demand shocks and serially uncorrelated cost and distortionary shocks, the optimal interest rate rule can be expressed in terms of a reaction to either the output gap or to inflation; that is, only one response coefficient is needed. Let $\psi_x = 0$; the optimal response to inflation is then equal to $\psi_\pi^* = \sigma\kappa/\lambda$. One can show that

$$\lim_{\psi_\pi \to \psi_\pi^*} \delta^* \to \infty.$$

When the benchmark rule is equal to the optimal rule and there are no aggregate demand shocks, the central bank should not be allowed any flexibility.

Equation (11) applied when there were no shocks to the Euler equation, corresponding to the case of a constant equilibrium real interest rate. In the presence of shocks to the equilibrium real interest rate (i.e., $\phi \neq 0$), the optimal penalty on deviations from the rule can be written as

$$\delta^* = \left(\frac{\lambda + \kappa^2}{\Delta}\right)\left(\frac{\lambda^2\sigma_u^2 + \kappa^2\sigma_\phi^2}{\sigma_e^2}\right) = \left(\frac{\lambda^2}{\Delta}\right)\tau^*,$$

where

$$\Delta \equiv \Lambda + \left(\lambda + \kappa^2\right)^2 \left(\frac{\sigma_\phi^2}{\sigma_e^2}\right) \geq \Lambda.$$

Thus, demand shocks ($\sigma_\phi^2 > 0$) call for putting less weight on deviations from the rule. This result is very intuitive—the specified rule does not allow for interest rate movements directly in response to demand shocks; an optimal policy would. Therefore, as demand shocks become a larger source of volatility, the optimal δ falls. If $\psi_x = 0$ and $\psi_x = \psi_x^*$ so that the assigned rule is consistent with the optimal response to inflation shocks, $\Lambda = 0$ and

$$\delta^* = \left(\frac{1}{\lambda + \kappa^2}\right)\left(\frac{\lambda^2 \sigma_u^2 + \kappa^2 \sigma_\varphi^2}{\sigma_\phi^2}\right) \geq 0.$$

In this case, the optimal value of δ is non-negative, independent of inflation shocks, but decreasing in the variance of demand shocks.

Jointly Optimal Goal- and Rule-Based Regimes

The special cases just considered showed how setting τ and δ both involve a similar trade-off between the benefits of reducing flexibility to limit distortions and the costs of reducing the ability of the central bank to pursue socially desirable stabilization policies. The dependence of the power of goal-based and rule-based measures on the relative volatility of underlying shocks is reminiscent of the classic Poole results on instrument choice (Poole 1970). Poole showed that an interest rate instrument performed better than a monetary aggregate instrument in the face of financial market shocks, while the reverse was true in the face of aggregate demand disturbances. In a similar manner, equations (8) and (9) suggest a goal-based performance measure may be best if shocks to aggregate demand dominate, while a rule-based measure may have advantages if shocks to inflation dominate. In general, Poole's analysis implies optimal simple rules will depend on the relative variances of the model's underlying shocks.[22] Similarly, one might expect that the weight to give to a goal-based performance measure relative to a rule-based measure may depend on the relative volatility of the model's shocks. The fact that, as shown by (8) and (9), the optimal τ is independent of demand shock volatility but decreasing in cost shock volatility while δ is decreasing in the volatility of demand shocks suggests there might be potential gains from using both forms of performance measures.

To assess the joint determination of the optimal values of τ and δ, I set $\kappa = 0.172$, consistent with a Calvo model of price adjustment with the fraction of non-optimally adjusting firms equal to 75 percent per quarter combined with log utility ($\sigma = 1$) and a Frisch elasticity of labor supply of 1. For the baseline, I set the standard deviations of all the shocks equal to 0.025. The parameters of the rule are set equal to their Taylor-values of $\psi_x = 1.5$ and $\psi_x = 0.125$. I then solve numerically for the values of τ^* and δ^* that minimize the unconditional expectation of social loss, given by (2). I set λ equal to the value appropriate if (2) is interpreted as a second-order approximation to the welfare of the representative household.[23] The analytic results for the optimal values of τ and δ taken individually showed that the variances of demand and cost shocks played a key role, so I investigate how variations in these variances affect the optimal power of the goal-based versus rule-based regimes.

To assess the relative roles of τ and δ when both are chosen optimally, I report the ratio of their optimal values as the variances of the disturbances vary. Figure 3.1 plots τ^*/δ^* as a function of the variances of the fundamental demand and cost shocks σ_ϕ^2 and σ_e^2.

22. See Walsh (2010), pp. 513–521.
23. This implies a value of λ equal to $(\kappa/\theta^p)(1 + \eta)/(1 - a)$, where θ^p is the price elasticity of demand faced by firms, η is the inverse wage elasticity of labor supply, and $1 - a$ is the elasticity of output with respect to labor. For $\theta^p = 9$, $\eta = 1$ and $a = 0.3$, this implies $\lambda = 0.0545$. See (21).

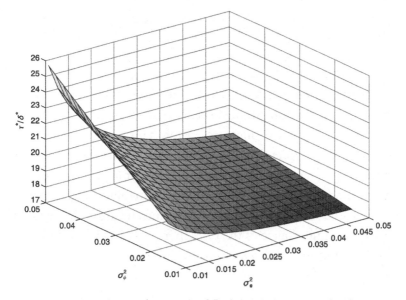

FIGURE 3.1: Ratio of optimal τ to optimal δ when jointly optimized as function of the variances of demand (σ_ϕ^2) and cost (σ_e^2) shocks.

Source: Author's calculations.

Both τ^* and δ^* are positive, indicating a role for goals and rules, but, as suggested by (8) and (9), the relative weight on goals as measured by τ rises as demand shocks increase in volatility, while the weight on rules as measured by δ rises as cost shocks become more volatile. For the parameters considered here, however, the weight given to deviations from the inflation target in assessing the central bank's performance is much larger than the optimal weight placed on deviations from the Taylor rule.

According to (8) and (9), an increase in $\lambda^2\sigma_u^2 + \kappa^2\sigma_\varphi^2$ —that is, an increase in the volatility of the distortionary shifts in objectives— would increase τ^* when $\delta = 0$ and δ^* when $\tau = 0$. In fact, these two equations imply the ratio between τ^* and δ^* is independent of the volatility of the distortionary shocks u and φ but depends on the relative variances of demand and cost shocks:

$$\frac{\tau^*}{\delta^*} = \left(\frac{\lambda + \kappa^2}{\lambda^2}\right)\left(\frac{\sigma_\phi^2}{\sigma_e^2}\right) + \frac{\Lambda}{\lambda^2}.$$

This continues to be true when τ and δ are optimally chosen jointly; they both increase with the volatility of the distortionary shocks u and φ, rising proportionately so that their ratio remains constant as $\lambda^2\sigma_u^2 + \kappa^2\sigma_\varphi^2$ increases. Thus, figure 3.1 is independent of $\lambda^2\sigma_u^2 + \kappa^2\sigma_\varphi^2$. While the optimal measure of performance places some weight on deviations from the inflation goal and deviations from the interest rate rule, the fundamental choice between a goal-based and a rule-based performance measure depends on the relative importance of the underlying shocks to private sector consumption and price-setting behavior.

Conclusions from the Simple Model

The simple model utilized in this section suggests that when political (or other) pressures cause transitory distortions to the objectives the central bank pursues relative to society's goals, there can be a role for both goal-based reforms and rule-based reforms. Both establish performance measures that affect the central bank's incentives and therefore affect policy choices. When each type of reform is considered in isolation, analytical expressions could be obtained for the optimal weight to place on achieving stable inflation and for punishing deviations from the Taylor rule. These expression for τ^* and δ^* showed that increases in the variance of shocks that distorted the central bank's objectives called for increasing the power of both types of accountability measures. Increased volatility of cost shocks reduces the weight that should be placed on inflation goals as limiting the flexibility to respond to these shocks becomes more costly. Under goal-based accountability, demand shocks do not affect the optimal power as the central bank already has an incentive to neutralize demand shocks. In contrast, demand shocks reduce the optimal power of the rule-based system since the Taylor rule does not allow for shifts in the equilibrium real rate of interest.

Goals and Rules in an Estimated Model with Sticky Prices and Wages

The previous section considered the use of goal-based and rule-based policy regimes using a very simple model in which some analytical results could be obtained and some results required a calibrated version of the model. In this section I consider the effects of τ and δ in an estimated new Keynesian model of sticky prices and wages based on Erceg, Henderson, and Levin (2000). As was clear from the expressions for τ^* and δ^* obtained in the previous section, their values will depend importantly on the relative volatility of different shocks. Thus, obtaining these values from an estimated model will provide a more realistic assessment of the performance of goal-based versus rule-based incentive systems.

The basic model is standard and details of its derivation can be found in Erceg, Henderson, and Levin (2000) or chapter 6 of Galí (2008). The model takes the following form:

$$y_t = E_t y_{t+1} - \left[i_t - E_t \pi_{t+1} - \left(1 - \rho_\chi\right)\chi_t \right] \tag{12}$$

$$\left(1 + \beta\delta_p\right)\pi_t = \beta E_t \pi_{t+1} + \delta_p \pi_{t-1} + \kappa_p \left(\omega_t - mpl_t + \mu_t^p\right) \tag{13}$$

$$\left(1 + \beta\delta_w\right)\pi_t^w = \beta E_t \pi_{t+1}^w + \delta_w \pi_{t-1}^w + \kappa_w \left(mrs_t + \mu_t^w - \omega_t\right) \tag{14}$$

$$\omega_t = \omega_{t-1} + \pi_t^w - \pi_t + e_{z,t} \tag{15}$$

$$mpl_t = -ah_t \tag{16}$$

$$mrs_t = y_t + \eta h_t - \chi_t \tag{17}$$

$$y_t = (1-a)h_t \tag{18}$$

$$g_t = y_t - y_{t-1} + e_{z,t}, \tag{19}$$

where y is output, ω the real wage, π inflation, π^w wage inflation, *mpl* the marginal product of labor, *mrs* the marginal rate of substitution between leisure and consumption, h hours, and g the growth rate of output. Aggregate productivity is assumed subject to a random walk process with innovation $e_{z,t}$, so output, the real wage, the marginal product of labor, and the marginal rate of substitution between leisure and consumption are all defined as log deviations from the permanent component of productivity. Other variables are expressed as log deviation from their steady state values (including zero steady-state rates of price and wage inflation). χ, μ^p, and μ^w are stochastic shocks to the marginal utility of consumption, price markups, and wage markups, all assumed to follow AR(1) processes with, for example, ρ_x denoting the AR(1) coefficient for χ and $e_{x,t}$ denoting its innovation. The first equation is a standard Euler condition linking the marginal utility of consumption in periods t and $t + 1$. The next two equations are reduced-form expressions for price and wage inflation, where δ_p and δ_w are the degrees of indexation in price- and wage-setting. The parameter η is the inverse wage elasticity of labor supply; $1 - a$ is the elasticity of output with respect to hours, the only variable input to production. To be consistent with the assumed unit root process in productivity, the elasticity of intertemporal substitution in consumption is set equal to one.

The elasticity of inflation with respect to real marginal cost is equal to

$$\kappa_p = \frac{\left(1-\varphi^p\right)\left(1-\beta\varphi^p\right)}{\varphi^p} \frac{1-a}{1-a+a\theta^p}$$

where $1 - \varphi^p$ is the fraction of firms optimally adjusting price each period and θ^p is the price elasticity of demand facing individual firms. Similarly, the elasticity of wage inflation with respect to the gap between the marginal rate of substitution between leisure and consumption and the real wage is

$$\kappa_w = \frac{\left(1-\varphi^w\right)\left(1-\beta\varphi^w\right)}{\varphi^w}\frac{1}{1+\eta\theta^w},$$

where $1 - \varphi^w$ is the fraction of wages optimally adjusting each period and θ^w is the wage elasticity of demand for individual labor types.

For estimation purposes, the model is closed with a specification of monetary policy, where the nominal interest rate i is treated as the policy instrument. I assume a standard Taylor rule with inertia of the form

$$i_t = \rho_i i_{t-1} + \left(1-\rho_i\right)\left(\phi_\pi \pi_t + \phi_g y_t\right) + v_t$$

where v is an exogenous policy shock.

Estimation

The model is estimated by Bayesian methods over the period 1984:1–2007:4, corresponding to the Great Moderation. A similar version of the Erceg, Henderson, and Levin model has been estimated over 1984:1–2008:2 by Casares, Moreno, and Vázquez (2011). I base my priors partially on their results, but I follow Chen, Curdia, and Ferrero (2012) in choosing prior distributions of beta for parameters constrained to be between 0 and 1 and gamma for parameters that should be positive. Output growth, inflation, wage inflation, and the nominal interest rate are treated as observables. Output is measured by chained real GDP deflated by the civilian population age sixteen and over. Inflation is measured by the log change in the GDP deflator, while wage inflation is the log change in hourly compensation in the non-farm business sector. The

TABLE 3.2: Prior and posterior distributions: Structural parameters

	Priors prior dist.	mean	s.d.	Posterior mean	5%	95%
Structural parameters						
η	gamma	4.34	0.25	3.7812	2.6792	4.6645
δ_p	beta	0.5	0.15	0.3690	0.3090	0.4410
δ_w	beta	0.5	0.15	0.2325	0.2000	0.2606
φ_p	beta	0.75	0.1	0.2081	0.0914	0.3218
φ_w	beta	0.75	0.1	0.1891	0.0703	0.2946
Monetary policy						
ρ_i	beta	0.83	0.1	0.5144	0.5000	0.5329
ϕ_π	gamma	2	0.25	2.7303	2.4659	2.9993
ϕ_g	gamma	0.35	0.05	0.4404	0.3822	0.5000
Disturbances						
ρ_χ	beta	0.9	0.2	0.9015	0.8692	0.9350
ρ_{μ^p}	beta	0.9	0.2	0.9886	0.9646	0.9999
ρ_{μ^w}	beta	0.9	0.2	0.1421	0.0100	0.2937
ρ_v	beta	0.3	0.2	0.4634	0.3611	0.5595
σ_z	invg	1.0	0.2	0.6567	0.5766	0.7324
σ_χ	invg	1.0	0.2	1.1921	0.9488	1.3864
σ_v	invg	1.0	0.2	0.4412	0.4109	0.4705
σ_{μ^p}	invg	1.0	3	1.2011	1.0027	1.3801
σ_{μ^w}	invg	1.0	3	4.9443	3.9333	5.9998

Source: Author's calculations

interest rate is the effective federal funds rate. All four observables are measured at quarterly rates. The values $\sigma = 1$, $\beta = 0.99$, $a = 0.36$, $\theta^p = 9$, and $\theta^w = 4.5$ were fixed, where the latter two values follow Galí (2013). Table 3.2 reports the prior distribution, means, and standard deviations, together with the posterior means and confidence intervals of the estimated parameters.[24]

24. The estimation period is chosen to exclude the post-2008 period during which the federal funds rate was effectively at zero. The implications of the zero lower bound for goal-based and rule-based performance measures are discussed in the concluding section.

Welfare Measures

In viewing central bank design as an issue of delegation, the objectives pursued by the central bank may differ from those of society, either because the central bank's evaluation of economic outcomes differs inherently from society's or because the central bank has been assigned objectives that differ from those of society. The former case corresponds to Rogoff's conservative central banker, a policymaker whose preference for low and stable inflation is greater than that of the public. The latter is the case considered in this paper, in which policymakers share society's preferences but have been assigned objectives that may differ from those of society. In either case, it is necessary to specify two sets of preferences: those taken to represent society's and those that underlie the central bank's policy choices.

In specifying these preferences, much of the monetary policy literature, including work on inflation targeting, takes the objectives of the central bank to be represented by a quadratic loss function in inflation squared (or squared deviations of inflation from target) and an output gap squared. These objectives are then also implicitly identified with those of society. Under a delegation scheme, society's and the central bank's objectives could each be represented by ad hoc quadratic loss functions, but the two loss functions may differ. Alternatively, in models based on the preferences of the individual agents populating the economy, outcomes can be evaluated in terms of their implications for the welfare of the representative household. If a welfare-based measure is used to represent society's preferences, the objectives of the central bank could take one of two basic forms. One could still represent the central bank's objectives by a standard quadratic loss function augmented by the performance measures assigned to the bank. Or one could assume the policymaker cares about the welfare of the

TABLE 3.3: Alternative welfare measures

		Society	
		Ad hoc	Welfare based
Central bank	Ad hoc	x	x
	Ad hoc w/ distorted output gap	x	x
	Welfare based		x
	Welfare based w/ distorted output gap		x

Source: Author's calculations

representative household, in addition to the performance measures that have been assigned. Each of these alternatives could then allow for distortionary shocks to the policymaker's output objective. Table 3.3 summarizes the combinations of objective functions that could be used to measure society's welfare and to represent the central bank's objectives. In the analysis of this section, six of the eight possible combinations of objectives will be considered; these combinations are indicated in the table. I have excluded the cases in which society's preferences are given by an ad hoc loss function while the central bank uses the welfare of the representative household to evaluate outcomes, as these combinations of preferences seem of limited relevance.

The ad hoc measure used to evaluate outcomes from society's perspective is taken to be

$$L_t^{s,adhoc} = \frac{1}{2} E_t \sum_{i=0}^{\infty} \beta^i \left(\hat{\pi}_{t+i}^2 + \lambda_x x_{t+i}^2 \right), \tag{20}$$

while the welfare-based measure is taken to be a second-order approximation to the welfare of the representative household, where the approximation is taken around the economy's zero-inflation efficient equilibrium.[25] In the context of the sticky-price, sticky-wage model, Erceg, Henderson, and Levin (2000) show that

---

25. I assume fiscal taxes and/or subsidies are in place to ensure the steady-state allocation is efficient.

$$L_t^{s,welf} = \frac{1}{2} E_t \sum_{i=0}^{\infty} \beta^i [(\hat{\pi}_{t+i} - \delta_p \hat{\pi}_{t+i-1})^2 + \lambda_x x_{t+i}^2 + \lambda_w (\hat{\pi}_{t+i}^w - \delta_p \hat{\pi}_{t+i-1}^w)^2], \quad (21)$$

where

$$\lambda_x = \left(\frac{\kappa_p}{\theta^p}\right)\left(\frac{1+\eta}{1-a}\right)$$

$$\lambda_w = (1-a)\left(\frac{\kappa_p}{\kappa_w}\right)\left(\frac{\theta^w}{\theta^p}\right).$$

Since the weight on output gap volatility in $L_t^{s,adhoc}$ is ad hoc, I employ the same value for λ_x in (20) as for λ_x in (21). Based on the estimated parameters reported in table 3.1, λ_x = 0.1486 and λ_w = 0.4061.

The central bank is assumed to minimize a loss function that is augmented by the performance measures which place additional weight on inflation volatility and deviations from an instrument rule:

$$L_t = L_t^{cb} + \frac{1}{2} E_t \sum_{i=0}^{\infty} \beta^i \left[\tau \hat{\pi}_{t+i}^2 + \delta(i_{t+i} - i_{t+i}^r)^2 \right],$$

where L_t^{cb} is the central bank's loss function in the absence of performance measures. Four alternative specifications for L_t^{cb} are used. These differ according to whether an ad hoc quadratic loss function or the welfare approximation is used and whether, for each of these loss functions, the central bank is concerned with x_{t+i}^2 or with the distorted gap $(x_{t+i} - u_{t+i})^2$. For example, if $u_t \equiv 0$ and the central bank employs an ad hoc quadratic loss function, policy will aim to minimize

$$\frac{1}{2} E_t \sum_{i=0}^{\infty} \beta^i \left[\hat{\pi}_{t+i}^2 + \lambda_x x_{t+i}^2 + \tau \hat{\pi}_{t+i}^2 + \delta(i_{t+i} - i_{t+i}^r)^2 \right]. \quad (22)$$

If the central bank's gap objective is distorted, policy will minimize

$$\frac{1}{2}E_t \sum_{i=0}^{\infty} \beta^i \left[\hat{\pi}_{t+i}^2 + \lambda_x \left(x_{t+i} - u_{t+i} \right)^2 + \tau \hat{\pi}_{t+i}^2 + \delta \left(i_{t+i} - i_{t+i}^r \right)^2 \right]. \qquad (23)$$

A similar distinction will arise if the central bank is concerned with minimizing (21) or (21) with x_t^2 replaced by $(x_t - u_t)^2$. Finally, the reference policy rule defining i_t^r is given by

$$i_t^r = 1.5\pi_t + 0.125 z_t, \qquad (24)$$

where z_t is a measure of real activity. Two alternatives for z_t will be considered: x_t, the gap between output and the efficient level of output, and y_t, output relative to the permanent component of output, interpreted as corresponding to output relative to trend.

Results

As a starting point, consider the case in which social loss is measured by the standard quadratic loss function given by (20), and the central bank's objective is (22). Assume $z_t = y_t$ in (24) so the reference policy rule includes inflation and the gap between output and potential as in the Reference Policy Rule proposed in H.R. 5018. The model given by (12) – (19) is solved over a grid of values for τ and δ under the optimal discretionary policy designed to minimize (22). For each combination, social loss measured by (20) is evaluated to obtain the values τ^* and δ^* that minimize social loss.

Row 1, column 1, of table 3.4 shows that $\tau^* > 0$ but $\delta^* = 0$ when a standard quadratic loss function in inflation and the efficiency output gap is used to represent both social loss and the central bank's preferences. Because there is no distortion appearing directly in the central bank's loss function, i.e., $u_t \equiv 0$ and the central bank cares about $\hat{\pi}_t^2$ and x_t^2, the only role for the performance measures is to address the dynamic inefficiency of discretionary

TABLE 3.4: Optimal τ and δ, Taylor Rule in π and y

| | Social loss | | | |
| | (1) Ad hoc (eq. 20) | | (2) Welfare (eq. 21) | |
Central bank loss	τ^*	δ^*	τ^*	δ^*
(1) ad hoc: π, x	4.04	0	1.37	0
(2) ad hoc: π, $x-u$	12.95	0	6.15	0
(3) welfare			0.33	0
(4) welfare in $x-u$			1.54	0

Source: Author's calculations

policy. Recall that Clarida, Galí, and Gertler (1999) showed that in the presence of serially correlated cost shocks, as is the case here, having the central bank place more weight on its inflation goal (relative to the true social loss function) would lead to improved outcomes.[26] In contrast, the rule-based performance measure receives zero weight.

Now suppose the distortionary shock u_t that affects the output goal pursued by the central bank is added, so that the central bank seeks to minimize (23). Since shocks to the central bank's preferences were not incorporated into the estimated model, I arbitrarily set $\sigma_u \equiv 1.0$ (1 percent). Going from row 1, column 1, of table 3.4 to row 1, column 2, shows that the optimal value of τ^* increases. As discretionary policy now suffers from the distortions in the central bank's output goal and those arising from discretion, the optimal power of the goal-based performance measure rises. As expected from the results from the simple model, adding this distortion significantly increases τ^* (from 4.04 to 12.95). The optimal δ^* is still equal to zero.

Results are similar when the welfare loss (21) is used to evaluate outcomes. Whether the central bank's objectives are based on the ad hoc loss function (22) (row 1, column 2) or (23) that

---

26. See also Tillmann (2012).

includes a distorted output gap objective (row 2, column 2), it is optimal to rely solely on the goal-based performance measure ($\tau^* > 0, \delta^* = 0$).

Now suppose the central bank cares about social welfare as well as its assigned performance measures. That is, the central bank attempts to minimize

$$\frac{1}{2}E_t\sum_{i=0}^{\infty}\beta^i[(\hat{\pi}_{t+i}-\delta_p\hat{\pi}_{t+i-1})^2\lambda_2 x_{t+i}^2+\lambda_w(\hat{\pi}_{t+i}^w-\delta_w\hat{\pi}_{t+i-1}^w)^2+\tau\hat{\pi}_{t+i}^2+\delta(i_{t+i}-i_{t+1}^r)^2]. \quad (25)$$

When the central bank cares about the welfare-based measure of loss, whether distorted by shocks to its output objective or not (rows 3 and 4, column 2), $\tau^* > 0$ and $\delta^* = 0$. Notice that the optimal power of the performance measure (τ^*) falls when the central bank cares about the welfare-based loss (compare row 1 and 2 to rows 3 and 4).

Figure 3.2 shows how τ and δ affect welfare-based social loss when the central bank also cares about the welfare-based loss function but with distortions to its output objective (corresponding to row 4, column 2, of table 3.5). Loss quickly becomes extremely large as δ increases above zero. It increases so quickly that the scale of the figure obscures the way loss varies with τ when δ is fixed at its optimal value of zero, making it hard to discern that $\tau^* = 1.54$. While setting τ equal to its optimal value reduces loss by 16 percent relative to the $\tau^* = \delta^* = 0$ case, increasing δ from o to just 0.05 when $\tau = 0$ leads to an increase in social loss by a factor of almost fifty.

The results reported in table 3.4 can be summarized briefly: for all combinations of loss functions for the central bank and the measure of social loss, whether the central bank's output target is distorted or not, the optimal weight to place on the goal-based performance measure (τ) is positive while the optimal weight to place on the rule-based performance measure (δ) is zero.

Now assume $z_t = x_t$ in (24) so that the reference policy rule includes inflation and the gap between output and its efficient

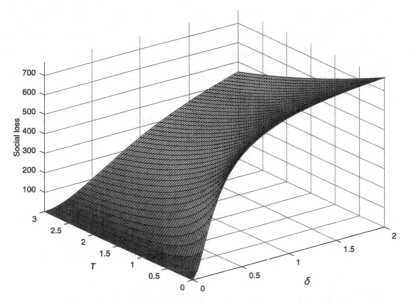

FIGURE 3.2: Loss rises quickly with δ when the reference policy rule depends on *y* (social loss given by (21) and central bank loss by (25) distorted by presence of *u* shocks to output gap objective).

Source: Author's calculations

TABLE 3.5: Optimal τ and δ, Taylor rule in π and *x*

| | | Social loss | | | |
| | | (1) Ad hoc (eq. 20) | | (2) Welfare (eq. 21) | |
	Central bank loss	τ^*	δ^*	τ^*	δ^*
(1)	ad hoc: π, *x*	6.44	1.19	0.24	0.70
(2)	ad hoc: π, *x−u*	11.26	2.38	0	1.50
(3)	welfare			26.21	11.36
(4)	welfare in *x−u*			36.05	12.22

Source: Author's calculations

level. In this case, the reference rule is defined in a manner that is more consistent with the underlying model. Results are shown in table 3.5. Now, δ* > 0 for all six different combinations considered. Row 1, column 1, of table 3.5 shows that when a standard quadratic loss function in inflation and the efficiency output gap is used to represent social loss and the central bank's preferences, it is optimal to employ both a goal-based system (i.e., $\tau^* > 0$) and a rule-based system ($\delta^* > 0$). Both performance measures are used in this case to address the dynamic inefficiency of discretionary policy. Adding the distortion to the central bank's output goal (row 2, column 1) increases the power of both performance measures. For this case with two distortions, the two performance measures serve to some degree as substitutes. For example, if either τ or δ is set to zero, there is a large reduction in social loss as the other increases from zero. The gain from setting τ optimally when $\delta = 0$ is approximately the same as that obtained by setting δ optimally when $\tau = 0$. However, if either is set at its optimal value, the further gain from employing the other performance measure is relatively small.

Rather than using an ad hoc loss function to assess outcomes as τ and δ vary, suppose the welfare-based loss function (21) is used to evaluate social loss. Assume policy is still determined by the central bank to minimize the ad hoc quadratic loss function (22) in $\hat{\pi}_t^2$ and x_t^2. Optimal values of τ and δ for this case are shown in rows 1 and 2, column 2, of table 3.5. The weights on both the goal-based and the rule-based performance measures fall relative to the case when the ad hoc loss function was used to measure social loss. The reduction in τ^* when welfare is measured by (21) rather than the ad hoc (20) is large, from 6.44 to 0.24 when $u_t \equiv 0$, while δ^* falls by over 40 percent. But perhaps more interesting is the result in row 2, column 2. If the central bank's output gap target is subject to stochastic distortion as in (23), the optimal scheme involves only the rule-based performance measure ($\tau^* = 0$). This result is consistent with the idea that a rule-based performance measure is a means of restricting central bank discretion. Figure 3.3 shows the percent reduction in social loss as a function of τ and δ. Loss clearly declines as δ rises from zero; in contrast, the reduction in loss is relatively flat as τ varies for a fixed δ.

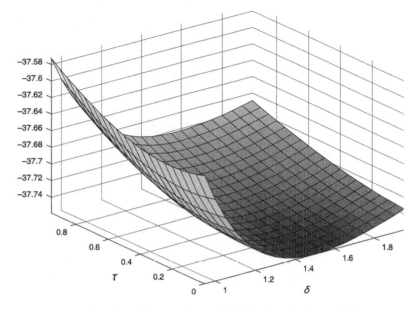

FIGURE 3.3: When the reference policy rule is based on $\hat{\pi}$ and x, social loss is given by (21) and the central bank's loss is (23), $\tau^* = 0$ and $\delta^* > 0$. (Compare with figure 3.2.)

Source: Author's calculations

In any case, the effects on loss as τ and δ vary are small. The results from the simple model indicated τ^* and δ^* would depend on the relative volatilities of the underlying shocks. Redoing the case corresponding to row 2, column 2, of table 3.5 with the standard deviation of aggregate demand shocks doubled causes τ^* to rise from 0 to 2.70 while δ^* falls to 0.70. The percent reduction in social loss as τ and δ vary for the case of more volatile demand shocks is shown in figure 3.4. Now, it is optimal to rely on both the goal-based measure and the rule-based measure of performance. This suggests the optimal performance measure may be highly dependent on the properties of the model's stochastic disturbances.

Rows 3 and 4 report results when the central bank cares about the welfare-based loss function (25). In the absence of a distorted

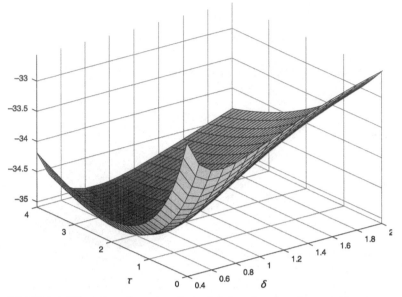

FIGURE 3.4: When the reference policy rule is based on $\hat{\pi}$ and x, social loss is given by (21) and the central bank's loss is (23), an increase in the volatility of aggregate demand shocks increases τ^* and reduces δ^*. (Compare with figure 3.3.)

Source: Author's calculations

output gap objective, both τ^* and δ^* are positive (table 3.5, row 3, column 2), and both are large. If the output gap target the central bank focuses on is distorted by u shocks so that $x_t - u_t$ rather than just x_t appears in the central bank's loss function, the optimal values of τ^* and δ^* both increase (see row 4, column 2), and in the case of τ^*, it increases quite significantly. Interestingly, when each performance measure is considered in isolation, the optimal weights are relatively small. For example, if $\delta = 0$ so that only the inflation measure is employed, the optimal weight to place on the goal-based measure is 1.45; when δ is also set optimally, $\tau^* = 36.05$. Similarly, if $\tau = 0$, the optimal value of δ is only 0.40; it increases to 12.22 when τ is set optimally. This is shown for δ in figure 3.5, which plots the change in social welfare as a function of δ for $\tau = 0$

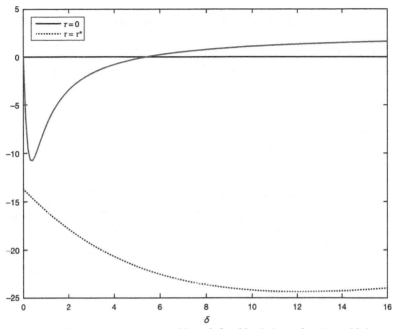

FIGURE 3.5: Percent change in social loss defined by (21) as a function of δ for τ = 0 and for τ = τ* = 36.05. Central bank's objective given by (25) distorted by presence of u shocks to output gap objective. Output measure in instrument rule is x.

Source: Author's calculations

and τ = τ*. Notice that if only the rule-based performance measure is employed (i.e., τ=0), social loss is higher than would occur with no performance measure (τ = δ = 0) for all δ > 5.4.

In general, the findings in table 3.5 suggest a role for both types of performance measures. However, in evaluating these results, an important consideration to bear in mind is that the rule-based performance measure analyzed here was taken to be the basic Taylor rule, with the coefficients on inflation and the output measure set equal to Taylor's original values. If these coefficients were optimized for the specific model used, it is likely that the optimal weight to put on the rule-based performance measure would rise.

Extensions and Conclusions

The central banking reforms initiated by the Reserve Bank of New Zealand Act of 1989 emphasized the importance of defining clear and sustainable goals for the central bank, combined with instrument independence in the conduct of policy. Such a system promotes accountability by establishing goals that are clearly defined and by giving the central bank the responsibility and ability to achieve these goals. Goal-based performance measures for central banks were motivated, in part, by a desire to constrain governments in their ability to influence monetary policy while allowing flexibility in the actual implementation of policy.

An alternative approach to reform focuses on constraining the central bank by establishing instrument rules as the means of measuring the central bank's performance. Requiring a central bank to justify its policy actions with reference to a specific instrument rule is a means of strengthening accountability by limiting the central bank's flexibility.

In a simple analytical exercise, I compared an inflation target and the Taylor rule as alternative performance measures. I showed that stochastic distortions to the central bank's goals, which could arise either from pressures external to the central bank or from the pursuit by the central bank of goals that differ from society's, justify a role for goal-based *and* rule-based performance measures. In using either performance measure, the need to limit distortionary shifts in objectives from affecting output and inflation must be balanced against the cost of reducing the bank's ability to engage in stabilization policies. Using a calibrated version of the simple model, I showed that an increase in the volatility of demand shocks relative to cost shocks increased the optimal weight to place on the goal-based performance measure relative to the rule-based measure.

The two approaches to central bank design were then evaluated using an estimated DSGE (dynamic stochastic general equilibrium) model with sticky prices and wages. Using the basic Taylor rule as the reference policy rule in the rule-based performance measure, along with Taylor's original coefficients, the definition of real activity used in the rule is crucial. When the rule is based on output deviations from potential, as in the recent proposal in the US House of Representatives, the optimal weight to place on deviations from the rule-based performance measure was always zero. In contrast, it was always optimal to employ a goal-based inflation performance measure. When the measure of real activity in the reference policy rule was the gap between output and its efficient level, it was generally optimal to place weight on both the goal-based and the rule-based measures of performance.

An important consideration in establishing any performance measure is its robustness. A reference policy rule that does not allow for shifts in the equilibrium real rate of interest, such as the one analyzed in this paper, is likely to produce poor outcomes if such shifts are an important source of macroeconomic volatility. An optimal rule would overcome this particular problem, but operational rules must be based on observable variables if they are to be of practical relevance, and the equilibrium real interest rate consistent with efficient production is unobservable. Optimal rules are also unlikely to be robust to model misspecification, an issue not addressed here. A reference policy rule that is optimal for a given model will presumably serve as a good performance measure within that model but may lead to poor results if the model is wrong or if the economic structure changes over time. Rule-based performance measures based on a rule optimized for a specific model would need, therefore, to be of low power. Of course, a simple rule, such as the Taylor rule, may be more robust across models and in the face of structure change than rules optimized for a specific model, and so a simple rule may serve as a useful, robust reference rule.

To simplify the analysis of the paper, I have ignored the constraint imposed by the zero lower bound (ZLB) on nominal interest rates.[27] The presence of the ZLB poses difficulties for both the goal-based and the rule-based performance measures. Neither provides a clear metric for what the central bank should be doing, or for how its performance should be judged, when the policy rate is at zero. This difficulty may, however, be less significant for the goal-based measure. A goal-based regime such as inflation targeting establishes a goal for the central bank but does not tie the hands of policymakers in terms of how policy is implemented to achieve the goal. For example, if the policy rate were at its lower bound with inflation below target, then a goal-based performance measure creates an incentive for the central bank to seek out new policy instruments in an effort to achieve its goal. A rule-based system may not be as effective in creating such incentives. A reference rule defined in terms of a single instrument may be of limited value during extended periods at the ZLB, as it does not provide any guidance to policymakers when the instrument value implied by the rule is unachievable. If the reference rule called for a negative interest rate, the central bank might seek to close the gap between i_t and i_t^r by directly focusing on the variables that affect i_t^r in an attempt to raise i_t^r above zero. In this case, either type of performance measure could promote policy innovations. However, because the rule-based measure is defined in terms of a specific policy instrument, and because it offers no guidance for how performance should be measured if that instrument is constrained, it may prove less likely to lead to the types of unconventional policies implemented by the Federal Reserve, the Bank of England,

---

27. I adopt the standard practice of referring to a zero lower bound for nominal interest rates, but the recent experience with negative nominal interest rates in Denmark, Sweden, and the eurozone suggests the effective lower bound may be below zero.

the Bank of Japan, and the European Central Bank during the past several years.

The focus in this paper has been on assessing policy performance in the presence of inefficient shifts in the central bank's objectives that potentially distort policy. Deviations of inflation from target or the policy interest rate from the recommendation of a Taylor rule were used as performance measures, creating incentives for the central bank to trade off minimizing these deviations against achieving other objectives. This is not the only role deviations from the Taylor rule can play. In the face of model uncertainty, Ilbas, Røisland, and Sveen (2012) show how appending deviations from the Taylor rule to the central bank's (non-distorted) loss function can contribute to policy robustness. In addition, the distortions considered in the present analysis do not affect the economy's steady-state equilibrium. Thus, policy objectives that create steady-state inefficiencies are ignored. Rogoff (1985) showed how placing additional weight on an inflation target could help overcome a systematic inflation bias under discretionary policy; a rule-based performance measure might play a similar role in addressing any systematic policy bias that affects steady-state inflation.

Finally, I have only considered traditional monetary policy objectives associated with controlling inflation and stabilizing an appropriate measure of real economic activity. As a consequence of the global financial crisis, central banks are now frequently tasked with responsibilities for macroprudential policies. An interesting question is whether a goal-based performance measure or a rule-based measure would best serve to promote accountability and good macroprudential outcomes. One significant difficulty in designing a goal-based performance measure in the case of macroprudential policies is the absence of a clear measure of the ultimate goal of policy. Inflation is both an ultimate goal of macroeconomic policy and an indicator that can be measured frequently to provide an ongoing assessment of policy. Achieving financial stability may also be an ultimate goal of policy, but there is no agreed-upon way to measure it. An index such as the ratio of credit-to-GDP may be a useful measure in this context, but it corresponds to an intermediate target. Assessing policy on the basis of movements in the credit-to-GDP ratio is much like using a monetary growth rate to assess the central bank's inflation performance. The usefulness of intermediate targets suffers if the link between the intermediate variable and the ultimate objective of policy is either uncertain or not well-understood. While it may be difficult to develop a goal-based performance measure for macroprudential policy, difficulties also arise in defining a rule-based measure. Macroprudential policies may involve the use of multiple instruments. In this case, basing accountability on how one particular instrument is used can easily distort policy by causing undue attention to that one instrument at the neglect of others. And even when attention is restricted to a single instrument—the setting of capital buffer requirements, for example—the state of research is such that there is no benchmark rule that has been extensively studied, is well understood, and could serve as a reference policy rule. The lack of the equivalent to a Taylor rule for macroprudential policy instruments is a severe limitation on the usefulness of a rule-based performance measure in the context of macroprudential policies.

COMMENTS BY ANDREW LEVIN

I'm very glad to serve as a discussant for this paper. In fact, I was looking back at my computer files, and I think the first time I discussed one of Carl's papers was at the Carnegie-Rochester conference in 2004. Like all of Carl's other papers, I really enjoyed reading this one. I like the fact that Carl always thinks of the international context, not just focused on what the United States does, but what we can learn from other central banks around the world in a very practical way. Carl also provides a very clear, elegant analysis, oftentimes using small, Keynesian models where it's possible to understand what's going on pretty clearly. In fact, I think that a major challenge in central banking is that the models that are intended to be reasonably realistic are so large as to become black boxes, which poses significant difficulties for central bank communication, transparency, and accountability. (In fact, one notable step forward recently was that the Federal Reserve Board has started publishing the FRB/US model that's often served as a benchmark for its analytical work.) At any rate, Carl's work is much more straightforward to grasp because it's typically focused on smaller, more stylized models. Moreover, I really appreciate that Carl includes some careful discussion of qualifications and limitations of his analytical results, rather than claiming to have solved everything in one paper as academic economists sometimes do.

So let me just highlight three of Carl's assumptions. First, there's no persistence anywhere in his model. There's no persistence in dynamics, and there's no persistence in the shocks, and that's what makes the analysis so elegant and the solution so simple. It effectively becomes a static problem. Moreover, there are no conditional commitments, because Carl's analysis is focused on the discretion problem, so there's no history dependence in the path of monetary policy. And there's no learning at all. In fact, that's the assumption that seems most limiting in this analysis, because the world just isn't that simple. We don't really understand the structure of the economy or the shocks that are hitting the economy in real time. And I think that's part of the reason why there's a lot of suspicion about central banks, because they're making such complex decisions under imperfect information, and there's a potential for the outcomes to be influenced by what's happening in the back room. And so the more that central banks can explain what they're doing, I think, the better. But again, the fact that we don't have complete information is really the fundamental rationale for central banks to be as transparent as possible.

Now let's turn more specifically to Carl's analytic framework. In this model, it's straightforward to determine the optimal targeting rule. And a key characteristic of that rule is it completely insulates the economy from aggregate demand shocks. The central bank directly observes any shift in the equilibrium real interest rate, because there's no imperfect information here, so policymakers can respond to such shifts by initiating a parallel shift in the actual real interest rate. Indeed, that characteristic of optimal monetary policy has been pointed out in John Taylor's work over the past several decades. By contrast, aggregate supply shocks do create policy trade-offs, and the optimal targeting rule balances those trade-offs appropriately.

The interpretation of the policy distortions in this model is a bit vague. But the basic premise is that the central bank's decisions may reflect "back room" influences such as having politically motivated conversations with the president that might not be revealed until many decades later. But these influences are purely transient, which makes the optimization problem static rather than dynamic. Now in reality, I think we're actually much more concerned about cases where these sorts of distortions are indeed persistent and induce markedly suboptimal deviations in the path of policy, of the sort that David Papell and Mike Dotsey discussed earlier. And then the central bank in effect has a distorted targeting rule, where those distortions essentially act like policy shocks and generate undesirable variability.

Now Carl considers two alternative approaches for the government—or, using Paul Tucker's terminology, "elected officials"—to influence the central bank's decisions. One approach is to incorporate an additional term into the central bank's loss function to give the central bank an incentive to place greater weight on putting inflation close to target and less weight on the central bank's own distorted objectives. The problem with this approach, as Carl has pointed out, is that this form of delegation doesn't place any weight on the economic activity goal, even though the output gap also matters for social welfare. And therefore, this approach is not ideal: at the same time that it diminishes some of the distortions resulting from back-room politics, this approach also skews the central bank's decisions away from the output gap toward a single-minded focus on inflation. I wonder if that defect could be solved by establishing what might naturally be called a dual mandate, that is, explicitly delegate both the inflation goal and the employment goal. After all, that's exactly the same as the form of the social welfare function. So then just delegate both goals, and let the weight go to infinity, and you can completely get rid of the distortions, and you're back to the fully optimal targeting rule.

Likewise with the delegation of benchmark policy rules, Carl's implementation skews the central bank's policy toward an instrument rule that doesn't fully offset aggregate demand shocks. But that problem can also be solved, because if you choose the rule carefully, you can fully replicate the optimal targeting rule. (In fact, Ben McCallum has made this point in numerous interchanges with Lars Svensson that many of you may recall.) Now the point is, by replicating the optimal targeting rule, and letting the weight, v, go to infinity, then this approach can also eliminate the policy distortions without skewing the policy stance in one undesirable direction or another.

Now moving on to some of the broader issues, I would assert that the real problem is not so much trying to restrict central bankers and put them into chains; rather, what's critical is the degree of transparency. And you see this in the very first sentence of the FOMC's Statement on Longer-Run Goals and Policy Strategy that was adopted in 2012 and that's been reaffirmed each year since then. The opening sentence of that statement reads as follows: "The FOMC seeks to explain its decisions to the public as clearly as possible." And I view that declaration as a binding commitment that the FOMC has an ongoing challenge to fulfill.

One specific issue, by the way, is that the FOMC has clarified its inflation goal as 2 percent in terms of the PCE (personal consumption expenditure) price index, so that's more or less a settled issue, at least for the time being. However, the FOMC is still not very transparent about its assessments of the maximum sustainable level of employment, and I think it's very important to start doing that. This is the $x - x^*$ that Carl emphasizes in his paper. Unfortunately, we don't even find out about the Fed staff's assessments of labor market slack until those documents are released after a five-year lag. I don't see why those assessments can't be made available in real time, because then, if analysts want to examine the implications of any particular policy rule, they can do so using the Fed's real-time assessments of the output gap, as well as making comparisons with the implications of other assessments such as those published by the CBO, the IMF, and the Organisation for Economic Co-operation and Development.

So the key premise is that policymakers need to explain their decisions in terms of a coherent policy strategy. In that regard, it's worth noting that the FOMC's Statement on Longer Run Goals and Policy Strategy is almost exclusively aimed at clarifying its longer-run goals. In fact, there's really only one clause in one sentence, namely, the indication that the FOMC "follows a balanced approach." In effect, what's still missing—and what's desired by the general public as well as academic economists, market investors, and members of Congress—is for the FOMC to explain its policy strategy more clearly.

Now there are two ways to do that. One of them is using forecasts, and that's the part where the FOMC regularly provides a substantial amount of information four times a year in the Summary of Economic Projections, including the outlook for GDP growth, unemployment, inflation, and the federal funds rate. I'll just highlight here that the essential problem is that forecasts depend crucially on the use of macroeconomic models. It might be a single model or a cluster of models, and the forecast might involve some judgmental adjustments (which tend to be remarkably opaque). Moreover, as we all know very well, such forecasts can be systematically and persistently wrong. Indeed, for the past five years in a row, the FOMC's projections for GDP growth have been much too optimistic. And it looks like that might happen yet again this year. Likewise, the trend for inflation has generally been downward over the past five years. But at every juncture, the FOMC's projections have been overly optimistic in predicting that inflation over the subsequent year or two would be coming back upward to its 2 percent target. And that was their outlook yet again in March of this year. I sincerely hope that outlook materializes, but it's not at all clear from the latest inflation data whether that will actually happen.

That track record simply underscores the pitfalls of relying too heavily on forecast targeting as the tool for determining and explaining the stance of monetary policy. The salient alternative, as John Taylor has emphasized, is to use simple policy benchmark rules that are designed to be reasonably robust in the face of model uncertainty. Of course, each of these tools—model-based forecasts and simple policy rules—have merits as well as shortcomings. Consequently, a sensible and prudent approach to monetary policy involves using both types of tools in making policy decisions and explaining those decisions. I hope that the FOMC would see the benefits of moving in that direction voluntarily, since that would likely be a better outcome than for Congress to adopt legislation with specific edicts about the FOMC's deliberative process and communications. However, if the Congress does decide that new legislation is warranted, then such legislation should be focused on ensuring that the FOMC provides sufficient information to the public to explain its decisions as clearly as possible.

GENERAL DISCUSSION

JOHN WILLIAMS: I really like this paper. I was one of the organizers of the conference in New Zealand. It's great to go to New Zealand in December. And it was a great opportunity to revisit the amazing accomplishments of the Reserve Bank of New Zealand in charting this course of inflation targeting twenty-five years ago all on their own as part of a much larger reform package in New Zealand.

I think though that the paper goes through kind of thinking through: Where are the distortions and what are the optimal policy taxes or subsidies? You have a distorted equilibrium and you're trying to come up with some countervailing distortions in terms of the penalty or the loss function the central bankers face.

I do go back to this twenty-five years ago in the invention of inflation targeting and think: What was the problem they were trying to solve? Here today, and we talked a lot about this, there's a perceived problem—I think George Shultz laid it out very nicely—about central bankers exceeding what they should be doing, and as a result making bad decisions. But if you do go back to twenty-five years ago, the problem was very high inflation in many countries, governments not holding central banks accountable, and central banks not taking responsibility or accountability for the high inflation. So in thinking about Carl's paper, we don't want to somehow lose that context in that discussion. In many ways, this goal-based approach was designed to make the central bank formally accountable for the one thing that a central bank actually can for sure do, and that's control inflation over the medium to long term. Central banks may want to be able to do a lot of other things, and sometimes they can, but that's the one thing that they should own, and that's one of the things I think that inflation targeting clearly did accomplish. And so if you think about all the costs and the damage to economies from very high and variable inflation in the US and Canada and Britain and New Zealand and in Australia and in every country you can think of, and basically the accomplishment of inflation targeting, of the accountability that's built around inflation targeting around the goal, I just think that thinking about any future kind of ways to put more accountability on a central bank that we don't lose sight of that, because that is something that I think was hugely successful and when we didn't have that accountability for a goal, it had a significant cost to society.

MICHAEL DOTSEY: OK, I want to say something that relates to both this paper and what Paul Tucker said before. It's sort of in defense of monetary rules of the past that were discarded.

So—the gold standard. Actually, the gold standard was not that bad of a rule, and if it really worked, it was a contingent rule. And if you had some huge shock come up, you could bail out. In fact, it's better than what the eurozone's got, because they don't have the contingency.

And the other one is monetary aggregates. Actually, it really wasn't tried. In fact, if they had done something like Ben McCallum's rule, which was discussed quite a bit fifteen to twenty years ago, that might have worked. So there are these events in history that became path-dependent, that said, "No, we're not going to do that. We're going to go toward using interest rates, but we're not going to use the gold standard." So you have to be more careful when you talk about it and assume these are dead ghosts that didn't work. Actually, one did work, and one could have worked better.

DAVID PAPELL: I think you need to be careful about drawing too much of a dichotomy between goal-based and instrument-based rules. The Taylor rule includes an inflation target which feeds into the intercept, and that intercept feeds into whether you would have deviations or not. Since you're embedding an inflation target, you're looking at—to my mind, at least—more accountability because you're seeing quarter-to-quarter whether what you're doing is going to move you toward that inflation target. And I think that's something you should think about in terms of the dichotomy between the rules.

JOHN TAYLOR: So, Carl, I see from your paper that when you have the right rule, you put all the weight on that rule. To me, that's really what we're talking about in the discussion of legislation. We do have a sense of what rules have worked pretty well—not optimal, exactly—and the Fed could base its strategy on those. And I think there are advantages also to having predictability, a strategy, and all that. Also, the legislation doesn't require the Fed to follow a particular rule, but a reference rule could help achieve predictability.

Another issue relates to the idea of "constrained discretion." As described in Carl's paper, the goal-based approach is a way to constrain not the central bank, but the government. And so it leaves no constraint on the central bank. And that's the problem with so-called constrained discretion. The terms may sound good, but it doesn't constrain discretion in any way, and so policy becomes a whatever-it-takes philosophy to get to the goals. That's what worries a lot of us now. It seems like it's completely up for grabs what the Fed and some other central banks will do. It's like Andy's reference to the Fed: strategy is mentioned, but there's no discussion of strategy. It's almost as if the focus on those long-run goals has let central bankers say, "Hey, don't worry about it. We've got those goals. Let us do whatever we want. It will be OK." And you get this highly discretionary setup.

CARL WALSH: Let me just respond to a couple of the comments. The framework of the paper is very simple to allow some analytical expressions to be obtained and to get a sense of what sort of factors would push you toward trying to put either more or less weight on the performance measures. The role of the shocks to the central bank preferences was to exactly get at—or at least have a channel for—the types of things that I think you're worried about, John. The central bank's preferences aren't, in some sense, tied down. If the central bank is potentially pursuing things that really are not in their mandate, one needs some way of judging their performance to hold them accountable.

But in the setup I've used, the big sources of bad policy, such as unachievable goals that lead to high rates of inflation, are absent. In some sense the model presumes you've solved the first-order problem, and now you're worrying about the second-order problem associated with getting stabilization policies right. And actually if you go back to either the classic Barro-Gordon paper on the time inconsistency of optimal monetary policy or Matt Canzoneri's paper on the inflation bias in the face of private information, you'll see they both concluded that with perfect information, you could just assign a specific rule to the central bank and tell them, "This is what you should do."

I think that the perfect information case is an environment in which we wouldn't be worried about things like performance measures and policy discretion. You could just say to the central bank, "Here is the list of contingencies, and in this contingency, you do this." But, that's the world of the model, where you can specify what all the contingencies are. In the real world, you can't, and then the issue is, what works best? Can you simply set out the overarching goals? Or, do you want to be more specific, and say, "We're going to evaluate you on the basis of how your instrument is moved relative to a benchmark rule?"

Now, as Andy pointed out, in the examples I examined, I didn't use an optimal rule. I just used the rule in the House legislation. If you design the optimal rule, then you'd want the power of the performance measure (the *delta*) to be very high. That is, if you know the optimal rule and if everything is observable, you can write down exactly what the central bank should do, and you hold them accountable for implementing that rule. The simple model is trying to capture the idea that we don't really believe we're in a world in which we know the best rule. In that environment, the question is: Which sorts of factors push you toward relying more on a rule to evaluate policy? And which factors push you more in a direction of focusing on the goals of policy to evaluate the central bank?

JOHN COCHRANE: I'd like to follow up with John Taylor's comment here. I think the model left out two of the most important considerations of goals. First, suppose the Fed just has an inflation goal, so its instructions are basically: do whatever you want to produce the desired inflation. Then the central bank can wake up and say, "We're buying stock in Paul Tucker's company, and we're going to mandate lending over here, because this is our macroprudential way to achieve the inflation goal." Do-what-it-takes with no limit on how is dangerous.

Second, an inflation target is also a commitment by the rest of the government, not just the central bank. I read this as the great success of New Zealand. Its inflation target was a joint monetary and fiscal policy accord. It said that fiscal policy would back up a 2 percent inflation, and only a 2 percent inflation.

DOTSEY: I think John raised an interesting point, but I'm not sure the paper actually addresses the point he raised. He sort of talked about how we get rid of some of the time inconsistency by designing these things. But I think you would want to solve—which I don't think you did—the full commitment problem, and then ask: What would I append in the time-inconsistent problem to sort of get me closer to that? I don't think you did that exercise.

WALSH: Well, in the estimated model I compare outcomes under alternative regimes by evaluating the combination of price inflation, wage inflation, and output gap volatility that the model implies is the correct measure of social welfare. I don't compare how well the performance measures do or how poorly they do relative to the fully optimal commitment policy.

REFERENCES

Alesina, Alberto, and Lawrence Summers. 1993. "Central Bank Independence and Macroeconomic Performance." *Journal of Money, Credit, & Banking* 25, no. 2: 157–162.

Athey, Susan, Andrew Atkeson, and Patrick J. Kehoe. 2005. "The Optimal Degree of Discretion in Monetary Policy." *Econometrica* 73, no. 5: 1431–1475.

Bade, Robin, and Michael Parkin. 1984. "Central Bank Laws and Monetary Policy." University of Western Ontario.

Baker, George P. 1992. "Incentive Contracts and Performance Measurement." *Journal of Political Economy* 100, no. 3: 598–614.

Baker, George, Robert Gibbons, and Kevin Murphy. 1994. "Subjective Performance Measures in Optimal Incentive Contracts." *Quarterly Journal of Economics* 109, no. 4: 1125–1156.

Barro, Robert. J., and David B. Gordon. 1983. "A Positive Theory of Monetary Policy in a Natural-Rate Model." *Journal of Political Economy* 91, no. 4: 589–610.

Benhabib, Jess, Stephanie Schmitt-Grohe, and Martin Uribe. 2001. "The Perils of Taylor Rules." *Journal of Economic Theory* 96: 40–69.

Billi, Roberto M. 2013. "Nominal GDP Targeting and the Zero Lower Bound: Should We Abandon Inflation Targeting?" Sveriges Riksbank working paper no. 270, June.

Blinder, Alan S., Michael Ehrmann, Marcel Fratzscher, Jakob De Haan, and David-Jan Jansen. 2008. "Central Bank Communication and Monetary Policy: A Survey of Theory and Evidence." *Journal of Economic Literature* 46, no. 4: 910–945.

Canzoneri, Matthew B. 1985. "Monetary Policy Games and the Role of Private Information." *American Economic Review* 75: 1056–1070.

Carlstrom, Charles T., and Timothy S. Fuerst. 2009. "Central Bank Independence and Inflation: a Note." *Economic Inquiry* 47, no. 1: 182–186.

Casares, Miguel, Antonio Moreno, and Jesus Vazquez. 2011. "Wage Stickiness and Unemployment Fluctuations: An Alternative Approach." *SERIEs* 3, no. 3: 395–422.

Chen, Han, Vasco Curdia, and Andrea Ferrero. 2012. "The Macroeconomic Effects of Large-Scale Asset Purchase Programmes." *Economic Journal* 122 (September): F289–F315.

Clarida, Richard, Jordi Galí, and Mark Gertler. 1999. "The Science of Monetary Policy: A New Keynesian Perspective." *Journal of Economic Literature* 37, no. 4: 1661–1707.

Crowe, Christopher, and Ellen E. Meade. 2007. "The Evolution of Central Bank Governance around the World." *Journal of Economic Perspectives* 21, no. 4: 69–90.

Cukierman, Alex. 1992. *Central Bank Strategies, Credibility and Independence.* Cambridge, MA: MIT Press.

Cukierman, Alex, Steven B. Webb, and Bilin Neyapti. 1992. "Measuring the Independence of Central Banks and Its Effect on Policy Outcomes." *World Bank Economic Review* 6, no. 3: 353–398.

Debelle, Guy, and Stanley Fischer. 1994. "How Independent Should a Central Bank Be?" *Carnegie Rochester Conference Series on Public Policy* 38: 195–225.

Dincer, N. Nergiz, and Barry Eichengreen. 2014. "Central Bank Transparency and Independence: Updates and New Measures." *International Journal of Central Banking* 10, no. 1: 189–253.

Drazen, Allan. 2000. *The Political Economy of Macroeconomics.* Princeton, NJ: Princeton University Press.

Erceg, Christopher, Dale W. Henderson, and Andrew T. Levin. 2000. "Optimal Monetary Policy with Staggered Wage and Price Contracts." *Journal of Monetary Economics* 46, no. 2: 281–313.

Evjen, Snorre, and Thea B. Kloster. 2012. "Norges Bank's New Monetary Policy Loss Function: Further Discussion." Norges Bank research working paper no. 11.

Frankel, Alexander. 2014. "Aligned Delegation." *American Economic Review* 104, no. 1: 66–83.

Galí, Jordi. 2008. *Monetary Policy, Inflation, and the Business Cycle: An Introduction to the New Keynesian Framework*. Princeton, NJ: Princeton University Press.

———— 2013. "Notes for a New Guide to Keynes (I): Wages, Aggregate Demand, and Employment." *Journal of the European Economic Association* 11, no. 5: 973–1003.

Ilbas, Pelin, Øistein Røisland, and Tommy Sveen. 2012. "Robustifying Optimal Monetary Policy Using Simple Rules as Cross-Checks." Norges Bank research working paper no. 2012-22: 30.

———— 2013. "The Influence of the Taylor Rule on US Monetary Policy." Norges Bank research working paper, 2013-04: 34.

Kahn, George A. 2012. "The Taylor Rule and the Practice of Central Banking." In *The Taylor Rule and the Transformation of Monetary Policy*. Edited by Evan F. Koenig, Robert Leeson, and George A. Kahn. Stanford, CA: Hoover Institution Press: 63–102.

Kydland, Finn E., and Edward C. Prescott. 1977. "Rules Rather than Discretion: The Inconsistency of Optimal Plans." *Journal of Political Economy* 85, no. 3: 473–91.

Levin, Andrew T., Volker Wieland, and John C. Williams. 1999. "Robustness of Simple Monetary Policy Rules under Model Uncertainty." In *Monetary Policy Rules*. Edited by John B. Taylor. Chicago: Chicago University Press.

Levin, Andrew T., and John C. Williams. 2003. "Robust Monetary Policy with Competing Reference Models." *Journal of Monetary Economics* 50, no. 5: 945–975.

Lund, Kathrine, and Ørjan R. Robstad. 2012. "Effects of a New Monetary Policy Loss Function in N.E.M.O." Norges Bank research working paper no. 10.

Poole, William. 1970. "Optimal Choice of Monetary Policy Instrument in a Simple Stochastic Macro Model." *Quarterly Journal of Economics* 84, no. 2: 197–216.

Posen, Adam. 1993. "Why Central Bank Independence Does Not Cause Low Inflation: There is No Institutional Fix for Politics." *Finance and the International Economy* 7: 40–65.

Rogoff, Kenneth. 1985. "The Optimal Degree of Commitment to an Intermediate Monetary Target." *Quarterly Journal of Economics* 100, no. 4: 1169–1189.

Rudebusch, Glenn D. 2002. "Term Structure Evidence on Interest Rate Smoothing and Monetary Policy Inertia." *Journal of Monetary Economics* 49, no. 6: 1161–1187.

Ruge-Murcia, Francisco J. 2014. "Do Inflation-Targeting Central Banks Implicitly Target the Price Level?" *International Journal of Central Banking* 10, no. 2: 301–326.

Svensson, Lars E. Ø. 2003. "What Is Wrong with Taylor Rules? Using Judgment in Monetary Policy through Targeting Rules." *Journal of Economic Literature* 41, no. 2: 426–477.

Taylor, John B. 1993. "Discretion versus Policy Rules in Practice." *Carnegie Rochester Conference Series on Public Policy* 39, no. 1: 195–214.

—— 2011. "The Rules-Discretion Cycle in Monetary and Fiscal Policy." *Finnish Economic Papers* 24, no. 2: 78–86.

—— 2012. "Monetary Policy Rules Work and Discretion Doesn't: A Tale of Two Eras." *Journal of Money, Credit, & Banking* 44, no. 6: 1017–1032.

—— 2013. "The Effectiveness of Central Bank Independence vs. Policy Rules." *Business Economics* 48 (July 2013): 1–21.

Taylor, John B., and John C. Williams. 2010. "Simple and Robust Rules for Monetary Policy." In *Handbook of Monetary Economics*, vol. 3. Edited by Benjamin Friedman and Michael Woodford: 829–859.

Tillmann, Peter. 2012. "Cross-Checking Optimal Monetary Policy with Information from the Taylor Rule." *Economic Letters* 117, no. 1: 204–207.

Tirole, Jean. 1994. "The Internal Organization of Government." *Oxford Economic Papers* 46, no. 1: 1–29.

Vestin, David. 2006. "Price-Level Targeting versus Inflation Targeting." *Journal of Monetary Economics* 53, no. 7: 1361–1376.

Walsh, Carl E. 1986. "In Defense of Base Drift." *American Economic Review* 76, no. 4: 692–700.

———— 1987. "Monetary Targets and Inflation: 1976–1984." Federal Reserve Bank of San Francisco *Economic Review*, Winter.

———— 1995a. "Is New Zealand's Reserve Bank Act of 1989 an Optimal Central Bank Contract?" *Journal of Money, Credit, & Banking* 27, no. 4, part 1: 1179–1191.

———— 1995b. "Optimal Contracts for Central Bankers." *The American Economic Review* 85, no. 1: 150–167.

———— 2003a. "Accountability, Transparency, and Inflation Targeting." *Journal of Money, Credit, & Banking* 35, no. 5: 829–849.

———— 2003b. "Speed Limit Policies: The Output Gap and Optimal Monetary Policy." *American Economic Review* 93, no. 1: 265–278.

———— 2010. *Monetary Theory and Policy*. 3rd. ed. Cambridge, MA: MIT Press.

————2015. "Goals and Rules in Central Bank Design." *International Journal of Central Banking* 11, no. S1: 1–45.

Woodford, Michael. 2010. "Optimal Monetary Stabilization Policy." In *Handbook of Monetary Economics*, vol. 3. Edited by Benjamin M. Friedman and Michael Woodford, chap. 14: 723–828.

CHAPTER FOUR

Institutional Design: Deliberations, Decisions, and Committee Dynamics

Kevin M. Warsh

Monetary policy is conducted by individuals acting by legislative remit in an institutional setting.

Great attention is paid to the individuals atop the largest central banks. Central bankers today are decidedly recognizable public figures. Some might even be called famous. Their newfound status, however, would make them thoroughly unrecognizable to their predecessors.

The central banks' responsibilities—the legislative remits with which they are charged—are also subject to considerable scrutiny. Monetary policymakers are tasked with keeping fidelity to their legislated mandates. Some, like the European Central Bank (ECB), are granted a single mandate, namely to ensure price stability. Others, like the Federal Reserve, are tasked with a so-called dual mandate, which includes ensuring price stability and maximum sustainable employment. The financial crisis resurrected yet another objective: ensuring financial stability.

Considerably less attention, however, is paid to the institutional setting in which the policymakers meet, deliberate, and ultimately decide on policy. These institutional dynamics alone are not determinative of the policy outcome. But I posit that the institutional dynamics influence policy decisions more than is commonly appreciated.

In business, academia, and government, people and policy converge in institutional settings. These settings matter considerably to the ultimate success—or failure—of an endeavor. An institution's setting is a function, in part, of its institutional design; that is, the way in which the entity is originally composed and comprised. But institutions are not static. They change with prodding, time, and experience. An institutional setting, thus, is also a function of the personalities populating it, actions undertaken, and cultures which endure.

Inside the marbled walls and grand columns of central banks lie rich histories and deep traditions. When new central bankers are sworn into office, they arrive with predispositions and preferences. But they get acclimated, in varying degrees, to the institutional setting. And for certain leaders, the institutional setting acclimates, at least somewhat, to them. Public policy decisions are ultimately affected by a mix of people, processes, ideas, and settings. Committees tasked with conducting monetary policy are not immune.

In my remarks, I will consider the institutional setting in the conduct of monetary policy. I review the academic literature, describe my own experience as a member of the Federal Open Market Committee (FOMC), and draw upon a recent study of the Bank of England's Monetary Policy Committee (MPC).

In 2014, I was asked by Governor Mark Carney, on behalf of the Bank of England, to undertake an independent review of the transparency of its decision-making. The report, *Transparency and the Bank of England's Monetary Policy Committee*, issued on December 11, 2014, assessed the transparency among monetary policy committees in advanced economies.[1] I benchmarked the Bank's transparency to its international peers and recommended certain reforms.[2] In the course of the review, I listened to the dis-

---

1. News release, "Bank of England announces measures to bolster transparency and accountability," December 11, 2014, http://www.bankofengland.co.uk/publications/Pages/news/2014/168.aspx; also, Kevin Warsh, "Transparency and the Bank of England's Monetary Policy Committee," Hoover Institution, December 17, 2014, http://www.hoover.org/research/transparency-and-bank-englands-monetary-policy-committee.
2. I owe special thanks to Lea Paterson and Amar Radia of the Bank of England for their valuable contributions, both to the report and to this research paper.

cussions of the MPC and met with most members who served on the committee since 1997. The assignment gave me a valuable—and rare—insight into the workings of the Bank's MPC and made for ready comparison to my own experience at the FOMC and that of my predecessors, captured in part by the published transcripts of FOMC meetings.

The MPC and FOMC have much in common: operational independence from the fiscal authorities, a commitment to price stability, and a strong reputation for integrity of its people and rigor in its analyses. But the institutional dynamics differ across these policymaking committees.

How consequential is a policymaking committee's institutional dynamics to its ultimate decisions? What happens when its people and practices meet amid uncertainty to deliberate and decide upon a policy choice? Is the committee fashioned to foster robust deliberations as part of its decision-making process? Or do the dynamics disincline its members from changing their a priori judgments? To what extent does the committee design foster groupthink? Or does it favor a diversity of views?

These questions cannot be answered definitively. But understanding the institutional dynamics inside monetary policy committees is likely as consequential to sound policy decisions as the skill of the people who lead the committees and the remits they are obliged to follow.

What causes institutions to succeed?

Scholars and practitioners in the fields of management and organizational design have much good work to share with central bankers. The lessons learned from these other disciplines are quite applicable to the evaluation of monetary policy committee dynamics.

Figure 4.1 illustrates the prerequisites for sound decision-making: high-quality inputs, optimal design of decision-making bodies,

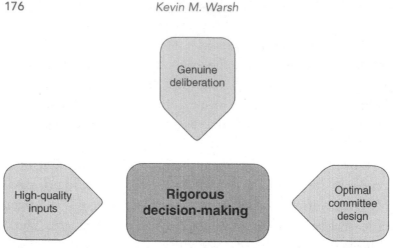

FIGURE 4.1: Key ingredients to sound decision-making

Source: Kevin Warsh, *Transparency and the Bank of England's Monetary Policy Committee*, 2014

and, crucially, an institutional setting that fosters genuine deliberation.

Decision-making and organizational success

Institutional dynamics have an important bearing on the long-term success of an organization.

In their survey of the academic literature, Mellahi and Wilkinson (2004) describe two broad models to account for organizational success or failure. One identifies "external factors" as the predominant force—failure of particular organizations is predominantly a symptom of an industry-wide decline of which management's control is limited.[3] An alternative theory emphasizes the importance of "internal factors," that is, the quality of management decisions and the institutional settings within which they are made.

3. As Mellahi and Wilkinson (2004) note, classic industrial organization literature traces the roots of industry-wide decline to Schumpeterian "creative destruction" (Schumpeter 1942).

The literature identifies numerous interrelated theories that link internal management inadequacies to organizational failure. These include:

- Janis's canonical Groupthink theory (1972, 1982), which highlights the tendency of small, homogenous management teams to make suboptimal decisions;
- Hambrick and Mason's Upper Echelon theory (1984), which links organizational achievements to the composition and background of an organization's senior management team;
- Staw, Sandelands, and Dutton's Threat Rigidity Effect theory (1981), which explains the tendency of management groups to stick rigidly to tried and tested techniques at times of threat and challenge, thereby increasing the risk of organizational failure among incumbents at times of secular change.

The common finding is to tailor institutional settings—that is, the design of decision-making processes and structure of decision-making groups—so that genuine deliberation prevails. This is particularly important in times of regime change in the data or policy paradigm.

That genuine deliberation should play a central role in decision-making is rooted in classical liberalism. John Stuart Mill (1859) championed the importance of free speech and discourse to intellectual progress. He advanced the belief that truth would emerge through the free competition of ideas in public discussion and debate. As Mill wrote in his classic *On Liberty*: "The general or prevailing opinion in any subject is rarely or never the whole truth; it is only by the collision of adverse opinions that the remainder of the truth has any chance of being supplied."

A core aim of deliberation is to achieve consensus among different parties. But, as noted by Barabas (2004) and others, deliberative processes should accomplish more than merely achieving consensus. Barabas defines "desirable" (or genuine) deliberation as that which succeeds not only in achieving consensus, but also in delivering intellectual progress: "Submissive consensus is clearly undesirable . . . [t]o be desirable, deliberation should improve knowledge so that participants come not only to a consensus, but also to an enlightened view of the problem at hand."

Genuine deliberation is, therefore, the process by which participants not only share information, but also learn from and influence one other. It is the crux of good decision-making processes within both public and private spheres, the "special sauce" to optimize policy.

As Schonhardt-Bailey (2013) describes in her comprehensive analysis of monetary policy deliberations: "Effective deliberation among . . . unelected experts who are being held to account is thus one of engagement and reciprocity where participants talk to one another and take up others' points." The institutional setting should allow genuine deliberation to flourish.

Identifying genuine deliberation: inquiry vs. advocacy

A useful starting point is to identify what effective deliberation should look like. A thorough assessment of the nature and importance of rigorous decision-making processes is provided by Garvin and Roberto (2001). They make a useful delineation between the process of "inquiry" and that of "advocacy."[4]

Inquiry is essential for successful decision-making and organizational success. As Garvin and Roberto put it: "Inquiry is a very open process, designed to generate multiple alternatives, foster the exchange of ideas, and produce a well-tested solution. . . . A process characterized by inquiry rather than advocacy tends to produce decisions of higher quality."

---

4. I treat "inquiry" and "deliberation" as largely synonymous.

Garvin and Roberto highlight the ways in which inquiry and advocacy differ:

Open and balanced sharing of information

People engaged in inquiry typically share information widely, typically in raw form, and allow participants to draw their own conclusions. Participants in an advocacy process, in contrast, often present information selectively, buttressing their arguments while withholding relevant conflicting data.

Critical thinking and assumption testing

Inquiry processes are ones of testing and evaluation. Effective decision-making groups step back from their arguments in order to confirm their assumptions by examining them critically. Participants do not shy away from asking hard questions. These indicia of critical thinking are not typically present in processes of advocacy, in which the discussions tend to be characterized by persuasion and lobbying.

Deliberation of multiple alternatives and encouragement of dissension

Inquiry cultivates and values minority views, and participants are comfortable raising alternatives. Inquiry processes tend to be characterized by thoughtful analysis of multiple alternatives, and usually avoid settling on the easy, obvious answer too quickly. Advocacy, by contrast, tends to suppress new ideas. Participants are passionate about their preferred solutions; that passion tends to harm their objectivity, limiting their ability to pay attention to opposing arguments.

Conflict is constructive, not personal

"Cognitive" conflict relates to the substance of the issues at hand. "Affective" conflict tends to be personal. Cognitive conflict is constructive, and often characterizes inquiry processes. It allows people to express differences openly and challenge underlying assumptions; participants in inquiry tend to be accepting of constructive criticism. Affective conflict, by contrast, harms the decision-making process. It more often involves personal friction, rivalries, and clashing personalities, and diminishes people's willingness to cooperate.

Active listening

Genuine listening and attentiveness to alternative points of view are typical of inquiry-making processes. Asking questions, probing for deeper explanations, and showing patience when participants explain their positions are all identified as evidence of active listening and are found in well-designed decision-making processes.

The Garvin and Roberto study echoes many of the themes advanced by Fishkin (1991) in his pioneering work on deliberation. He identifies five characteristics of productive deliberations:

- *Informed:* arguments should be supported by appropriate and accurate claims;
- *Balanced:* arguments should be met by contrary arguments;
- *Conscientious:* participants should talk and listen with civility and respect;
- *Substantive:* arguments should be considered solely on their merits, rather than being given weight (or not) based on how they are made, or by whom they are made;
- *Comprehensive:* all points of view held by significant portions of the population should be given attention.

Fishkin used these principles to design a range of experiments conducted in both the United States and the United Kingdom. He demonstrates that well-designed deliberative processes can lead to better outcomes.

Barabas (2004) also stresses the need for deliberation processes to be well-designed if they are to advance intellectual progress, singling out criteria such as the quality and breadth of information provided to decision-makers and the degree of open-mindedness of participants as important contributors to success. He concludes: "Deliberation increases knowledge and alters opinions, but it does so selectively based on the quality and diversity of the messages as well as the willingness of participants to keep an open mind."

In sum, for organizations to thrive over time—in the private or public sector—the institutional setting must ensure genuine deliberation.

Committee dynamics: When do monetary policy committees succeed?

The trend toward committee-based decision-making is among the major developments in the conduct of monetary policy. Committee dynamics—be they related to structure, composition, or culture—can therefore have an important bearing on policy outcomes.

There is considerable literature on optimal design of monetary policy committees (see, for example, Sibert 2006, Maier 2010, and Reis 2013). And there is an emerging consensus that well-designed committees tend to make better-quality decisions than individuals. Perhaps the best known research in the monetary policy arena is that of Blinder and Morgan (2005), which shows that groups tend to outperform individuals in a simple monetary policymaking game.[5]

5. The Blinder and Morgan work was replicated in the United Kingdom by Lombardelli, Proudman, and Talbot (2005).

TABLE 4.1: Elements of Optimal Committee Design[7]

1. Clear objectives and independence	• Clearly defined goal and efficient instructions • High degree of central bank independence
2. Size	• Not much larger than five members
3. Measures to avoid free-riding	• Easy identification and evaluation of individual contributions
4. Polarisation and group-think	• Institutional encouragement of independent thought
	• Diversity of backgrounds and experiences • Mix of internal and external members • No fixed speaking order to avoid information cascades

Source: Kevin Warsh, *Transparency and the Bank of England's Monetary Policy Committee*, 2014; Philip Maier, "How Central Banks Take Decisions: An Analysis on Monetary Policy," in *Challenges in Central Banking: The Current Institutional Environment and Forces Affecting Monetary Policy*, eds. Pierre L. Siklos, Martin T. Bohl, and Mark E. Wohar (Cambridge, UK: Cambridge University Press, 2010).

Maier (2010) summarizes several hypotheses to explain the rationale for the superiority of committee decisions. These include the potential gains from the pooling of information from different sources and the advantages of processing information from a group comprising different skills and experiences. Other benefits of committee-based decision-making include the provision of "insurance" against the extreme preferences of any one individual.

Committee decision-making, however, is not without potential drawbacks. These include the inefficiency of sharing and processing information among large groups and the risks of the emergence of groupthink. In addition, committee-based decision-making is also often described as prone to inertia, although the empirical evidence is less clear-cut.[6]

Given that committee-based decision-making processes can incur benefits and costs, the matter of committee design is consequential. The superiority of smaller committees with members of

6. Blinder (2002) finds that committees are no more inert than individuals when making decisions.

diverse experiences is a recurring theme. As Sibert (2006) states: "[M]onetary policy committees should have a clear objective, publish individual votes and not have many more than five members. They should be structured so that members do not act as part of a group, perhaps by having short terms in office and members from outside the central bank."

Similar assertions are made in Maier (2010), whose conclusions on optimal committee design are summarized in table 4.1.

From theory to practice: design features of monetary policy committees

What do policy committee dynamics actually look like in practice?

The leading central bank monetary policy committees are designed somewhat differently from one another. As table 4.2 shows, the number of decision-makers, decision-making protocol, and principals in attendance diverge markedly among leading central banks.

A healthy dose of caution should be applied before presuming a direct read-across from the experience of the Fed with the Bank of England, or indeed of any other central bank. But, as Schonhardt-Bailey (2013) describes the policy process: "[M]onetary policy made in a committee setting . . . involves the aggregation of individual preferences of policymakers into a collective decision." So, it is important to consider how the "aggregation of individual preferences" differs by virtue of the institutional arrangements of the MPC and FOMC, which will be discussed in the balance of the paper.

MPC evaluation

The institutional dynamics of the Bank of England's MPC are favorable to genuine deliberation and sound decision-making.

7. As outlined by Maier (2010).

TABLE 4.2: Comparison of committee designs

	Bank of Canada	Bank of England	Bank of Japan	European Central Bank	Federal Reserve	Norges Bank	Reserve Bank of Australia	Reserve Bank of New Zealand	Sveriges Riksbank	Swiss National Bank
Frequency of scheduled meetings (per year)	8	8[a]	14	8[a]	8	6	11	8	6	4
Number of decision-makers (or voting members)	6	9	9	21[b]	12	7	9	1[c]	6	3
Decision-making protocol	Consensus	Vote	Vote	Vote	Vote	Consensus	Vote	Governor	Vote	Consensus
Principals[d]/others in attendance	6/approx. 5	9/6	9/approx. 15	25/approx. 25	19/approx. 60	7/10	9/approx. 5	n/a	6/approx. 20	3/10

Source: Kevin Warsh, *Transparency and the Bank of England's Monetary Policy Committee,* 2014

(a) The ECB and Bank of England have announced an intention to move to eight monetary policy meetings per year rather than twelve, as is recent practice.

(b) As of January 2015.

(c) Monetary policy decisions at the RBNZ are made by the governor.

(d) The number of principals is defined as the number of members of the committee who participate at meetings.

The MPC meets many of the criteria for an optimal monetary policy committee, including its relatively small size. Membership of the MPC is drawn from a diverse group—five of the nine members are "internal," typically with prior central banking experience; the remaining four are "external," appointed by the chancellor of the exchequer. The four externals serve a maximum of two three-year terms, and are typically drawn from varied backgrounds, including academia, business, and financial markets.

In my view, the MPC's design facilitates effective deliberation, due in part to the relatively small number of people in attendance at the policy meetings. There are typically around fifteen people present at the MPC's monthly policy meetings—the nine committee members, a representative of Her Majesty's Treasury, and five senior staff members of the Bank's monetary analysis area.

More generally, the one-member, one-vote structure of the MPC, and the associated strong ethos of individual accountability on the committee, ensure that it is possible to identify and evaluate individual contributions. As Sibert (2006) notes: "The solution to groupthink is to get group members to stop thinking and behaving as group members."

As Maier (2010) puts it: "In many ways, the Bank of England's committee structure follows best practice: it has a clear goal, it is made up of diverse members (academics, business representatives, and central bankers) and it is not too big. Also, individual contributions can be identified and evaluated, and its members are encouraged to think for themselves."

Informed by my access to the MPC, I was struck by the nature and quality of the discussion inside of the committee room. I listened to many examples of genuine and effective deliberation, especially during the first day of the MPC's two-day meeting.[8]

8. MPC meetings were structured so that the first day of discussions included a review of economic and market developments. The second day focused largely on the policy deci-

During the first day of discussion, the debate was free-flowing and open, the tone usually courteous and informal. Members routinely queried each other intently on the bases for their opinions, and played devil's advocate as they sought to understand the trends in the economy and financial market developments. Members exhibited behavior indicative of robust inquiry and evaluation processes.

Members sought to test, dismiss, or advance competing hypotheses to solve puzzles in the economic data. The discussion was marked by balanced arguments among participants, who appeared genuinely open to alternative theories of the case. Participants also appeared willing to accept constructive criticism of their proffered analyses.

No less revealing was the markedly different discussion of the second day of the committee meeting, which largely matched the Garvin-Roberto "advocacy" criteria. By then, most members had fully considered the economic data and heard views of their colleagues. They were prepared to explain their individual judgments on the appropriate stance of policy. While the first day was genuinely deliberative, the second day was decisional. And when compared with the ad hoc informality of the first day, the second day was orderly, almost formal in comparison. Members often read from pre-written set pieces to explain their policy decisions. Most members were in full advocacy mode. They tried to persuade others of the merits of their positions. Members defended their positions and marshalled particular, sometimes selective, data to buttress their preferred policy stances. Members tended to devote their speaking time to advocating their positions, seeking to influence the views of their colleagues in anticipation of future policy decisions.

---

sion itself. This scheduling of events is expected to change, based in part on the Bank of England's adoption of reforms proposed in my independent review.

In sum, the MPC is endowed with certain institutional attributes that lend themselves favorably to robust deliberation.[9] And the robustness of the discussion is highly conducive to sound policy decisions. Of course, it is no guarantee.

FOMC evaluation: committee dynamics

The FOMC's institutional design is not inconsistent with sound practice. But there are certain institutional aspects of the FOMC which differ somewhat from best practice, at least as identified in the literature.

By statute, the FOMC includes twelve voting members. When fully constituted, seven of the twelve voting members of the FOMC serve as members of the Board of Governors, each nominated by the president and confirmed by the Senate with terms up to fourteen years in duration, subject to renewal. Five of the voters, presidents of a rotating cadre among the Reserve Banks, are chosen by geographically diverse Reserve Bank boards, subject to the approval of the Board of Governors.

Policy deliberations, however, occur in a much larger institutional setting. Nineteeen people convene in the discussion (voters and non-voters alike) and a total of about sixty people are in attendance, including a range of subject-matter experts on key aspects of the economic and financial landscape.

While the Reserve Bank presidents are supported by large, independent staffs of economists to help inform their forecasts and policy judgments, I would note that the economic models and forecasting tools are substantially similar across the Federal Reserve System. This explains, in part, the remarkable conformity of the so-called dot plots in the projections from FOMC participants.

9. In my report to the Bank of England, I sought to advance the cause of transparency without undermining its favorable institutional dynamics.

But the FOMC's institutional setting is different, not only in size, from the optimal committee configuration. Its deliberations and decisions also follow a different institutional pattern. One simple mechanism for evaluating the breadth of views is to review trends in dissent: that is, the number of FOMC members who voted against the majority policy stance.

By both FOMC tradition and practice, the bar for lodging a dissenting vote is high. Neither Chairman Greenspan nor Chairman Bernanke ever cast a vote in the minority. In contrast, the governor of the Bank of England was outvoted on nine occasions since 1997. And governors of the Federal Reserve, unlike Reserve Bank presidents, only rarely dissented in casting of votes. In the past decade, for example, there has been only one instance of dissent by a sitting governor.

This also represents a notable difference with the MPC, where the one-member, one-vote principle is diligently respected by both internal and external members of the MPC and the public at large. Indeed, approximately half of MPC meetings to date have included at least one dissenting vote.

Voting behavior, however, is an imperfect measure of the Fed's institutional dynamics. "Counting the votes" does not give a full accounting of the quality of deliberations or decisions. Among other reasons, FOMC participants in the deliberations include Reserve Bank presidents, only some of whom actually cast votes at each meeting. More important, the conduct of monetary policy is not a simple, binary choice made in isolation between tighter or looser monetary policy. It involves a process of continuous decision-making by central bankers based on changing assessments of historical and contemporaneous data, forward-looking forecasts, and changing understandings of the transmission channels of monetary policy.

For these reasons, study of the actual discussions by policymakers is useful.

The Fed created a valuable trove of transcripts through which more information can be gleaned about how the institutional design actually operates in practice. Following significant congressional scrutiny and public pressure in 1993, the Fed agreed to publish lightly edited transcripts of FOMC meetings with a five-year delay. And, by ultimately releasing transcripts dating to 1976—when participants had virtually no expectation that verbatim transcripts would ever see the light of day— the Fed created a useful natural experiment to evaluate committee dynamics.

FOMC evaluation: transcripts and academic research

The Fed's committee dynamics can be better understood by evaluating the text of the transcripts themselves. With studies seeking to make sense of millions of spoken words, this is a daunting and imperfect exercise.

Still, recent academic research meaningfully advances our understanding of the Fed's deliberations. New research techniques are employed to distill more careful assessments of the FOMC participants' preferences, including systematic textual analysis, language-mapping algorithms, and other more subjective coding of transcript data. No surprise, Fed policymakers far more often reveal their differing judgments on economic variables in their discussion around the table than in their actual votes. Nor should we be surprised that the academic research is divided on the effect of the existence of the transcripts themselves on the FOMC's institutional dynamics.

Meade and Stasavage (2008) find evidence that the Fed's post-1993 transcript policy led to deterioration in the quality of FOMC deliberations. In the authors' formulation, policymakers are motivated to achieve two goals in the policymaking process: making optimal policy decisions and garnering a good reputation in public (often associated with conformity with the prevailing consensus).

The existence of public transcripts, even with a lag, caused FOMC participants to voice less dissent in the meetings themselves and to be less willing to change policy positions over time. For example, the number of dissenting opinions expressed by voting members fell from forty-eight (between 1989 and 1992) to twenty-seven (between 1994 and 1997).

I would note that another important phenomenon may have also contributed to greater conformity in the FOMC's deliberations: the growing reputation of Chairman Greenspan during the period. This is not inconsistent with the authors' formulation, of course—participants may well care how they are perceived. But it is less obvious whether the more stifled debate is owed largely to the changed transcript-release policy.

Schonhardt-Bailey (2013) provides a comprehensive assessment of policy deliberations in the conduct of US monetary policy. She subjects the transcripts to rigorous quantitative and qualitative textual analysis and conducts in-depth interviews with many FOMC participants. In addition, she takes account of the environment in which the deliberations occur. This includes the "quality of deliberations"—that is, whether the committee discussions consist of "argued reasoning" and a "reasonably frank exchange of views" or "pre-prepared, canned" remarks.

She concludes that the publication of transcripts likely had some impact on FOMC deliberations: "[O]ur results provide support for a conclusion that over time a greater emphasis emerged on set-piece interventions by members. This could be a result of the publication of the transcripts after 1993, as the knowledge of the expected publication of the transcripts drove the real deliberation out of the FOMC meetings and into unrecorded 'pre-meetings,' with the FOMC becoming the place for reading of prepared texts. If so, then we have evidence to support the negative impact of what we might call 'extreme transparency' of policymaking. We do, however, observe that the timing of the shift in the nature of deliberation in the FOMC does not readily fit with the surprise decision in 1993 to publish the transcripts . . . Our overall conclusion here is that while the decision on the publication of the transcripts quite possibly contributed to a change in the style of deliberation, other causes also seem to have been at work."

What other factors might be involved?

My experience at the FOMC suggests that there are several institutional dynamics that influence the nature and quality of deliberations. The "tone at the top" set by the chairman surely impacts the discussion inside the committee room. It is worth considering whether the leader of the committee crowds-in or crowds-out the discussion. The collegiality of the members themselves also matters. This is not just a matter of amity. The deliberative process is enhanced when participants believe they are able to influence the judgments of their colleagues. The willingness to entertain unorthodox views, and to hear perspectives from participants with dissimilar backgrounds, also can prove fertile ground for deliberation.

Hansen, McMahon, and Prat (2014) attempt to identify the factors of greatest significance. They find evidence that published transcripts drive both greater discipline (i.e., stronger preparation to make contributions to meetings), but also greater conformity (i.e., herding of views to minimize reputational harm). They conclude that "the net outcome of these two effects appears to be positive . . . [we] therefore find that the evidence from the 1993 natural experiment points toward an overall positive role for transparency."

The authors' results are more supportive of the benefits of transcripts than previous studies. Their conclusion rests, in part, on identifying the effect of transcripts by comparing the contributions of inexperienced FOMC members ("rookies")—who are likely to feel the discipline and conformity effects more sharply because less is known about their abilities—before and after 1993. They assume that the power of the discipline and conformity effects on behavior is related to the number of years of experience on the FOMC.

This assumption is not wholly consistent with my assessment. Rookie status and the associated risk-aversion and/or eagerness to impress do not tend to last long at the FOMC. After an introductory period, most quickly achieve whatever comfort and influence they will have in the institution's environment. Those who are comfortable breaking with consensus do just that, while others tend to conform to the prevailing views.

Hansen, McMahon, and Prat (2014) are cognizant of the risk that public transcripts may drive some of the FOMC's deliberations outside of the formal FOMC meeting. So the authors make an understandable assumption: "[They] take as a given that the whole FOMC does not meet outside of the meeting to discuss the decision."

In my experience, there is no attempt by FOMC members to avoid the transcripts per se, but policy deliberations happen on a rather continuous basis. Given the large number of FOMC participants and the even larger number of staff in attendance at meetings, some discussions inevitably happen more routinely in small groups. The Government in the Sunshine Act—a law designed to ensure the public's right to know of policy discussions—is diligently followed.[10] But hallway discussions by two or three members of the committee are not uncommon. Moreover, the Board of Governors (as distinct from the FOMC) typically meets biweekly to discuss, among other things, the state of the economy and the establishment of so-called discount rates. While distinct from the FOMC's policy decision, these discussions by the Board of Governors are not totally unrelated to FOMC policy discussions.

My judgment is consistent with much of the evidence from the academic literature: transcript publication contributed to the

10. See http://www.federalreserve.gov/aboutthefed/boardmeetings/sunshine.htm for more.

changing nature of the FOMC meeting, including less robust deliberation and increased use of prepared speeches by participants. But other factors related to the operating dynamics of the FOMC are also likely to have been associated with less robust deliberations, including the greater perceived deference by members to the views of the chairman.

Conclusion

Monetary policy is made neither by rule nor by unfettered discretion. It is made by committee. And the institutional dynamics of the committee are of considerable consequence to making sound policy decisions amid uncertainty. Institutional settings may attract much less attention than the individuals leading central banks—or the legislative remits that central banks are assigned—but they may be no less important to delivering sound policy outcomes for the benefit of the overall economy.

COMMENTS BY PETER FISHER

Without rehashing what Kevin said and wrote: yes, institutional settings, design, and dynamics matter. We're all going to sign up for that. I'm going to try to be a little less sanguine and a little less polite than my good friend Kevin. I may also try your patience by pointing out that legal scholars and legal philosophers have been working on the question of rules versus discretion and substance versus process for centuries—centuries before the economics profession existed. Notwithstanding the risk of condescension about lawyers, there's some thinking about rules that you have to comply with and an appreciation of the process/substance distinction which I find lacking—at least at some central banks today.

I thought I would talk about effective decision-making bodies I have known, and ineffective ones, not by name but by attributes. Even though I had almost ten years at the FOMC table, reflecting on Kevin's paper helped move my thinking about individual versus group accountability at central banks and now I am less sure of my preference. I thought I understood the awkwardness of group accountability when more than once I saw the FOMC gravitate toward no one's first choice and virtually no one's second choice, and we ended up with third-best outcomes. But now I'm also worried about individual accountability of a pseudo-nature, which I'm afraid is the regime we now have and that I think Kevin was alluding to.

Let me compare and contrast a team of Navy Seals and the US Congress as decision-making bodies, and let's assume the best of each of them. A number of differences come to mind. Size of team is certainly one. But for me, what jumps off the page is how they approach the question of objectives. A commando team has a clear, single objective, and they work together to overcome multiple constraints. We don't tell them that it's equally important not to injure civilians, and to capture your target, and to gather some intelligence. We don't say those are all three equally important, just go figure it out. Their commanding officer should tell them which is most important, which is the objective and which the constraints.

Now, we don't expect Congress to do that. We expect Congress to be a war of objectives, a competition for resources. And as Paul Tucker knows, my good friend Henry Richardson, a philosopher at Georgetown, spent much of his career merely on the question of whether we can reason about ends—whether we can have reasoned discourse about competing objectives. He's an optimist about this, but it's a near thing. If it's that hard, it can't be very easy.

So, with these two examples in mind, let me note attributes that I think are particularly important in good decision-making bodies. These are, first, a single objective and multiple constraints; second, what I'm going to call "Bayesian candor"—meaning honesty about the unpredictability of the future and about the best way to come to grips with that; and third, my new thoughts on individual vs. group accountability, individual input but collective accountability for the outcome.

Single objective/multiple constraints. I think most problems—I don't want to say all—where you think you've got multiple objectives can be better approached as having a single objective and multiple constraints. I think that can happen with monetary policy. I see that effective decision-making bodies have a shared single objective that they're committed to, however they formulate it, and other "competing objectives" are conceived as constraints.

Bayesian candor. Effective decision-making bodies don't waste a lot of time regurgitating facts to one another. Being good Bayesians (whether they know the work of Thomas Bayes or not), they are candid about their priors and work to unpack new information symmetrically. That is, as Thomas Bayes taught us, we should both think about the possibility that new information confirms our prior, and be open to the possibility that new information is not consistent with our prior—is either anti our prior or independent of our prior. My experience is that this is the best antidote to groupthink, because it requires you to think hard about the symmetry of the risks. You don't let new information just confirm your prior. You also accept the possibility that new information may not be consistent with your prior. Being a good Bayesian also helps separate the problem of forecasts from the problem of judgment about what to do about the forecasts: there's X amount of uncertainty in our forecast, and we're now going to have to make a judgment about what to do about that.

Individual vs. group accountability. In my view, effective decision-making bodies tend to practice individual input but collective accountability for the outcome. I don't see a lot of great decision-making bodies go out and say, "Well, I actually voted in the majority but I didn't really agree with point seven in the thing we released." And this is where my appreciation of group versus individual accountability is evolving. There's something about inputs, individual accountability for candid inputs and a symmetric consideration of the risks separated from priors, and a collective accountability for output that I think represents best practice.

Now before comparing these attributes to central banks, in the Bayesian spirit I should admit my own priors, especially in present company. Credit Suisse tells us that, as they measure these things, wealth on the planet has doubled the last fifteen years.[11]

---

11. "Global Wealth Report 2014," Credit Suisse Research Institute, October 2014. See also Josh Zumbrun and Carolyn Cui, "Glut of Capital and Labor Challenge Policy Makers," *Wall Street Journal*, April 24, 2015.

Does anyone here think that the productive potential of assets on the planet has doubled in the last fifteen years? I think not. And the conclusion I come to is that something very odd has happened to monetary conditions. Now some of us may view this as a sign of a great success of monetary policy. I'm admitting my prior that it's something that deeply disturbs me. If I looked back at ancient Rome and saw that the wealth of the Roman republic had doubled in fifteen years, I would be confident that something odd had happened to monetary conditions. So, that's one of my priors.

So how does the Fed stack up, or central banks in general stack up, to the idea of a clear, single objective and multiple constraints? Not very well. I find this interesting because my own reading of section 2A of the Federal Reserve Act is that there *is* a single objective, not something that we call a dual objective. A first-year law student would not be able to turn this into a dual mandate. To do that, you have to get a room full of distinguished economists to torture the English language this much.

Section 2A says that the Federal Reserve *shall maintain—shall*, that's the imperative, that's the mandate, elementary statutory construction tells you to pay attention to what's coming next because this is the thing that you must do, you have no option, you are compelled to—*shall maintain* the long-run growth of the monetary and credit aggregates commensurate with the economy's long-run potential to increase production, so as to promote effectively the goals of—and we have three—maximum employment, stable prices, and moderate long-term interest rates. Would a careful lawyer think you could conform to this mandate by manipulating long-term interest rates as low as you possibly can in order to make people who have control of financial assets better off? No, I don't think you could. I don't think if you put [Fed counsel] Scott Alvarez on a witness stand, he could contort this statement to such an outcome.

Although I try your patience with a lawyer's analysis of the objective, section 2A does have a single objective and three measures of success. But the Fed doesn't read it that way. The FOMC decided to rewrite it and call it a "dual" objective, a "dual" mandate, two different things that are constantly at war with one another—which leaves wide open the question: what is the rule and what is the discretion?

Now, to Bayesian candor. I think there's certainly a lot of work on forecasts inside most central banks, but in my ten years at the FOMC table and the subsequent fourteen reading transcripts and minutes, I haven't seen a lot of work on the third variable in the Bayesian calculation. I've seen some effort at defining priors. I've seen incorporation of new evidence. I have not seen a systematic effort to try to capture the possibility that the new information does not confirm our prior but is either antithetical to it or completely independent of it. The single best thing that decision-making bodies do is to call BS on each other and to know how to unpack their forecasts.

Finally, collective accountability for the outcome. I don't think we have that now. We have several hundred words produced to explain a point-in-time description of the mood of a committee, and every member then has their own forecast and their own dot. The single most important output of monetary policy is the expected path of short-term interest rates, and yet the current FOMC feels free to allow every man and woman to have their own expected path. They don't even coalesce around a path, let alone a forecast, or a view of the objectives, or the constraints. Everyone gets their own view of the reaction function. Everyone gets their own view of the objectives. Everyone gets their own view of the facts. Everyone gets their own forecast. For me, this does not remotely square with effective decision-making.

Let me just end by saying that I think a single objective and multiple constraints is a discipline we should aspire to. We should take seriously democratic accountability. And before we write new laws, we should try to adhere to the ones we have.

GENERAL DISCUSSION

GEORGE SHULTZ: As you're talking, I'm thinking of a contrast in your description of the national security arena because there are great similarities but there are also some differences. In the first place, in the national security arena there's great concern about any overlaps between intelligence and policy. You're always worried that intelligence people get too close to policy people and they start cooking the intelligence to suit what people want, so you make a big effort. I remember the first National Security Council meeting I ever went to when I was secretary of the treasury. Dick Helms was the director of CIA. He briefed, he answered questions, and then he got up and left the room. He would not be in the room when policy was discussed. He stayed at the White House in case he was called back in for something but he made no policy intrusion. So I think it's not quite the same because people may brief decision-makers on the facts and whatnot, but they come with opinions, probably more than in the national security field, and they probably push into the intelligence more. There's probably more interaction. But I would put forward as a general proposition that it's good to keep these things separate because if people presenting the intelligence get infected with the policy, almost without knowing it, they'll skew it. That's one problem.

Then you have a mission of some kind, and whoever is there from the military will almost inevitably say, "Before I can tell you whether I can do the mission, you have to tell me with some precision what the mission is." Then you decide what you're going to do. One of the great diseases in this area occurs when you've thought about your mission carefully, you've designed your equipment and everything to accomplish it, you go out and you do it, and then you say, "We got this done. Now let's go out and do something else." You develop what is called mission creep, and pretty soon you're doing things that you didn't plan to do and you fail. The original mission succeeded but you've allowed yourself to get drawn into things that were extraneous and didn't work. Probably some of the same problems exist in economic policymaking; at least as I experienced them, they do. You want to have people who will give you intelligence who are insulated somehow from the policy process. Then you're not always thinking about big, broad policy but you're more focused. It seems to me that with mission creep you change your mission by what you do; you change the situation. You have to be very alert to that or you'll find yourself sideways.

Another thing I couldn't help but reflect on is what you call Bayesian candor. I don't see how you can have Bayesian candor or any other kind of candor if everything is going to be transcribed and publicized. You've got to go to somebody and say, "What do you think?" and have an exchange in private. If you can't have that kind of exchange, you won't be able to trust people. One of the things you should try to do, it seems to me, in the policy arena, is develop a trusting relationship with your counterparts. When I was secretary of state, I called it "gardening." That was one thing I tried very hard to do—to develop relationships with people so that they trusted me, which meant that if they said something to me in confidence, I wasn't going to blare it to the press the next day and embarrass them. It was private. There's a lot to be said for private discussions where you're not sure but you try something out, and you don't want to be embarrassed about it later. So I think these transparency provisions that have been hooked onto the Fed are counterproductive.

It also seems to me in our economy these days that we are plagued with uncertainty and the regulatory maze out there. It keeps changing. It would be nice to know what the Fed is going to do. If five different governors go out and make five different speeches, you say, "What is going on here?" I should think there would be some respect for a decision that's made and some curbing of people who go out and express different views because it confuses the people trying to interpret what this very powerful institution is going to do and it clouds the message you're trying to deliver.

BINYAMIN APPELBAUM: I'm curious. Both Kevin and George have raised the idea, which one always hears from Fed officials, that things would be better if you guys weren't required to have transcripts published five years later, if things that you said didn't eventually become public. I'm so puzzled by that. You all seem like strong, independent, forceful thinkers, and you see things like Ben Bernanke since leaving the Fed has become much more combative in his public remarks than he ever seemed to be in the transcripts. What is it about having your remarks published five years later that so constrains your ability to express your views? Why should that be a factor that suppresses debate among people of intellect and conviction?

KEVIN WARSH: So let me take a stab at Binya's question and offer a couple comments on George's comments. So Binya, first, for better or worse, I never felt terribly constrained inside the Fed's board room. Nor was I terribly prepared. [Laughter.] I mean, it would have required significant time to write balanced, beautiful prose to prepare for a typical FOMC meeting. Instead, I've been jotting notes on note cards since I was George and John's student twenty-five years ago. So I don't think it's laziness on my part. Instead, I would reflect and react based on the discussion inside of the room. You can read a lively debate, for example, between [Treasury] Secretary [Timothy] Geithner and me about how to handle Bear Stearns in the 2008 transcripts which are now public.

Outside of the financial crisis, my experience suggests (and Andy and Bill and others here have sat around the FOMC table) that genuine deliberation—a real give-and-take—does not commonly prevail. I said to a long-serving colleague who sat next to me at the FOMC meetings, "I just heard the long prose of what so-and-so said about the state of the economy and his purported policy preference, and I can't decipher either his analysis or conclusions."

To which my colleague replied, "Exactly."

So I don't want to speak for George, but I am a huge champion of transparency and want to ensure that our central bank explains its decisions forthrightly. Why did we make the decisions we did? But I worry the transcripts now provide only a superficial transparency. Genuine, thought-provoking conversations invariably happen somewhere, and they must. And so in the name of inviting the world into every titillating comment inside of the FOMC room, we may not have actually improved transparency. We may have obfuscated the real issues, and moved the genuine deliberations elsewhere. So instead of John and Charlie and I debating in front of our colleagues the hard questions about productivity, instead during the coffee break, I say to John, "Hey, what do you really think is going on with total factor productivity?" And he offers me his view in candor. This isn't contrary to the Government in the Sunshine Act. It's because policymakers are trying to resolve tough economic riddles. So we have an absolute obligation to the public to get the right answer as best we can, for effectively communicating, for being totally transparent in our decisions. But when policymakers arrive and get acclimated to central banks, they observe what their peers are doing, and as I talk about in the paper, some decide to pull their punches, especially post-1993. The existence of the transcripts is not the only reason, but I think it's part of the explanation. But you shouldn't take that as an excuse to suggest policymakers should be hiding the secrets of the Federal Reserve. They—the public—need to know, and they

have a right to know. But we should understand: real deliberation is essential, too.

Just a couple points on George's comments. First, they—the
Fed—tries to preserve the independence of the forecasting process, so there is a staff forecast. And Andy and Bill were intimately involved with it. As best as I can observe from my perch,
policymakers try not to interfere. It doesn't mean that, in his day,
Don Kohn wouldn't ask about some assumption staff was making about something or another. But the forecast tries to arrive
from the economists and staff to the board as *their* forecasts.
And in the minutes, the Fed tries to distinguish the staff forecast from that of the policymakers. So I do think there are real
attempts to preserve that independence. And I don't want to come
across as anything other than totally respectful of that process.

But I think Peter brings up a separate point, which is: in the
name of transparency, everybody has a forecast. We have the
staff forecast, and twelve Reserve Bank forecasts, and governors are running their forecasts. The amazing thing about the
forecasts, all independent, is that the forecasts are all on top of
each other. That's really quite a puzzling development. So one
very cynical way to conclude is the staff forecast is the modal
forecast, and everyone else is doing incremental sensitivities to
it, because in the institution of 27,000 people, there may be a
groupthink as to how the economy works, or fear to express
an independent view. Hence, these forecasts predicted in 2009
that the economy in 2010 would be booming. The same thing
occurred in 2010: the forecasts promised that the economy in
2011 would be booming. Similar consensus for 2011, 2012, 2013,
2014, and 2015. And yet, we've still been growing around 2 percent for seven years, far below forecasts throughout the period.
The groupthink, I fear, contributed to a systematic error.

It reminds me of something George and I have talked about
previously: how to mitigate the groupthink in organizational

settings. In the national security arena, after a series of errors, authorities try to create a red team and a blue team, to challenge one another, and try to understand what happened. Are the same chronic errors being made year after year after year? Does the Fed need to call a time out? Or is it just bad luck seven years in forecasting in a row? So I'd suggest that policymakers have plenty to learn about the reasons for their errors. We should be very tough on ourselves, and examine critically why the Fed seems to be making the same sorts of errors systemically in its forecasts.

And just one final point about communication and about transparency. I think the objective should be effective communication. The objective isn't that every word that's ever been said should be shown on television. The purpose of effective communication is to try to separate cacophony from real insight, noise from signal. And a judgment has to be made. And in the name of transparency, I worry that central banks around the world have fallen into the trap of communicating everything that crosses their minds. And I don't think that that's the right way forward. So I would suggest that we think of communication with that very important modifier.

PETER FISHER: Going back to Binya's question, I was there in 1993 when the transition came, when everyone woke up and realized that there were verbatim transcripts. As the decision was being made to publish them and go forward with the new regime, several of us spent some time looking at transcripts and looking at minutes. It was my view then that the minutes were better than the transcripts at telling you what happened. The transcripts were full of rather raw and funny (odd) references that were hard to decipher. Someone would say "this big" and wave their hands in the air, and the transcript would say "this big." I am afraid that in the name of increasing the transparency, we increased noise to signal.

MICHAEL BORDO: I want to go back to the history of the Fed a
bit. And if you look at the FOMC when [William] McChesney
Martin was the chairman, there were a lot of dissents. I went
through all those transcripts, in the fifties and sixties, and what I
found is that in the way he ran his committee, everybody would
speak first, and then he'd say something at the end, and then
they'd vote. And when you look at the votes, there were often
four or five dissents. He didn't quit over them. That was just the
way he ran the committee. It was a very congenial committee.
Then Arthur Burns came along; his view was totally different.
He didn't want any dissents. He was an authoritarian. And that's
when things started to change. And again with Volcker, he had
some dissents, but the dissents were perceived to be a threat to
him. In fact, I think he quit over them. Then Greenspan managed the meetings in such a way that there wouldn't be any dissents, and Bernanke did the same thing. So what your paper
told me is it really matters who's running the committee. The
culture of these committees really is important. And if you look
at history, you really see some interesting contrasts.

CHARLES PLOSSER: Sure. I just want to echo what Michael just
said. The notion of governors not dissenting is in fact a fairly
recent phenomenon. And I think, from my perspective, it's not
a good one.

But I want to go back. There have been so many interesting
things said here that it's really hard to know where to start. But I
wish the FOMC was more like the MPC or the old Fed when it
comes to dissent and the transparency of the debate.

PAUL TUCKER: We do too.

I do wish it was more like that. I think that's actually a credit
to transparency, and is preferable to hiding behind so-called
consensus decision-making. And I, too, think there ought to
be fewer meetings. I've often said the FOMC ought to have a

press conference after every meeting, and there ought to be four meetings a year. And that would be sufficient to make long-term policy decisions. The more frequent the meetings, the greater is the pressure to react to short-term and often transitory events.

The other thing I think is true is about the nature of the debate. Like you, Kevin, I was never really afraid to say what was on my mind. The transcripts never impaired me. But I would say that the debates that we have in FOMC are not necessarily debates at a single meeting. Debates go on and on and on. And many of the prepared statements and the comments that FOMC members are making are in the context of a much longer discussion where there's give and take. Maybe the give and take doesn't always occur in one meeting, but over a number of meetings—maybe even years if you think about the inflation target debate. The debate occurs in reaction to staff memos. It occurs in reaction to what your colleagues have said maybe in the last meeting, where there were some questions left on the table. So I think that there is real debate that goes on. Maybe it's not the most efficient or as extemporaneous as it might be, but I think a lot of healthy debate in fact does go on.

The last point I want to make is that I find the emphasis on the importance of consensus a bit troubling. Everybody gets behind the decision, everybody agrees with it, and you move on. I'm not sure that's the right way to think about monetary policymaking. I actually think that consensus and the pressure for consensus decision-making is the enemy of transparency, is the enemy of good communication. The desire to not have any dissent and to get everybody on the same page means that FOMC policy statements and our communications become so vacuous, so vague, so uninterpretable, just so everybody can sign onto it, that it actually turns out to be very bad communication, and something that nobody's happy with. So I think you'd be better off from a communications standpoint to be more clear about what the statement really says and get the people behind it who agree with it. The committee and the public should not worry so much if a governor dissents, it should be acceptable. They should not be concerned if there are three, four, or five dissents. Uncertainty and disagreement among nineteen very bright people should be the norm and accepted, especially in difficult circumstances. I just think that pressure for consensus can be counterproductive and lead to a kind of forced group-think. I am fond of a comment by Walter Lippmann who said that where all men think alike, no one thinks very much.

So I think excessive stress on consensus can be the enemy of good and clear communication. And I don't think monetary policymaking is the same as national security. This is not something where we're going out to fight a war. I think consensus can actually mask not just the communication of [what] the policy is, but it can mask the policymakers' true uncertainty about what we know and what we don't know. And when you think that the FOMC or monetary policy is, "Oh, everybody agreed with it, so it must be right." Well, what do we know? We know it's probably not right. We may not know how wrong it is for five years, but we know it's probably not right. Forecasts are almost always wrong. And if we were making our policy decisions based on those forecasts, they will be incorrect as well.

What people want, and particularly what the financial markets want, is certainty. They want clarity and certainty of what the Fed's going to do. We don't know as policymakers what's going to happen in the future. And being honest about that uncertainty is an important part about the debate. Non-consensus votes can actually be revealing and informative. That's all part of the process. Yes, it's cumbersome. Yes, it's obviously not terribly efficient in some ways. But it is what it is. That's the reality of the world that we live in. And I think that we don't do ourselves a service when we try to make it an autocratic process.

I mean, why have a committee at all? Why not just appoint a person and let him make all the decisions? I don't necessarily think that's an efficient way to do it, either. But to have a committee where you want diverse views to try to hash out a decision, and then try to hide all that, defeats the purpose of having a committee in the first place. Public confidence in the Fed is essential and the committee structure with differing views helps build confidence in the institution. The alternative is a model that depends solely on the views of one powerful individual. That model detracts from the institution but is a tension that exists and the one promulgated by the media and others when they constantly refer to the Greenspan Fed, the Volcker Fed, or the Bernanke Fed. Ben Bernanke wanted to de-personalize the Fed; he believed that the public's trust should be in the institutions, not simply the individual. It is unfortunate that he didn't make more progress toward that goal.

JOHN WILLIAMS: I think that Kevin's paper and presentation—and I agree with Peter's point that your presentation was more pointed than the paper—is really important. I think that first of all, Kevin had this unique opportunity to observe firsthand the Federal Reserve at its critical stages, seeing how it really works from—and I'm going to make a point on this—from a governor's perspective. [Laughter.] Because I think there are some differences. In addition, Kevin has had the opportunity to listen after the fact to the Bank of England's MPC discussions and policy meetings and understand—really understand—how those work. I learned a lot from talking to you about this earlier, and I've learned a lot from this paper. And I think this is the kind of thing I give John credit for organizing this conference. We should be thinking through these issues and questioning the structure of our policy meetings. In this regard, I'm going to bring up a couple things that I think are particularly relevant.

The first is—you didn't talk about this, and maybe Andy and Bill are going to chew me out about this—but the phrase I use to describe how the Federal Reserve works is called the "strong staff model." The staff of the Board of Governors, the hundreds and hundreds of PhD economists and lawyers [laughter] basically are the permanent component, if you will, if I'm going to do a time-series econometrics term here, are the permanent component of the Federal Reserve System. They're the ones who actually have all the information, they're the ones who have all the resources, and they're fantastic at their jobs. The governors come and go. The governors currently have no personal staff resources to them, although I think that is changing somewhat and is part of the bill that's being considered in the Senate. That's very different from how it works at the twelve Federal Reserve Banks. We have dedicated staff supporting us in preparation for FOMC meetings. I have twenty-seven PhD economists. Same goes for Charlie, when he was in Philadelphia with Mike and others, an incredible team. And what do we do a week before the FOMC meeting? We have all those things that Kevin wished he was having. We have those open debates. We have the closed-room discussions—so it's true of all the other banks too—where we constantly challenge each other. And I'll add—apparently, there's no sense at my bank that you can't tell the president of a Federal Reserve Bank that he's completely wrong and doesn't understand anything. And that's a good thing. So I think that in fact, what's interesting about our structure is a lot of what you're talking about is either happening on the third floor of the Federal Reserve Board—that's where the staff are hashing out a lot of issues and the memos and everything—but it's also happening at the twelve Federal Reserve Banks. So really, I come to the FOMC meeting, and I do have prepared remarks. I try to respond to what's happening at the meeting. But I come into

the meeting after having read through all the memos and briefings, having thoroughly talked to people about this, and have
thought through a lot of these issues. And so I think there is a
difference in terms of how we work, because unlike the Bank of
England, the external—because as I understand, Paul correct
me—the external members don't have this kind of dedicated
staff in the way that we do.

TUCKER: Not in the way that regional Federal Reserve Banks do.
But individual policymakers each have a small staff supporting them. I, as a governor, had an economic adviser as well as
a private secretary (a central banker), and the four "externals"
are supported by their own unit, as well as having access to the
main staff directorates.

WILLIAMS: Right. So I think there is a difference there in how
our structures work. The second thing I wanted to bring up is
the publication of transcripts. To me, it's simply not an issue.
I couldn't care less that my words will be made public in five
years. Five years to me is an eternity. I go out and speak regularly about the economy and monetary policy, for better or for
worse, and I took, Kevin, your remarks that it was a good thing.
[Laughter.] For me, what's important is that we've got to get the
policy right. Peter, I don't know if you said it, Kevin you said that,
we've got to get the policy right. So transcripts don't bother me.

What bothers me is actually the minutes. So what's happened
with the minutes is actually very different from what you've
talked about. Today, the minutes are incredibly detailed. You
know, in the Fed we love all these words like "a few," "some,"
"many," all of these things, and everybody, whether in the
media, or in the markets, is fixated on how many people said
what according to the minutes. It's like they are recording how
many thought the sun rises in the east, versus the sun rises in
the west. So we're literally now in a situation, where if I don't
say, "Q1 growth was weak," it might say in the minutes, "A few

members thought Q1 growth was weak." What were the rest of us thinking? That it was strong? I don't know. So we're getting ourselves into this kind of transparency that is getting in the way to having meaningful conversations. But I do think that the points you raised in your paper and in the discussion around this—these are things that we really should be thinking a lot more about. And I've heard Charlie say this. I've heard others say this. The goal is not transparency. The goal is clarity. The goal is making monetary policy more effective.

TUCKER: First of all, to Kevin and Peter, this is incredibly stimulating, really wise words from both of you, if I may say so. And for what it's worth, even though I've never attended an FOMC meeting, I've been hearing accounts of FOMC meetings for about a quarter of a century and I absolutely recognize the distinctions you describe and, at least from the perspective of those of us in the Bank of England when we were granted independence in 1997, they're deliberate. We wanted a very different style of committee. We thought—and, more important, Gordon Brown and Ed Balls thought—that a truly one person-one vote committee was a precondition for independence.

But I want to come back to a couple of points that George Shultz made. One was about separating the role of the staff from that of the policymaker. The UK set-up most definitely reflects that, but with the opposite conclusion in terms of the staff forecasts. There is not one. Because if the staff made the forecasts, every time they presented the labor market data to you, or the GDP data, or anything else, there would be a risk that their forecast would color their interpretation of the data, because they would be invested in *their* forecast. And during my time that created a battle (with a small "b") within the Bank of England, because the staff thought that they would have more rewarding jobs if they produced a staff forecast. And our view was, we would really like your jobs to be more rewarding, but we're even

more keen on you giving us a reading of the monthly and quarterly data that is as objective as possible, plus in a one person-one
vote committee we need to forge a collective forecast if we can,
as that process exposes our underlying views of what is going
on in the economy. I don't know whether you attended those as
well, Kevin, but there are half a dozen or so half-day forecast-
round meetings each quarter. These are the most remarkable
meetings. It is the opposite of the strong staff model. The UK
model absolutely depends upon each of the policymakers serving fairly long terms. The regional Fed presidents do so here,
but I have a concern that in the United States, governors are
serving shorter terms. This relates to what I was talking about
this morning. Given the extensiveness of the power of today's
central banks, I think a decent case could be made for service
on central banking policy bodies coming late in life, with long
terms that everyone served, and then straightforward retire-
ment from active life—like Supreme Court justices. I think that
with these super-powerful institutions, society has to protect
itself from policymakers leaving office early and having other
things they want to do rather than gardening, which, as I say, is
how things are for our top judges. Coming to the point, I think
that what I've just described is absolutely antithetical to a chair-
centered committee.

In the same vein, in today's world, which is very different
from even only twenty years ago, in order to get governors to
serve longer, my guess is that it is important that they do have
a staff.

The other points I wanted to pick up were about transparency
and transcripts. I think this whole debate about transparency
and transcripts, seeing exactly who says what to whom when,
is actually very closely linked to this morning's discussion. The
more the goals are properly framed, the more the central bank
is constrained to reveal its strategy. If that is correct, it reduces

the imperative of the public, journalists, Congress, Parliament seeing everything policymakers have said to each other in order to keep a check on whether the central bank has departed from its objective and is up to something else. The less scope there is for slacking, the less you need to guard against it by having, if you like, tape recordings, transcripts, of everything. That is not a decisive case against transcripts, but it illustrates how the design of regimes has to be holistic.

In the case of the Fed, I think a very important part of the existing regime is that no more than three governors can meet without minutes being published. A worthwhile concern lies behind that, but it means that the kind of deliberation that John and Charlie describe in their institutions is almost impossible. The upshot is that, under Kevin's account, there is in effect a double constraint, where deliberation doesn't happen in the FOMC meeting, and it can't happen outside the meeting without breaking the law. That's the kind of issue that those interested in Fed reform should be debating at the moment.

The final thing I would say about the minutes is that right at the outset of the life of the UK's MPC, when I was part of the secretariat, we decided—i.e., Eddie and Mervyn and the rest of us—very explicitly not to use code words such as "measured pace" or anything like that. We were concerned that code words could become slogans with their own life, where the committee wouldn't be able to keep control of what they meant. There is a risk that you get locked into such code words. As secretary, I was under instruction to just write in English: don't try and fall back on slogans month after month, to represent the discussion. Charlie summed it up: clarity.

The point of saying that is that it is another manifestation of how the design of policy regimes is (or should be) holistic. In a chair-dominated committee, the ordinary members can signal that they will vote against the chair. Consensus can then end up being forged through drafting of inherently ambiguous language, with members each finding what they want in the words but also with the meaning being determined by the interpretation of financial markets. By contrast, in one person-one vote committees, you get more minority votes (which should not be thought of as "dissents" because they are not dissenting but, rather, expressing their policy preference). But that kind of approach could not work with a very large committee, such as the FOMC.

ANDREW LEVIN: I thought this was a brilliant paper. I'm really glad that you wrote it. Hopefully you'll write sequels. I guess that I've often heard the phrase that the Federal Reserve is among the most transparent central banks in the world. And when I hear that phrase I get frustrated, because it doesn't seem accurate. And I think one rationale that's given for saying so is that the FOMC is practically unique in producing complete meeting transcripts that are published five years later. But the release of those transcripts is completely different from what we were discussing this morning about the need for the FOMC to explain the rationale for its decisions to the public in a timely way. The transcripts have nothing to do with that at all. Therefore, I'd just like to add a few constructive suggestions about where there could be room for improved clarity of explanation.

First, why doesn't the Federal Reserve bring in an outside expert like Paul Tucker or someone else from the Bank of England? Or Lars Svensson? Or Carl Walsh? To my knowledge, many central banks around the world have regular initiatives where they bring in a recognized expert like Kevin to look at how things are done on the forecasts, on the policy process, on how the research is organized, how the research can be more policy-relevant. And that has not happened at the Fed, and it should happen, and it can happen. And it shouldn't have to happen because Congress requires it. It should be voluntary.

Second, I fully agree with John Williams that the staff plays a crucial role at the Federal Reserve. At the European Central Bank, the staff forecast is published four times a year in the ECB monthly bulletin. There's no reason why the Federal Reserve couldn't voluntarily start to do that. Those are all things that can be worked out. But if the Fed wants to be on the frontier of transparency and clear communication, I think that would help a lot, because right now the FOMC minutes only include one or two paragraphs of general qualitative description about the staff forecast. And then Fed watchers are just looking closely at those few words trying to make some inferences about the staff forecast.

Third, the Fed should publish quarterly monetary policy reports. In fact, the Supreme Court provides a reasonably good analogy for this approach. The FOMC needs to have a policy strategy that provides the rationale for its specific decisions. And the FOMC chair is generally the natural person to figure out that strategy, except in rare instances where a chairperson might be too far from the consensus view and hence wouldn't be able to draft the explanation for the committee's decision. And that happens with the Supreme Court once in a while, too. But the chair would generally oversee the drafting of the majority view. And then there can be concurring opinions from committee members who broadly agree with the majority view but maybe have a few qualms. And then there could be dissenting opinions, and those dissenting opinions could be joined together, just like with the Supreme Court. With this sort of approach, the public would be able to see the rationale for the decision as well as the diversity of views, and the deliberations in a sense would become much more transparent through that kind of document.

So these are all ways that I think the Federal Reserve could very substantially improve the clarity of its monetary policy communications.

MICHAEL DOTSEY: A very quick comment on Kevin's remark regarding John Williams giving a speech and moving the two-year rate, yet he might not be moving his colleagues. To me that signals two things—the great credibility that the Fed has and the uncertainty in the market. You're continuously updating your beliefs as you get new information, which is a greatly preferred position to that of a Swiss National Bank, for instance. Right now the market is ignoring it, because they have no more credibility. By the way, Peter, that last remark is my personal one, not that of my employer. [Laughter.]

JOHN COCHRANE: I'd like to relate this to the discussion about rules we were having this morning. Peter said something very important: effective committees agree on a goal. Yet when I look at the Fed I see the opposite picture. The huge debate is really about: What are the goals? I made a little list: inflation, unemployment, employment, labor force participation, and all these broken down by many demographic groups, output gaps, financial stability, asset prices, credit spreads, stocks, the health of big banks, inequality, credit access, and who knows what else. The Fed is fighting about what are the goals, and the goals are rapidly expanding. As I mentioned this morning, perhaps the most crucial part of a rule such as John Taylor's is the implied list of things that the Fed should *not* pay attention to, should not target, and for which the Congress will not hold the Fed accountable.

Of course, it's much more effective if goals and limits come from within the institution, and the institution owns them, rather than having goals shoved down its throat. Among other problems, the institution is likely to subvert externally demanded goals.

Inflation is an interesting example. You said "price stability," mirroring the language of the legislation governing the Fed. The Fed has artfully interpreted that to mean 2 percent inflation forever. The Fed has invented its own goal. Whatever Congress passes may well be ignored.

I've never been to an FOMC meeting, and I've never been to a Bank of England meeting, but I've been to a meeting that actually functions pretty well—the University of Chicago faculty meeting, where we decide who gets tenure and who doesn't get tenure. A few features seem important and relevant here. First: dissent without reprisal. You can disagree, and offer dissenting opinions, but in the end after the vote is taken, you close ranks and take joint responsibility. We don't re-argue old cases, we don't bear grudges for contrary opinions—or at least doing so, which does happen, is regarded as petulant bad form. We don't later say, "Well, I voted against it," or "I pointed out how bad that paper was." Or, "Now he's a superstar, aren't you ashamed you voted no?" As a result, people do their homework, discuss the papers, think about the case, and revise their opinions when colleagues argue effectively. As a result, cases are argued on the merits, not logrolled: you vote for my candidate, and I'll vote for yours.

This outcome is a result of culture, not rules. That's how it worked at Chicago, but other places are not so effective. People don't read papers, or decide the fix is in and just go along, or logroll.

Second, you're constantly talking about the goals. In most cases, we're really not talking about whether Paul should get tenure or not, we're talking about what are our standards for tenure. The decision at hand is usually decided, but most of the discussion is about resetting the standards for the next decision.

And that argues against something Kevin mentioned. More frequent meetings are useful, even when there's no data, because we've got to keep talking about: What are the goals, what are we really here for?

FISHER: Quickly, I dropped out of my notes the thought that part of what I think effective bodies do, is they know when they're having a dialectic discussion clarifying the objective, and they can separate that from an argument about the forecasts or a judgment call. They know when they're refining the objective. And that's in part my answer to Charles, which is if I thought that the dissent and the noise and the decision coming out was a rounding error, I'd be less worried. I'm afraid, as John was just saying, it's actually about objectives. And that feels very destructive. And so I'm fine with robust argument, and I'm fine with dissent in principle, but it feels like a jump ball on what the objective function is.

PLOSSER: Well, I was going to say I agree. I think a lot of what is being discussed is about the objectives, and the vagueness of the mandate doesn't help. Mandates that are vague and, perhaps, not even achievable leave room for much debate over policy decisions.

WARSH: Yes, in fifteen seconds, a response to John Williams's last comment: So there's nothing wrong with the meetings themselves, but the meetings beget expectations that there will be outputs: a new forecast, a statement for the press (Binya and the rest of the media), a new policy outcome even based on preciously little data that emerged in the inter-meeting period.

REFERENCES

Barabas, Jason. 2004. "How Deliberation Affects Policy Opinions." *American Political Science Review* 98, no. 4: 687–701.

Blinder, Alan S. 2002. "Through the Looking Glass: Central Bank Transparency." CEPS working paper no. 86. Princeton University, December.

Blinder, Alan S., and John Morgan. 2005. "Are Two Heads Better than One? Monetary Policy by Committee." *Journal of Money, Credit, & Banking* 37, no. 5: 789–811.

Fishkin, James. 1991. *Democracy and Deliberation: New Directions for Democratic Reform.* New Haven, CT: Yale University Press.

Garvin, David A., and Michael A. Roberto. 2001. "What You Don't Know About Making Decisions." *Harvard Business Review* 79, no. 8: 108–116.

Hambrick, Donald C., and Phyllis A. Mason. 1984. "Upper Echelons: The Organization as a Reflection of Its Top Managers." *The Academy of Management Review* 9, no. 2: 193–206.

Hansen, Stephen, Michael McMahon, and Andrea Prat. 2014. "Transparency and Deliberation within the FOMC: A Computational Linguistics Approach." Centre for Macroeconomics, London School of Economics and Political Science.

Janis, Irving L. 1972. *Victims of Groupthink: A Psychological Study of Foreign-Policy Decisions and Fiascoes.* New York: Houghton Mifflin.

Janis, Irving L. 1982. *Groupthink: Psychological Studies of Policy Decisions and Fiascoes.* 2nd ed. New York: Houghton Mifflin.

Lombardelli, Clare, James Proudman, and James Talbot. 2005. "Committees Versus Individuals: An Experimental Analysis of Monetary Policy Decision Making." *International Journal of Central Banking* 1, no. 1: 181–205.

Maier, Philip. 2010. "How Central Banks Take Decisions: An Analysis on Monetary Policy." In *Challenges in Central Banking: The Current*

Institutional Environment and Forces Affecting Monetary Policy. Edited by Pierre L. Siklos, Martin T. Bohl, and Mark E. Wohar. Cambridge, UK: Cambridge University Press: 320–356.

Meade, Ellen E., and David Stasavage. 2008. "Publicity of Debate and the Incentive to Dissent: Evidence from the US Federal Reserve." *The Economic Journal* 118, no. 528: 695–717.

Mellahi, Kamel, and Adrian Wilkinson. 2004. "Organizational Failure: A Critique of Recent Research and a Proposed Integrative Framework." *International Journal of Management Reviews* 5–6, no. 1: 21–41.

Mill, John Stuart. 1859. *On Liberty.* 2nd ed. London: Savill and Edwards.

Reis, Ricardo. 2013. "Central Bank Design." *Journal of Economic Perspectives* 27, no. 4: 17–44.

Schonhardt-Bailey, Cheryl. 2013. *Deliberating American Monetary Policy: A Textual Analysis.* Cambridge, MA: MIT Press.

Schumpeter, Joseph A. 1942. *Capitalism, Socialism, and Democracy.* New York: Harper & Brothers.

Sibert, Anne. 2006. "Central Banking by Committee." *International Finance* 9, no. 2: 145–168.

Staw, Barry M., Lance E. Sandelands, and Jane E. Dutton. 1981. "Threat Rigidity Effects in Organizational Behavior: A Multilevel Analysis." *Administrative Science Quarterly* 26, no. 4: 501–524.

CHAPTER FIVE

Some Historical Reflections on the Governance of the Federal Reserve

Michael D. Bordo

Since the financial crisis of 2007–2008, there has been considerable interest in reform of the Federal Reserve System. Many blame the Federal Reserve for causing the crisis, for not handling it well, and for mismanaging the recovery. Criticisms include: keeping the policy rate too loose from 2002 to 2005 and thereby fueling the housing boom: lapses in financial regulation that failed to discourage the excesses that occurred; the bailouts of insolvent financial firms; the use of credit policy; and conflicts of interest between directors of the New York Federal Reserve Bank and Wall Street banks.

The Dodd-Frank Act of 2010 made some minor changes to Federal Reserve governance: removing the voting rights of Class A Reserve Bank directors for selection of the president and vice president of the Reserve Bank; and changing the Federal Reserve's lender-of-last-resort policy—limiting the use of 13(3) discount window lending. Some have urged that the reform process go further, e.g., Conti-Brown (2015) argued that the Reserve Bank presidents be appointed by the president while the recent Shelby bill includes requiring this change only for the president of the New York Federal Reserve Bank.[1]

For helpful comments I would like to thank Peter Ireland, Mary Karr, John Cochrane, Allan Meltzer, and the participants at the Central Bank Governance and Oversight Reform conference held at the Hoover Institution, May 21, 2015.

1. Similar calls for reform of Fed governance were proposed in congressional bills in 1977 and 1991, which did not pass.

A similar cacophony of criticism and calls for reform of the Fed occurred after the Great Contraction of 1929 to 1933, which President Franklin Delano Roosevelt blamed on the banks and the Federal Reserve. This led to a major reform of the Federal Reserve System in congressional acts in 1933 and 1935.

In this paper I examine the historical record on Federal Reserve governance and especially the relationship between the Reserve Banks and the Board from the early years of the Federal Reserve to the recent crisis. From the record I consider some lessons for the current debate over reform of the Federal Reserve.

Establishment of the Federal Reserve System

A signature aspect of the Federal Reserve System is its federal / regional structure and governance. The Federal Reserve Act of 1913 was passed following a long deliberation over reform of the US financial system after the Panic of 1907. The panic was the straw that broke the camel's back, following a series of banking panics that plagued the post–Civil War national banking system. The US banking system was characterized by considerable instability involving frequent banking panics since Andrew Jackson's veto of the charter of the Second Bank of the United States. Its causes included the prohibition on interstate branch banking[2] and the absence of a lender of last resort. The reform movement that followed the 1907 panic called for the creation of something like a central bank, but there was considerable opposition to a European-style central bank which had all of its financial power concentrated in the financial center. The Aldrich-Vreeland Act of 1908 created a network of National Reserve Associations, which were modeled on the plan of the private clearing houses in many US cities. Clearing houses issued a form of emergency currency ("clearing house

2. This was not the case in Canada, which never had a banking crisis (Bordo, Redish, and Rockoff 2015).

loan certificates") during panics and on a number of occasions successfully allayed the panic (Gorton 1985). The Aldrich-Vreeland Act also established the National Monetary Commission (NMC), which was to study the monetary experience of many countries and make recommendations for a reform of the US banking system.

The NMC in 1912 put forward a plan for a regional central bank system called the Aldrich Plan. It was based on an earlier plan suggested by Paul Warburg, an influential German-born banker, which was in many ways an American adaptation of the Reichsbank. The Aldrich bill called for the establishment of a National Reserve Association, headquartered in Washington, D.C. The association's branches would be located throughout the United States and serve member commercial banks. The association would issue asset-backed currency and rediscount eligible paper consisting of short-term commercial and agricultural loans for its members at a discount rate set by the national association's board of directors. The discount rate would be uniform throughout the country. The association would also be able to conduct open market operations (Bordo and Wheelock, 2010).[3]

The Aldrich plan was defeated in Congress. After the election of 1912, when the Democrats took power, it was greatly revised to include a stronger role for the government. The resultant Federal Reserve Act of 1913 represented the Wilsonian compromise, which gave a role in the system to the regional commercial banks (Main Street), the money center banks (Wall Street), and the federal government (Karr 2013).

The Federal Reserve System differed markedly from Aldrich's proposed National Reserve Association in terms of structure and governance. Rather than a central organization with many branches,

3. Neither the Aldrich plan nor the subsequent Federal Reserve Act considered adopting nationwide branch banking. The political economy of the US banking industry was very successful in blocking that reform until the end of the twentieth century. Hence, given the fractured US banking system, a regional reserve bank system was a reasonable arrangement (Calomiris and Haber 2014, Bordo, Redish, and Rockoff 2015, Bordo and Wheelock 2010).

the Federal Reserve System consisted of twelve semi-autonomous regional reserve banks and the Federal Reserve Board, which had a general oversight role. Whereas the Federal Reserve Board was made up of five members appointed by the president and chaired by the secretary of the treasury, the reserve banks were owned by their member banks and the governors (after 1935 called presidents) were appointed by local boards of directors, consisting of nine directors. Three of the directors (Class A, who were primarily bankers) are elected by the Reserve Banks; three of them (Class B, to be non-bankers) are also elected by the Reserve Banks; and three (Class C, to be non-bankers) are appointed by the Federal Reserve Board. The member banks are required to purchase stock in their local Reserve Bank.

A key difference between the Federal Reserve Act and the Aldrich plan was that the individual Federal Reserve Banks set their own discount rates (subject to review by the Federal Reserve Board), and each bank was required to maintain a minimum reserve in the form of gold and eligible paper against its note and deposit liabilities. The demarcation of authority between the Reserve Banks and the Board in Washington was not clearly spelled out in the Federal Reserve Act. This led to serious problems in the 1920s and 1930s.

The Early Years: 1914 to 1935

The Federal Reserve Banks opened their doors in December 1914 just in time for the outbreak of World War I in Europe. The war meant that the Fed faced a very different environment than its framers envisaged and consequently it changed its operations in novel ways. Because of the war, most countries left the gold standard. Also, once the United States entered the war, the Fed began discounting commercial bills backed by government securities. Also, as the war progressed the Fed pegged short-term interest rates to help the Treasury finance the war. This meant that it gave up its independence to the Treasury.

At the end of the war, in 1918, the Federal Reserve kept its discount rate low at the Treasury's behest. This fueled a massive commodities price boom and inflation. Faced with declining gold reserves in late 1919, the Federal Reserve Banks (with approval by the Board) raised discount rates. This led to a serious deflation and recession, which Friedman and Schwartz (1963) termed the Fed's first policy mistake for waiting too long to cut its rates. The recession also led to severe criticism of the Federal Reserve, causing it to cut back on the use of discount rates as its key policy tool and shifting it toward the use of open market operations.

Conflict among the Reserve Banks and between the Reserve Banks and the Board began quite early over the lack of cooperation in setting discount rates and conducting open market operations. This occurred because the Act wanted the Reserve Banks to conduct their own monetary policies to influence economic conditions in their own districts and because the Board's coordinating authority was not clear—i.e., whether the member banks had to follow the Board's instructions.

To create a coordinating mechanism, the Reserve Banks, without the Board's consent, set up the Governors' Conference in 1921 to coordinate both discount rate and open market operations. In April 1922, the Reserve Board asserted its authority and disbanded the Governors' Conference, in its place setting up the Open Market Investment Committee (OMIC) to coordinate open market operations at the national level. It was composed of the governors of the Reserve Banks of New York, Chicago, Boston, Philadelphia, and Cleveland.

As it turned out, Governor Benjamin Strong of New York became the de facto leader of the OMIC. According to Friedman and Schwartz (1963), the OMIC under Strong was very successful at stabilizing the US economy and producing what they called "the high tide of the Federal Reserve." Nevertheless, many of its actions were resented by the seven Reserve Banks that were not on the committee and by the Board, which often felt that its authority was being challenged (Eichengreen 1992). Also, although the Board had ultimate authority on setting rates and conducting open market operations, individual Reserve Banks could opt out.

Several famous examples of conflict provide a strong flavor of the steep learning curve that the system faced in its early years. The first episode was in 1927, when Strong arranged a meeting on Long Island between himself and the governors of the central banks of England, France, and Germany. At this summit it was agreed that the New York Reserve Bank would lower its discount rate to help the Bank of England in its struggle to stay on the gold standard. The Board was not part of the negotiations. After the meeting there was a vociferous debate at the Board and in the other Reserve Banks about going along with the rate cut. In the end, the Board reluctantly approved Strong's action, but the Chicago Reserve Bank held out. The Board subsequently forced Chicago to cut its rate.

Adolph Miller of the Board, the only professional economist in the system, later argued that Strong's policy fueled the Wall Street stock market boom which led to the Great Depression, a view adopted much later by Herbert Hoover in his memoirs.

The second notable example of discord was in early 1928 when New York and Chicago disagreed over raising rates to stem the stock market boom. In the end, a tightening open market policy was followed (Wheelock 2000).

The third example was in 1929 when the Board and New York disagreed over how to stem the Wall Street boom. The Board wanted to engage in moral suasion to ration credit against loans to finance stock market speculation. New York and the others on OMIC doubted such a policy would work and pushed for raising discount rates. The Board blocked New York ten times until it finally acquiesced in the early summer of 1929, when it was too late.

The fourth example was after the Wall Street crash in October 1929. The New York Reserve Bank under Governor George Harrison unilaterally engaged in open market operations to provide liquidity to the New York money market to prevent a banking panic. His actions were criticized by the Board for not following protocol. Later in November, Harrison's request to engage in further easing policy was blocked by the Board, undoubtedly worsening the recession.

In March 1930, the Board disbanded the OMIC and created the Open Market Policy Committee (OMPC). It contained all twelve Reserve Bank governors. According to Friedman and Schwartz, this was a huge mistake because the larger committee, without the leadership of Benjamin Strong, who died in October 1928, was unable to be decisive. Its defects became apparent as the Depression worsened and the Fed failed to stem a series of worsening banking panics.

By the spring of 1932, under pressure from the Congress, the Federal Reserve began a massive open market purchase program led by Harrison of New York. It was quickly successful in reversing the recession but it was short-lived. Reserve Bank governors began to worry that their gold reserves were declining toward the statutory limits. Some governors and the Board also worried that the purchases would lead to speculation, an asset price boom, and inflation. Once Congress went on recess, the purchases stopped (Friedman and Schwartz 1963, Meltzer 2003).

The final and most serious example of discord in the system was in the first week of March 1933, during the final panic of the Great Contraction. The panic, unlike the three preceding ones, involved a speculative attack against the New York Reserve Bank's gold reserves. Some argue the attack reflected the market's belief that newly elected President Roosevelt would take the United States off the gold standard (Wigmore 1987). The attack led to a depletion of the New York Reserve Bank's gold reserves toward the statutory limit, after which it would have to cease conducting lender-of-last-resort actions. The New York Fed turned to the Chicago Reserve Bank, which had ample gold reserves, and requested a temporary loan of gold. Chicago turned New York down. The Board refused to intercede. The crisis worsened and was only ended when Roosevelt took office and declared a banking holiday.

Friedman and Schwartz cite these examples in their indictment of the Federal Reserve for causing the Great Contraction. They believed that had Benjamin Strong lived, he would have effectively used the OMIC to prevent the mistakes that followed his death. They were in favor of the consolidation of power in the Board that followed in 1935.

Eichengreen (1992), using the tools of game theory, demonstrated that had the Reserve Banks and Board coordinated policy during the above examples of discord, the US economy would have been much more stable. He also supported the consolidation of the system in 1935.

On the other hand, Brunner and Meltzer (1968), Meltzer (2003), and Wheelock (1991) argued that the real problem that the Federal Reserve faced wasn't structural but resulted from the theory of monetary policy it followed. They argued that the Federal Reserve as a whole followed the "real bills doctrine" and a variant of it called the Burgess-Riefler-Strong doctrine. According to this doctrine, the Federal Reserve should focus on two indicators of the stance of the economy: member bank borrowings and short-term interest rates. They argued that from 1930 to 1933, because rates were low and member bank borrowing was low, the Federal Reserve viewed its policy as largely accommodative and hence did not see the need for further loosening. Meltzer argued that Strong and most Reserve Bank governors as well as members of the Board believed in this flawed doctrine. Hence, according to them the Roosevelt consolidation of the Federal Reserve was not really necessary.

One counterfactual question that arises is: How would the structural problems of the Federal Reserve have been corrected without a major reorganization? In addition, as the above authors argue, the Federal Reserve didn't really change its (flawed) model of monetary policy until after the Great Inflation. So what forces could have pushed the Fed to improve its policymaking in the mid-1930s in the absence of the reorganization?

Reform of the Fed

The Great Contraction was blamed on the banks and the Federal Reserve, especially the New York Reserve Bank. This led to major reforms of the 1913 Federal Reserve Act. The first reform was the Glass-Steagall Act of 1932, which among other things greatly broadened the collateral that Reserve Banks had to hold against their notes and deposits, which allowed them more flexibility in their discounting policy. The 1933 Glass-Steagall Act split commercial from investment banking and created the Federal Deposit Insurance Corporation (FDIC). It also changed the name of the OMPC to the Federal Open Market Committee. The twelve Reserve Banks remained members of the FOMC; the Federal Reserve Board was given clear authority over initiating open market operations, but the Reserve Banks still had the option of opting out of actions recommended by the Board.

The most significant changes to the act occurred in the 1935 Banking Act. Much of the legislation was drafted by Marriner Eccles, Roosevelt's choice to be chairman of the Board, and Lauchlin Currie, his aide at Treasury. Eccles was a Keynesian before Keynes's *General Theory* (Meltzer 2003). Eccles wanted the federal government to control the levers of both fiscal and monetary policy to raise aggregate demand. His plan was to remove the Reserve Banks completely from Federal Reserve decision-making and make them branches of the Board in Washington. However, his bill was blocked by Senator Carter Glass, one of the framers of the original act, and so the final legislation maintained an important but subsidiary role for the Reserve Banks.

The 1935 act replaced the Federal Reserve Board with the Board of Governors of the Federal Reserve System. The president appointed seven governors, subject to Senate approval. The secretary of the treasury and the comptroller of the currency were removed from the Board. All twelve Reserve Bank presidents (demoted from the title governor) remained on the FOMC but only five could vote (one of which was the New York Reserve Bank president[4]). The other four voting presidents served on a rotating basis. The voting procedure to nominate Reserve Bank presidents was unchanged. Other important changes were to the supervision and regulation of member banks, which came under the purview of the Board, then to be delegated to the Reserve Banks. Also, the responsibility for international economic policy shifted from the New York Reserve Bank to the Board.[5]

Once the bill was passed, power irrevocably shifted from the Reserve Banks to the Board of Governors. However, from the mid-1930s until 1951, the Federal Reserve was subservient to the Treasury and monetary policy was geared to pegging interest rates at a low level to facilitate Treasury funding. The Federal Reserve acted independently only once, in 1936–37, when it doubled excess reserves to prevent the commercial banks from fueling another speculative boom. This action, according to Friedman and Schwartz, led to

4. From 1936 to 1942, New York rotated with Boston. New York was assigned a permanent place in 1942.
5. The unit banking system was left untouched. A plan by the large money center banks to allow nationwide branching was blocked by the lobby of the small banks. The compromise was the creation of the FDIC (Calomiris and White 1994).

a severe recession in 1936–37.[6] During World War II the Federal Reserve, a de facto branch of the Treasury, served as an engine of inflation to finance the war effort.

Board of Governors Reserve Bank Relations: 1951 to 2006

A run-up of inflation in the late 1940s led the Federal Reserve System to push for independence from the Treasury to be able to raise interest rates. President Allan Sproul of New York led the campaign, which was finally successful in the Federal Reserve Treasury Accord of March 1951. (See Meltzer 2003, chapter 7, and Bordo 2006 for the dramatic details.) William McChesney Martin became chairman of the Board in 1951. Under his tutelage there was considerable harmony between the Board and the Reserve Banks with the possible exception of the debate in the 1950s between the Board and New York over "bills only" (whether open market operations should be conducted only in short-term Treasury bills or also in bills of longer duration). The Board wanted bills only; the New York Fed preferred longer-dated securities. In the end, the Board won.

In the early Martin years, before 1965, the FOMC was run in a very collegial manner and the Reserve Bank members, especially President Alfred Hayes of New York, had a considerable say. The Fed was most concerned with maintaining low inflation and maintaining a balance-of-payments equilibrium to preserve the Bretton Woods system. Problems began in 1965 with the beginning of the run-up in inflation that would become the Great Inflation. Under pressure from the administration to follow expansionary monetary policy to ease the Treasury's financing of the Vietnam War

---

6. The Treasury's decision to sterilize gold inflows also had a negative impact on the economy (Meltzer 2003).

and President Lyndon Johnson's Great Society, the Board, whose members became increasingly influenced by the Keynesian thinking of the economics profession and the administration, followed "even-keel policies" which led to monetary expansion and a buildup of inflation (Meltzer 2010).

During these years the Federal Reserve Bank of St. Louis under President Darryl Francis played an important role as a "maverick" Reserve Bank.[7] Francis and his research director, Homer Jones (former teacher of Milton Friedman at Rutgers University), adopted the modern quantity theory views of Friedman and continually criticized the Board for its inflationary policies based on its targeting of "net free reserves" (excess reserves less borrowings) and the targeting of short-term interest rates to control the "tone and feel of the money market." Researchers at St. Louis presented powerful evidence against the free reserves doctrine (Meigs 1976). They made a strong theoretical and empirical case for the Fed to focus on targeting monetary aggregates and total reserves. They argued that if the Fed controlled the money supply, it could reduce inflation. Francis and Jones's advocacy did not sway the Board in the 1960s. Indeed, some members wanted to stifle dissent and have the entire system speak with one voice. But this was not strictly enforced, either by Martin or by his successor, Arthur Burns (who was considerably less forgiving of dissent).

Monetarist ideas began to influence the Fed during the 1960s and 1970s when the research staff at the Board, following St. Louis's lead, began to present monetary aggregates data, and in the Humphrey-Hawkins Full Employment Act of 1978, when Congress required that the Fed present successively lower target ranges of money growth to gradually reduce inflation and to justify significant departures from the targets. The St. Louis approach was

---

7. Francis's predecessor at St. Louis, D.C. Johns, was also a pioneer advocate for monetary targeting in the 1950s, as was President Malcom Bryan of the Atlanta Fed. See Wheelock (2000) and Hafer (1997).

finally vindicated in 1979 when President Carter appointed Paul Volcker as chairman of the Board with the mandate to break the back of inflation and inflationary expectations. Volcker took a page from the St. Louis script, drastically cutting money growth and allowing interest rates to rise dramatically in a clear departure from the Fed's traditional targeting of short-term rates.

After the Volcker shock, inflation and inflationary expectations dropped by the mid-1980s. Other seminal contributions to the monetary policy debate in the 1970s and '80s that came from the Reserve Banks included rational expectations and the vertical Phillips curve (Mark H. Willes in Minneapolis); the case for a price level and /or an inflation target, which came from Cleveland (W. Lee Hoskins); and the case against Federal Reserve participation in exchange market intervention on the grounds that it conflicted with credibility for low inflation, which came from Richmond (J. Alfred Broaddus) and Cleveland (Jerry Jordan). Thus, the Reserve Banks had a strong voice in the making of policy during the Great Inflation and the Great Moderation.[8]

The Financial Crisis and Beyond

The Crisis of 2007–2008 was managed by the FOMC and the New York Reserve Bank. They quickly developed extensions to the discount window mechanism to overcome the problem of stigma (the term auction facility) and many facilities that provided credit to the sectors of the plumbing that lay beneath the shadow banking system. They also extended the Bretton Woods–era swap network to the central banks of the advanced countries and prevented a global liquidity crisis (Bordo, Humpage, and Schwartz 2015). During this

---

8. In this period, President Gary Stern (Stern and Feldman 2004) raised a growing concern about the rise of "moral hazard" in the Fed's lender-of-last-resort policy, which since the Penn Central bailout in 1970 and that of Continental Illinois in 1984 had established the "Too Big to Fail doctrine." Also see Bordo (2014).

period several Reserve Bank presidents (Jeffrey Lacker of Richmond, Charles Plosser of Philadelphia, Thomas Hoenig of Kansas City, and Richard Fisher of Dallas) expressed their concerns over the growing use by the Fed of credit policy which is a form of fiscal policy, over the bailouts of insolvent non-bank financial intermediaries and the general extension of section 13(3) of the 1935 Banking Act, which allowed the Board of Governors to extend the discount window to non-banks in the face of "unusual and exigent circumstances." They were concerned that these policies posed a threat to the Federal Reserve's independence.

After the crisis, these issues were brought up in the Financial Crisis Inquiry Report of 2010. Another issue that got considerable play was a conflict of interest between the directors of the New York Reserve Bank and some Wall Street firms after it was disclosed that a director of the Fed simultaneously was a partner at Goldman Sachs. Another critique of the New York Fed's governance was the close connection between Fed leaders and Wall Street. This reflects factors such as a common financial culture and the revolving door between staff and officials at the New York Fed and Wall Street. This makes it difficult to keep an arm's-length distance between the central bank and the financial markets. This has been a perennial critique that goes back to the clandestine Jekyll Island meeting held in 1910 that created the original Aldrich Act.

As a consequence, the Dodd-Frank Act of 2011 made a significant change to the voting procedures of the Board of Directors of the Reserve Banks. No longer would Class A directors (bankers) be allowed to vote for the president of the Reserve Bank.

Other reforms relevant to the Federal Reserve that came out of Dodd-Frank were the prohibition of 13(3) lending to large non-bank financial institutions and a requirement that the Federal Reserve could only use 13(3) to rescue groups of institutions after clearance by the Treasury.

There has been a continuous backlash against the Federal Reserve since the crisis. Congressman Ron Paul called for abolition of the Fed and a return to the gold standard and free banking. Other members of Congress have advocated auditing the Fed's monetary policy deliberations and requiring the president of the New York Bank to be appointed by the US president subject to Senate approval—a move that would strengthen the administration's influence on the Board. Peter Conti-Brown, a lawyer, argued at a recent Brookings Institution conference (March 2015) that the Federal Reserve Act was unconstitutional because the president of the United States had to go through two layers of bureaucracy to remove a Reserve Bank president for cause. To do so would involve, first, requesting the Board of Governors to request the removal to the Reserve Bank's board of directors; and then the Reserve Bank's board of directors would have to agree.

Conti-Brown makes his case based on a Supreme Court decision in 2010. He proposes to make the Reserve Bank presidents subject to summary appointment and dismissal by the Board of Governors and require that the Reserve Banks become branches of the Board of Governors, i.e., he wishes to go back to the original Eccles Plan of 1935.[9] Doing so would, as Carter Glass realized eighty years ago, make the Board a direct agent of the federal government.[10]

Does the case against the Reserve Banks make economic sense? To this author it does not. History suggests that the federal/regional nature of the Fed is one of its great sources of strength. Reserve Banks have long brought fresh viewpoints to the policymaking table. The

9. His second best solution is to make the Reserve Bank presidents subject to presidential appointment.

10. Richard Fisher (2015) proposed reforms to Fed governance more favorable to the Reserve Banks, including: rotating every two years the vice chairmanship of the FOMC away from the New York Fed to all of the Reserve Banks; having the systemically important financial institutions (SIFIs) supervised and regulated by Federal Reserve staff from a district other than the one in which the SIFI is headquartered; and giving the Reserve Bank presidents an equal number of votes as the Washington-based governors, except for the chairman.

Reserve Bank research departments, starting with St. Louis in the 1960s, have been behind many of the positive improvements that have occurred in Fed policymaking. These include the ending of the Great Inflation, the Great Moderation, and the advent of credibility for low inflation and the inflation target. These improvements before 2002 greatly enhanced the independence and effectiveness of the Fed.

In addition, the Reserve Bank presidents continue to bring valuable and diverse information and opinions to FOMC meetings that would not be as readily available if the committee consisted entirely of US presidential appointees (Goodfriend 2000). The Beige Book contains valuable real-time information that might be lost if the Reserve Banks had their powers significantly curtailed.

One wonders if a monolithic central bank with its board appointed by the US president could have made these accomplishments. The experience of other advanced country central banks in the twentieth century suggests not. The Bank of England, the Banque de France, the Bank of Japan, and the Bank of Canada were subservient to their treasuries until after the Fed made its historic changes in the 1980s, which served as an example to them. The only two exceptions were the Swiss National Bank, which has always had a culture of price stability and also a federal structure like the Federal Reserve (Bordo and James 2008) and the Bundesbank, which was founded based on the stability culture of maintaining stable money (Beyer et al. 2013).

Some Lessons from History

The key lesson that comes from this historical survey is that the federal/regional structure of the Federal Reserve should be preserved. The Reserve Bank presidents should not be made US presidential appointments subject to Senate confirmation or subject to summary appointment and dismissal by the Board of Governors.

This would only make the Federal Reserve System more politicized and would greatly weaken its independence.

Federal Reserve power was greatly increased by the Dodd-Frank Act, which put the chairman of the Fed on the Financial Stability Oversight Council. It has the power to designate non-bank financial entities as systemically important financial institutions (SIFIs) and to require stress tests administered by the Federal Reserve.[11] In addition, the Federal Reserve, like other central banks, has elevated the goal of financial stability (to head off asset price booms and other sources of systemic risk that could lead to a financial crisis) to the same level as its traditional functions of preserving macro-stability and serving as lender of last resort. To accomplish this new mandate, the Fed would use new tools of macroprudential regulation. This increase in power, in a sense creating a financial and economic czar, by itself poses a threat to the Fed's credibility and independence and to American democracy.

This is not to say that reforms to the Federal Reserve are not necessary. Above all is the need for improvements in governance and safeguards against conflicts of interest (especially at the New York Reserve Bank). Other areas for reform include: the recognition that the structure of US banking has changed radically since 1913 toward a more concentrated, universal, nationwide branching system; the more rapid turnover of Federal Reserve governors (ever since the Great Inflation reduced their real incomes), which undermines the longer-term perspective toward policymaking which the original framers hoped for; the revolving door between the governors and the financial industry, which makes them more subject to regulatory capture; and the withering of many of the Reserve Banks' original functions (e.g., check-clearing), reflecting ongoing financial innovation. Another reform long overdue is to geographically redistribute the Reserve Banks to reflect the

11. The Dodd-Frank Act also created the Consumer Protection Agency, which is housed at the Board but is not subject to its control.

massive changes in the distribution of the US population since 1913.[12] Many of these reforms would increase the Fed's accountability and provide less radical remedies to the Fed critics than downgrading the regional Reserve Banks. They would also strengthen the voice of Main Street within the Fed, in counterbalance to Wall Street and federal power.

An independent Federal Reserve committed to maintaining low inflation and macro-stability and to serving as lender of last resort is a safeguard against economic instability and a prerequisite to sustained economic growth. Following rules-based monetary policy and lender-of-last-resort policy would greatly enhance that outcome.

12. Belongia and Ireland (2015) posit that the number of Reserve Banks could be reduced from twelve to five (Atlanta, Chicago, Dallas, New York, and San Francisco), all of which are major financial and business centers. Also, they would make the presidents of these five Reserve Banks permanent voting members of the FOMC.

COMMENTS BY MARY KARR

I should say, "And now for something completely different." I feel a little bit in the minority here as I am the only non-economist and lawyer in the room, so I take a slightly different tack. I also, since I am a current employee of the Fed, feel compelled to say that these are my own views and not the views of the Reserve Bank of St. Louis, Jim Bullard, or anyone else. And having said that, I think that Michael's paper really presents quite an informative summary of how legislation in the aftermath of financial crises has changed the structure and role of the Federal Reserve System. When I refer to the Federal Reserve System, I am collectively referring to the Board of Governors and the twelve Reserve Banks. And I am in overall agreement with much of what he has to say—actually, almost all of what he has to say. His focus is on the Fed's core monetary policy mission, and the discussion of the contribution of individual Reserve Banks, particularly since the sixties, strongly supports the role of independent voices within the Fed. I think you got a little bit of that today from John and Charlie when they talked about the Reserve Bank FOMC prep process and the kind of free-for-alls that tend to go on in research departments as they debate policy outcomes.

So I think the question facing us is how best to retain independent voices. Assuming independent voices are a good, which I do, how best to retain those within the Fed. Prior legislation, as particularly as Michael has described it, addresses structural reorganization, and usually the context has been some further centralization of authority in Washington as a means to improving monetary policy and supervisory outcomes. But even among economic historians and economists, as I've listened today, there is still debate as to whether issues related to the Fed's conduct of monetary policy were a result of structural defects or mistakes in theory. And as he further notes, mistakes of theory have persisted throughout the history of the Fed, at least until the Great Inflation and maybe until today. Some would argue that they still persist. My background is in law, not economics, so I can't address those issues, and I'm not even going to try to. But my role in the Reserve Bank—and I've been at the bank since 1991 as general counsel and also as corporate secretary—so my career at the Fed has focused in large degree on issues that relate to Reserve Bank governance and the relationship of the Reserve Banks to the Board of Governors.

So as Bordo notes, the system was, is, and always will be a creature of legislative compromise, unless Ron Paul has his way, and we're abolished. And I would note that Ron Paul has been arguing that from long before the most recent financial crisis.

So that those who are interested in the Fed operate with a base of knowledge, I will contribute a few observations of my own about system governance. In my view, the structure of the Federal Reserve System ultimately reflects sensitivity to the problem of having a central monetary authority in a federal system of government and in a democratic system of government. So Congress to date has maintained a central bank that isn't [central], as my friend and colleague Dave Wheelock has noted. And as Mike pointed out, it has an independent agency in D.C., the government part of the Fed. It has the financial center part of the Fed on Wall Street, and other Reserve Banks located throughout the country to preserve independent voices from Main Street.

Where do we get our political accountability? Well, the independent agency in Washington has significant control over the operations of the Reserve Banks. And through that control, we remain accountable to the Board, the entity whose governors are subject to presidential appointments and Senate confirmation. So some examples of that control are found in the Federal Reserve Act. I think Mike mentioned general oversight and supervision of the Reserve Banks, which goes back to the beginning. Another power that goes back to the beginning is the power to remove any officer or director of the Reserve Bank. We all serve at the pleasure of the Board of Governors.

Additionally, Reserve Banks' powers were based on the powers of national banks under the National Banking Act. So as Mike noted, Dodd-Frank amended a provision to provide that only the Class B and C directors—those who may not be bankers—now appoint the Reserve Bank presidents and first vice presidents. This process illustrates again that the Fed is a creature of delicate balances. Those appointments have to be approved by the Board of Governors of the Federal Reserve System. Once again, the Reserve Bank Board is accountable to an authority that has political accountability directly as a federal agency.

And then in further overlapping control, the [members of the] board of directors of each Reserve Bank are directed to supervise and, at least in the St. Louis Fed bank, do direct and supervise the bank. There's this myth that bankers control the Fed, and the Fed was created by—and to benefit—bankers. But from the beginning, there has been a complex scheme for the selection of Reserve Bank directors that is not well understood. Directors are classified into groups and serve staggered terms of three years. By Board policy, they're limited to two terms. So after six years—maximum seven if they fill in a vacancy—they're termed out of office. The elected directors, the three A's and three B's who are elected by the member banks, are each selected by subgroups of the member banks. Each Reserve District groups its member banks into small, medium, and large. And each of those groups selects one banker and one non-banker to the Reserve Bank board. So the charge that the Fed exists or is dominated by the large banks is based on a fundamental misunderstanding of Reserve Bank governance. Of the nine directors on each Reserve Bank board, only three may be bankers. And of those three, only one may come from among the largest banks in the district. So when the Federal Reserve System was created, I think the bankers shared my view and actually lobbied the drafters for the creation of an entity called the Federal Advisory Council. Each Reserve District appoints one banker, who cannot be a director, to serve for three one-year terms on an advisory council that meets with the Board of Governors four times a year to advise on questions related to the economy and banking regulation.

Mike concludes by suggesting that Reserve Banks' locations might deserve review since they were based on the economy and the population in the United States as it was in the beginning of the last century and, obviously, that's changed quite a bit. Some might consider that beneficial. This may not be necessary, because in addition to the twelve banks, the Reserve Banks have addressed geographic and economic changes in multiple ways going back to the beginning of the Fed, principally through a network of twenty-four branch offices scattered around the country, each with its own advisory board of seven directors—seven or five, I guess, in the case of Minneapolis—who provide input into the economy.

He also notes that perhaps improvements in governance and safeguards against conflicts of interest might be desirable. My only reaction to that, as someone who has thought about this for a long time, is that I'm not sure whether the perceived failures of governance and the perceived conflicts were structural and thus subject to legislative correction. I would submit that they weren't, but that's my personal opinion. And with that, I've concluded.

GENERAL DISCUSSION

PAUL TUCKER: This has been fascinating listening to this, and I have a question to both of you. Listening to Mary's account of how the regional Federal Reserve Bank heads are constituted, I find it hard to recollect a speech by any Fed chairs about these subjects. That strikes me as odd. Why not talk about the design of the regime, about governance, as well as about the economic conjuncture, etc.?

MARY KARR: I think it's complex. And I think it's not a subject that very many people care about. A few years ago—and I'm trying to remember when it was—the GAO [Government Accountability Office] was directed to do a study of Fed governance, and they came around and they interviewed people in every Reserve Bank, presidents, board secretaries, about governance. And they had exactly the same reaction that you did, Paul, which is, "Gee, we didn't understand all this stuff. Why don't you be more effective at telling your story?" I don't have a good answer for that. It is complex. And I think one of the answers is probably that not very many people care. Michael?

MICHAEL BORDO: Yes, but since the crisis, suddenly they did care.

KARR: Yes, they care for a little while.

TUCKER: So I think my point is, any organization that is so powerful knows that things are eventually going to go wrong. And they know that questions about governance are going to come up. And you try to do the best you can so things don't go wrong. But you have to try all the time to make sure that your organization is understood, so that you get criticized for the right things rather than based on misunderstandings.

KARR: Well, I think so, too. When I came to the Fed in 1991, the big book about the Fed was *Secrets of the Temple.*[13] The mood internally was: keep your head down and don't say much. And that was before we released results of any kind of monetary policy action. The FOMC met, and the market guessed what it did. I've seen a lot of change since 1991, and we've been moving in all kinds of ways toward greater transparency. I'm not always sure—as someone pointed out later—that transparency equals clarity. This is an area where we haven't done as much.

WILLIAMS: I just Googled "GAO report, Federal Reserve." Here is the headline by ABC News on the GAO report: *Federal Reserve Report Rife with Conflict of Interest.*

KARR: Which one was this?

WILLIAMS: That's the 2011 GAO report. So what actually happens when people talk about this in the media, is they take everything they can find, and we read through this, and basically try to find what the story is.

TUCKER: The UK's not so different. [Laughter.]

WILLIAMS: So it is one of these issues. We go out, and we explain the purposes and functions. We do all this stuff, and here is the GAO, which is coming out and saying this is a very good system. But it's actually reported as "rife with conflicts of interest," because there are bankers on the board and stuff like that. If you Google it, all of our speeches and the things that we talk about are not going to show up. But the GAO report does.

GEORGE SHULTZ: I listened, Mary, to your reassuring comment about how people get appointed to the regional banks. It was very reassuring. So it eases my worry about independence of the regulator and the regulated. But I did have an experience that sticks with me. When the New York Fed was open, I had a candidate. Alan Greenspan and I had the same candidate. We

13. William Greider, *Secrets of the Temple: How the Federal Reserve Runs the Country* (New York: Simon & Schuster, 1989).

talked about it. And we both knew the Secretary of the Treasury. We never even got in the conversation. We were totally out of it. The New York financial people appointed the guy. There was no question about it. They got their man.

KARR: I can't speak for the presidential selection process at the New York Fed. I can only speak for the process that I've seen in my own Reserve Bank. I've seen two, and in each case our board was very active in seeking the best possible candidates, communicating directly with the Board of Governors about the search process as it went forward. Clearly, the Board of Governors and the Reserve Banks have to agree. There are some interesting stories—maybe you know them, Michael, as the historian—about lengthy stalemates in some Reserve Districts over appointments where the board of directors and the Board of Governors could not come to an agreement. It's an interesting thing.

CHARLES PLOSSER: So George knows, you can't get appointed as president of a Federal Reserve Bank without the Board of Governors approving it. They have ultimate veto power. So even if the bankers on the New York board of directors wanted someone in particular, the Board of Governors had to be complicit in some sense.

KARR: Absolutely. They have a veto.

PLOSSER: So the standoff is the rare case.

KARR: Yes, where you have a board of directors who has the fortitude to withstand pressure from the Board of Governors for a while.

SHULTZ: Alan Greenspan and I, we couldn't even get in the conversation.

KARR: Was he chairman then?

JOHN TAYLOR: This is when he was chair.

KEVIN WARSH: So this is just my experience of the last period. It is true statutorily that the appointments are subject to the approval

of the Board of Governors, so candidates like John would come
through as they are. But my experience suggests that it would
be very difficult, and it would be reasonably unprecedented in
modern times, for the Reserve Bank's preferred choice not to
ultimately be accepted by the Board of Governors.

KARR: But I think there's a long dance that goes on to get to that
point with some governors and staff and Reserve Banks.

UNKNOWN SPEAKER: I was going to say, it seems like if you look
after this crisis and after the New York crisis, and you see these
criticisms of the Reserve Banks, it's just one Reserve Bank. It's
New York. And in 1933 it was New York, even though there was
all this tension going on in New York. But the focus of the populace was against New York. And the focus of the populace today
is against New York. So there is something about New York, and
it's because Wall Street's there, etc. So the question is: What is
the evidence that New York is the bad hat? I don't know.

TAYLOR: A lot of people think there's evidence.

PLOSSER: It is true that New York is different. And there are lots
of ways one could characterize that. Paul's question was: Why
isn't there more effort to educate the public about the Federal
Reserve System?

The very last speech I gave as a president was titled, "An
Appreciation of the Fed's Twelve Banks." It was about a lot of
those subjects. And actually I gave more than one such talk,
but it happened to be the last one. So I think your question is
an interesting one, which is: Why haven't you seen Ben [Ber-
nanke] or Janet [Yellen] or [Paul] Volcker or whoever, people
at the Board of Governors, more proactive in describing the
strengths of the system? I think it goes back to what Michael
described as the long history of tension between the Board of
Governors and the Reserve Banks. There are many people at the
Board of Governors who view the Reserve Banks as a nuisance,
who would just as soon see us go away. And that tension is not

a recent phenomenon—it has been there for a long time. I think there's part of the institutional ethos or culture at the Board and in Washington, that they're not anxious to defend the system as it stands and particularly the Reserve Banks. So it's kind of up to the Reserve Banks to defend themselves in many cases. In fairness, Ben, on occasion, did that. But it's rare. When the governors are pushed, they tend to do that. So I think the Reserve System ends up making that problem for itself, which I think has a long history and is unfortunate.

JOHN COCHRANE: This seems like a question ripe for international comparison. Let's ask Paul: Are you convinced? Do Scotland, Wales, and Northern Ireland each get their own bank and maybe the Channel Islands too? I got a chuckle out of Paul, I think. The Bundesbank did a pretty good job as a single bank. So, do other central banks, that do not have this complex organization and regional structure, do better or worse than the Fed? Europe seems to be heading in our direction, actually. They have a European Central Bank and many national central banks. But I don't get the sense that the central banks of Greece and Italy are founts of great ideas in macroeconomics in the same way that St. Louis and Minnesota have been.

The defense so far has been that the Fed was set up as it is to disburse political power regionally, and to keep the fragmented banking system alive. Here the comparison with Canada is apt, as it's often said Canada has a single banking system, and that it has therefore had far fewer crises than the United States. Canada also does not have this system of regional central banks. The US system then evolved into geographically separate macroeconomic research departments that came up with independent ideas. This evolution was not at all part of the original idea. But I'm also skeptical that lots of federally supported macroeconomic research, by full-time federal government employees, is the best way to produce distinct and innovative ideas.

To sum up, international comparisons would be useful. As far as I know, no other country does it our way, and it's not obvious that our outcomes are so much better than those of every other country.

ANDREW LEVIN: Well, just two comments. The first is, having been outside the Fed now for the last several years and talking to people in the outside world, I can say that the Fed oftentimes comes across as very defensive. The answer always seems to be: "Well, if it ain't broke, don't fix it. It's been working that way for a hundred years." And of course, Mike Bordo is a good friend of the Federal Reserve System, so if his paper concludes that it would be a good idea to revisit these questions for the first time in a hundred years, that conclusion should be taken very seriously. And I really wish that the Federal Reserve would voluntarily look into these issues and conduct its own studies, publish those studies, and give serious consideration to how things could be improved.

And this also connects to what Kevin said about the size of the FOMC. I think that having nineteen participants around a table makes it pretty difficult to have a truly deliberative process. Now if the Federal Reserve Bank presidents all got together and voluntarily said, "We could shrink from twelve down to seven," one significant benefit would be to improve the deliberative quality of the FOMC's decision-making process. That would be exactly the kind of constructive approach that I wish we would see sometimes.

My second comment is that a federal judge made a ruling in a Freedom of Information Act case on March 31. It was an important ruling that bears directly on these constitutional issues. Specifically, the FOIA has an exemption to safeguard the relationship between banks and their supervising agencies. And the Federal Reserve Board actually pleaded that exemption, and the federal judge granted it. Here are the exact words of the judge:

"As the Board points out, the fact that it can require examination of the Federal Reserve banks is no different than any other financial institution subject to mandatory supervision by a federal regulator. . . . If a financial institution cannot expect confidentiality, it may be less cooperative and forthright in its disclosures. There's no reason to believe the Federal Reserve Banks would not react the same way."

Now maybe the plaintiff will appeal that decision, and the appeals court will overrule the judge's verdict. But the fact that FOIA only applies to federal agencies and not to the regional Federal Reserve Banks is a real problem. Every federal agency has an inspector general, but the Federal Reserve Banks do not, and that's also a serious problem. And so again, the Fed should voluntarily be looking at ways to move forward with constructive reforms and not just keep repeating, "This is the way we've always done it."

PETER FISHER: I had seventeen years at the Fed and five of them in the legal department. The supervisory work the Reserve Banks do on other banks is done under authority of the Board.

KARR: I think he's talking about a request to review the Board of Governor's examinations of Reserve Banks.

FISHER: That's the Board keeping stuff confidential, not the Reserve Banks keeping stuff confidential.

KARR: But that's the Board relying, probably at the request of the Reserve Banks—

LEVIN: Unfortunately, I'm not an attorney. But if you read the judge's verdict, he certainly seems to be saying that a Federal Reserve Bank may be less cooperative and forthright in its disclosures to its supervisor, meaning the Board of Governors, and it's kind of shocking to see such an opinion coming from a federal judge.

FISHER: But that's an argument a Board of Governors lawyer made to the judge.

KARR: Yes.

TAYLOR: So I just have a question. The broader, difficult issue is about regulatory capture, and there are many ways that can occur. There's the revolving door, for example, but the appointment process is one that people worry about. It seems to me that the checks you're describing are formally there, but there are many other influences that can affect appointments, and they do.

KARR: There are.

TAYLOR: We know it, and George has given an example.

KARR: There are, but I think New York is a different case. And I can't speak about the New York Fed and potential regulatory capture. We've certainly seen accusations of that from former examiners in the press over the last couple of years. For most of the Reserve Banks, I would say—and John and Charlie, chime in—but the supervision of financial institutions is a delegated function from the Board. One of the things that the Board has done in the aftermath of the financial crisis is reasserted itself in the supervision of the largest financial institutions and decreased the amount of delegation and the amount of freedom of action of entities like the New York Fed. And I think part of that is to deal with this perceived issue of regulatory capture. For the rest of us, I would argue, who aren't in New York and supervising the money center banks, it's a much different issue. I suspect that was true in Philadelphia and maybe San Francisco. Our Reserve Bank presidents are not involved in supervision. The Board of Governors, by policy, now wants to be involved in the hiring and firing of a senior supervisory officer, as I recall. Isn't that correct, John?

WILLIAMS: Yes.

KARR: So there have been some changes to try to address some of these issues by the Fed itself.

BORDO: I want to pick up on something that John Cochrane said which I think is really prescient. When the Federal Reserve was founded we had a unit banking system, totally fragmented. We had it until the 1990s. Now we have moved in the direction that other advanced countries have long been with nationwide branch banking. In the United States, it is not quite nationwide branch banking, but it is getting there. An implication of this is that one of the original purposes of the Federal Reserve Act was for the regional Federal Reserve Banks to oversee and conduct monetary policy with their local member banks and serve as semi-autonomous central banks. This was because of the fact that capital markets were not integrated and so there was a case for separate regional monetary policies. By contrast, today we have a fully integrated nationwide capital market and we have nationwide banks mainly headquartered in New York. Now who is in charge? The New York Fed? So in a sense we are back to the earlier 1920s struggle between the New York Fed and the Board. The other Reserve Banks are kind of peripheral to this game. And that is where some of today's governance problems come from.

SHULTZ: Let me tell all you New Yorkers something. We're different! We're not like Washington, we're not like New York. San Francisco's different! [Laughter.]

REFERENCES

Belongia, Michael, and Peter Ireland. 2015. "Don't Audit the Fed, Restructure It." e21, Economic Policies for the 21st Century, Manhattan Institute, May.

Beyer, Andreas, Vitor Gaspar, Christina Geberding, and Otmar Issing. 2013. "Opting Out of The Great Inflation: German Monetary Policy after the Breakdown of Bretton Woods." In *The Great Inflation,* edited by Michael D. Bordo and Athanasios Orphanides. Chicago, University of Chicago Press.

Bordo, Michael. 2006. "Review of *A History of the Federal Reserve, vol. 1* (2003) by Allan H. Meltzer," *Journal of Monetary Economics* 53, no. 3: 633–657.

Bordo, Michael. 2014. "Rules for a Lender of Last Resort: An Historical Perspective." *Journal of Economic Dynamics and Control* 49, issue C.

Bordo, Michael, Owen F. Humpage, and Anna J. Schwartz. 2015. *Strained Relations: US Foreign-Exchange Operations and Monetary Policy in the Twentieth Century.* Chicago: University of Chicago Press.

Bordo, Michael, and Harold James. 2008. "The SNB from 1907 to 1946: A Happy Childhood or a Troubled Adolescence?" In *The Swiss National Bank 1907–2007,* edited by the Swiss National Bank. Zurich: Neue Zurcher Zeitung Publishers.

Bordo, Michael, Angela Redish, and Hugh Rockoff. 2015. "Why Didn't Canada Have a Banking Crisis in 2008 (or in 1930, or 1907, or . . .)?" *Economic History Review* 68, no. 2 (February).

Bordo, Michael, and David Wheelock. 2010. "The Promise and Performance of the Federal Reserve as Lender of Last Resort, 1914–1933." In *A Return to Jekyll Island: The Origins, History, and Future of the Federal Reserve,* edited by Michael Bordo and William Roberds. New York: Cambridge University Press.

Brunner, Karl, and Allan Meltzer. 1968. "What Did We Learn from the Monetary Experience of the United States in the Great Depression?" *Canadian Journal of Economics* 1, no. 2: 334–48.

Calomiris, Charles, and Stephen Haber. 2014. *Fragile by Design: The Political Origins of Banking Crises and Scarce Credit.* Princeton, NJ: Princeton University Press.

Calomiris, Charles, and Eugene White. 1994. "The Origins of Federal Deposit Insurance." In *The Regulated Economy: A Historical Approach to Political Economy,* edited by Claudia Goldin and Gary Libecap: 145–188. Chicago: University of Chicago Press.

Conti-Brown, Peter. 2015. "The Twelve Federal Reserve Banks: Governance and Accountability in the 21st Century," Brookings Institution, Hutchins Center Working Paper no. 10, March.

Eichengreen, Barry. 1992. "Designing a Central Bank for Europe: a cautionary tale from the early years of the Federal Reserve System." In *Establishing a Central Bank: Issues in Europe and Lessons from the US,* edited by Matthew B. Canzoneri, Vittorio Grilli, and Paul R. Masson. Cambridge, UK: Cambridge University Press.

Fisher, Richard W. 2015. "Suggestions after a Decade at the Fed: Remarks Before the Economic Club of New York." New York City, February 11.

Friedman, Milton, and Anna J. Schwartz. 1963. *A Monetary History of the United States, 1867 to 1960.* Princeton, NJ: Princeton University Press.

Goodfriend, Marvin. 2000. "The Role of a Regional Bank in a System of Central Banks." *Federal Reserve Bank of Richmond Economic Quarterly* 86, no. 1.

Gorton, Gary. 1985. "Clearinghouses and the Origin of Central Banking in the United States." *Journal of Economic History* 45, no. 2: 277–283.

Hafer, A.W. 1997. "Against the Tide: Malcolm Bryan's Experiment with Aggregate Targets in 1959 and 1960." Southern Illinois University at Edwardsville. Working paper no. 98–1010.

Karr, Mary H. 2013. "Structure and Governance: Providing Oversight and a Window to Main Street." *History of the Federal Reserve Bank of St. Louis.* FRED.

Meigs, A. James. 1976. "Campaigning for Monetary Reform: The Federal Reserve Bank of St. Louis in 1959 and 1960." *Journal of Monetary Economics* 2 (November): 439–54.

Meltzer, Allan H. 2003. *A History of the Federal Reserve, vol. 1, 1913–1951.* Chicago: University of Chicago Press.

Meltzer, Allan H. 2010. *A History of the Federal Reserve, vol. 2, Book 1, 1951–1969.* Chicago: University of Chicago Press.

Stern, Gary H., and Ron J. Feldman. 2004. *Too Big to Fail: The Hazards of Bank Bailouts.* Washington, DC: Brookings Institution.

Wheelock, David C. 1991. *The Strategy and Consistency of Federal Reserve Monetary Policy, 1924–1933.* New York: Cambridge University Press.

Wheelock, David C. 2000. "National Monetary Policy by Regional Design: The Evolving Role of the Federal Reserve Banks in Federal Reserve System Policy." In *Regional Aspects of Monetary Policy in Europe.* Edited by Jurgen Von Hagen and Christopher Waller. Boston: Kluwer Academic Publishers.

Wigmore, Barry. 1987. "Was the Bank Holiday of 1933 Caused by a Run on the Dollar?" *Journal of Economic History* 47: 839–856.

CHAPTER SIX

Panel on Independence, Accountability, and Transparency in Central Bank Governance

Charles I. Plosser, George P. Shultz, and John C. Williams

PART 1

Balancing Central Bank Independence and Accountability

Charles I. Plosser

It's been a fascinating day with very interesting discussions on a wide range of issues. In my remarks I'm going to take two things as given. The first is, the United States needs a central bank. It would be a very interesting discussion to consider alternative arrangements, but I'm not going to go there. And besides that, most countries today operate under fiat money regimes, and fiat money, of course, means that money has value because the government says it has value. Central banks for the most part are responsible for maintaining the purchasing power and value of a fiat currency. Of course in the United States, the way the Fed does that is by buying and selling securities in the open market to control the growth of money and credit. And that authority to buy and sell securities in the open market gives the central banks, and the Fed in particular, extraordinary powers to intervene in financial markets, not only through the quantity of things that they buy, but through the types of assets that they choose to buy.

Now the second premise that I'm going to take as given is that it is desirable to have a healthy degree of separation between government officials who are in charge of spending and those who are in charge of printing the money. That is to say that a healthy degree of independence for a central bank is a valuable characteristic. And I think it's just good governance. History tells us that when central banks lack that political independence, outcomes are on average worse, often much worse. Printing money just becomes an easy substitute for tough fiscal choices, and that's not a good thing. So this healthy degree of separation between government expenditure decisions and the printing of fiat currency is just wise; I'm going to take that as given as well.

Now over the years, as we've heard listening to Michael [Bordo] and the others, unhappiness with the Fed comes and goes. We see episodes where the Fed is reviled or praised, and sometimes at the same time. But the recent criticisms, I think, largely stem from policy actions or choices of the Fed itself, as the Fed has pushed the envelope of traditional monetary policy. These include the obvious things we've talked about—bailouts of individual financial institutions, such as Bear Stearns and AIG; six years of essentially zero-policy interest rates; aggressive large-scale asset purchases that quadrupled the size of the Fed's balance sheet, and not just of Treasury securities but of mortgage-backed securities to support the housing market. Those decisions about the types of assets purchased, I believe, are a form of credit allocation by the central bank, and thus are more akin to fiscal policy than monetary policy. But regardless of the justification for any of these actions, what these actions have done is raise serious questions in many people's minds about the tremendous discretionary power that rests with the central bank. This has led to calls for reform of our central bank to enhance oversight and, perhaps, alter its governance.

So how, in a democratic society, do you design an institution that has considerable authority to do what it needs to do, including sufficient independence, but also is accountable and constrained in the use of its authority? Part of the problem in many of the proposals put forward in Congress and elsewhere is that they seek accountability through greater political control and interference. And from my perspective, that risks robbing the central bank of much of its needed independence. For example, making Federal Reserve Bank presidents political appointees, or opening up monetary policy deliberations to real-time political or policy audits by the GAO (General Accountability Office) are, I think, potentially very damaging to the Fed's independence going forward.

So the way I look at this is, we should look at ways to limit the scope of authorities or responsibilities rather than impinge on the central bank's operational or political independence. So I'm going to highlight three ways I think of pursuing such restrictions on a central bank. First, narrowing the mandate for monetary policy. The broader the mandate, the more opportunity there is for discretion and, indeed, more discretion means there's more opportunity for more mischief. Discretion allows for the opportunity to make good decisions, but it also creates the opportunity for making really bad decisions. Indeed, broad mandates contribute to the view— and, in my view, the mistaken view—that central banks are capable of solving all manner of economic ills, and thus making it difficult to hold them accountable or measure their success. I'm reminded of the old saying: responsible for everything and accountable for nothing. The second way to restrict central bank actions is through the type of assets that can be purchased or sold, thus constraining the composition of its balance sheet and the range or scope of its market interventions. And the third way is to ensure appropriate discipline and accountability through more transparent communication of a monetary policy strategy, and this is where rules can play a vital role.

So let me talk first about goals and objectives of the Federal Reserve. The mandate from Congress has evolved over time. Its latest incarnation was set in 1977. The mandate, as Peter [Fisher] read to us earlier, says that the FOMC "shall maintain *long-run* growth of monetary and credit aggregates commensurate with the economy's *long-run* potential to increase production so as to promote effectively the goals of maximum employment, stable prices, and moderate, long-term interest rates (italics mine)." Now Peter thought this mandate was actually very narrow. But he also noted that the interpretation of the mandate, whether it be by the Fed itself or by Congress, is actually quite vague and broad. It seems to have become the accepted wisdom that this mandate means the Fed should stabilize short-term fluctuations in employment while maintaining long-term price stability. I'm going to leave it to others to opine whether that's the only interpretation that this language could offer, or even if it's the best one. I think that's open for question. But I would suggest that it's in fact the vagueness of this mandate itself that's part of the problem.

The general interpretation of the mandate has allowed wide discretion for the Fed to pursue different objectives at different times, thus making communication of a coherent monetary policy strategy challenging at best. Indeed, the active pursuit of an employment mandate has been, and continues to be, problematic for the Fed. Many—or most—economists would at least be dubious of the ability of monetary policy to predictably manipulate employment with any precision in the short run. There is a strong consensus among economists that in the long run, monetary policy does not determine employment. And indeed, the FOMC's 2012 statement of longer-term goals and objectives acknowledges this. The statement explicitly says, "The maximum level of employment is largely determined by non-monetary factors that affect the structure and dynamics of the labor market." So the committee acknowledges that it does not know the maximum level of employment at any point in time and acknowledges that even conceptually it changes over time. So the committee for those reasons said it was inappropriate to quantify a numerical goal for the employment mandate. All that was great. Yet from my perspective, the committee seems to act and talk as if it does have a target, and that monetary policy can always achieve it. The language that the Fed often uses tends to equate the long-term unemployment rate from the quarterly Summary of Economic Projections (SEP) of FOMC participants with maximum employment. And yet that's not the same thing as maximum employment attainable at any point in time. They are very different concepts. Indeed, the concept of maximum employment differs depending on the model one uses.

From my perspective, what's worse is there seems to be a view that not only is there an employment target, but other details of the labor market are also part of the mandate, and monetary policy can be used to determine those as well. Wage growth, participation rates, part-time versus full-time employment are some of the examples that come to mind. I know of no good economic theory or empirical evidence that explains the relationship between any of these labor market characteristics and monetary policy, although I'm sure somebody could come up with one. Now many people are advocating we have another mandate, financial stability, whatever that means, and that be added to the list of goals. That would further muddy the waters, and I'll have a little bit to say about that later.

So it's the vagueness of the mandate which has given wide latitude to the Fed to exercise great discretion over what it thinks is important, when it thinks it's important, and the instruments it uses to achieve a particular objective. For example, massive purchases of MBS (mortgage-backed securities) were undertaken in the hopes that significant subsidies to the housing sector relative to other industries would have beneficial results on aggregate employment, more so than just simply purchasing treasuries. Now you can debate whether this is an accurate empirical statement of what would actually be accomplished by such purchases. I don't think we have much evidence of that. But on the other hand, you could also debate whether such decisions to subsidize one industry in favor of another should belong to the central bank in the first place. Now of course, one can argue that monetary policy can't avoid affecting relative prices and allocations. Even in the best of worlds that's probably true. But I think it's important to consider, in thinking about the institution, the limits to the interventions that should be allowed and the types of goals that should be assigned to an independent central bank.

So when establishing the longer-term goals and objectives for any organization, whether it be the Fed, but particularly one that serves the public—I think Carl [Walsh] was making this point earlier—it's important that those goals be achievable. It's important that you assign an organization or institution goals that it can achieve. Assigning unachievable or unattainable goals to an organization is a recipe for failure, because it will fail at it. And for the Fed, and central banks more generally, failure contributes to a loss of confidence in the institution and thus its legitimacy.

My fear is that over the last quarter century or so, the public has come to expect way too much from central banks and way too much from monetary policy in particular. This has been quite evident around the world in the recent crisis, where the public and elected officials have relied on central banks to solve all manner of economic woes. I believe this is the wrong direction to take central banks, giving them more and more and more scope for both discretion and responsibility for our economic well-being. I'm reminded of Milton Friedman's admonishment in his presidential address to the AEA (American Economic Association) way back in 1967 when he said, "We are in danger of assigning to monetary policy a larger role than it can perform, in danger of asking it to accomplish tasks it cannot achieve and, as a result, in danger of preventing it from making the contribution that it is capable of making." Those are very wise words, I think, and we need to revisit them in the context of current monetary policy and institutions.

So as you can guess by now, I think the aggressive pursuit of broad and expansive objectives is quite risky. It could have undesirable repercussions down the road, including undermining the public's confidence in the institution, its legitimacy, and its independence. Indeed, I think the changes and reforms being discussed in Congress are the early salvos in just such a process. And it's worrisome, from my perspective. Expansive and vague mandates also make it difficult for the public to hold a central bank accountable, as it allows for policymakers to shift the goalposts, so to speak, to justify their policy choices. This aggravates the problem of accountability, because it muddles the metrics for success. Thus my earlier reference to "responsible for everything but accountable for nothing" is, I think, very apt.

So in order to narrow the focus of the Fed and create a more limited purpose central bank, I conclude that it would be appropriate to redefine the mandate to focus solely, or at least predominantly, on price stability. A single, primary mandate would help focus attention and reduce discretion to pursue other, perhaps unachievable goals and make it easier to hold the Fed accountable for its policies. It would also provide some protection for the Fed from demands arising from other interests outside the Fed or even inside the Fed that desire the Fed to pursue other objectives just because it can.

Another way of limiting the sorts of interventions a central bank can undertake is to more narrowly constrain the assets it can hold on its balance sheet, thus constraining the markets in which it can in fact intervene and purchase assets. This is not an uncommon restriction, and it's implemented in different ways in different countries. The ECB (European Central Bank) has a different set of restrictions than the Fed does. The Fed, of course, is already restricted in some degree by what it can do with its System Open Market Account (SOMA). The Fed is allowed to hold only US government securities or agency obligations that are fully guaranteed by the government of the United States. This has permitted, however, the widespread, large-scale purchases of MBS. As we know, however, section 13(3) lending was used to circumvent even those restrictions, because it allowed the Fed to purchase many assets from Bear Stearns and JP Morgan and AIG, for example, "under unusual and exigent circumstances."

Now the FOMC has actually indicated in its so-called exit principles that it does desire to return the SOMA to an all-treasuries portfolio. I think that's an admirable goal. Unfortunately, given the size of the MBS portfolio and the inclination of the FOMC not to engage in outright sales of MBS, it may not happen in my lifetime. But we can get there. Now this recommendation to return SOMA to an all-treasuries portfolio does not necessarily impact the ability of the Fed to lend to depository institutions through the discount window, and thus to continue to play a role as the lender of last resort. What remains is the authority under section 13(3), which was used extensively during the crisis, to lend to JP Morgan, Bear Stearns, and AIG. Now those instances, in my view, were not true lender-of-last-resort activities. Lender of last resort is intended to provide, as we've talked a lot about today, liquidity to otherwise solvent or sustainable institutions based on strong collateral, not to prop up failing institutions by accepting poor collateral. Of course, in times of crisis, as we've talked about, the distinction between insolvency and illiquidity can be a difficult thing to determine.

I think there needs to be a new approach to emergency lending, and so in that regard, I go back to where Paul [Tucker] started us this morning about how do we define the rules of the game in emergencies. I worry a little bit that crisis management has now become the sine qua non of central banking. All of a sudden we now believe that if we can't solve the emergency lending problems, central banks aren't worth much to us. Crisis management and financial stability have taken on renewed importance, perhaps to the detriment of other roles that central banks should play. This is an important topic and the trade-offs faced by central banks as they acquired ever broader mandates have yet to be fully understood.

I think a way to go about emergency lending or bailouts is not to fully integrate fiscal policy with monetary policy, because these are fiscal policy decisions. I have suggested that the way to go about it is to establish a new accord between the Treasury and the Fed. So what you could do is have an environment where, in an emergency, it is the Treasury that ends up taking the responsibility for saying, "We're going to bail out or rescue or buy some private assets in order to rescue institutions to promote financial stability," however they want to define that term. And that would be OK, as it is a fiscal policy action. Then the Treasury could turn around and tell the Fed, "We'd like you to execute this strategy for us." That's fine. But what needs to be decided, from my perspective, is the Treasury agrees *ex ante* that within some period of time— say six months, one year, or some predetermined window—the Treasury will swap those assets on the Fed's balance sheet that are private assets for treasuries. It would just be a swap. That frees the Fed to conduct monetary policy without the baggage of the credit allocations brought about through the acquisition of private assets. The Treasury would take over responsibility for the bailout and the credit exposure rather than the central bank. So I think that's one way to begin drawing some lines about how you could go about having the Fed play an operational role when needed but also, *ex ante*, protecting it on the flipside to return its portfolio to all treasuries.

Finally, I'll just briefly make my third point regarding transparency and systematic policy, because I made it already. Earlier we talked about a monetary policy report, about transparency and communication. I do feel that the Fed can and should be accountable and one way to do so is to describe its monetary policy strategy. I don't think discretion is a strategy. I think that using rules and benchmarks to convey information about how the committee sets policy would be very useful. And doing that through a monetary policy report that used various rules as benchmarks and guidelines and then force the committee, force the FOMC, to explain its actions in the context of those benchmarks could be a very healthy step in the right direction.

I think the public has come to expect too much from central banks and has come to question the breadth of powers that they seem to possess. I think this is dangerous for the Fed and dangerous for the economy. And if the public loses confidence in the Fed, the central bank is at risk of losing its independence and legitimacy. So rather than micromanaging the governance, auditing policy decisions in real time, or undermining its independence, it would be better to establish, in my view, a more limited-purpose central bank, whose activities and responsibilities are more narrowly defined, whose scope for discretion is more limited, and yet whose independence is protected.

PART 2

Central Bank Transparency: Less is More

George P. Shultz

I've listened to what Charlie has to say, and all I can say is, "Amen." [Laughter.] I'd only add one little problem: I don't think the Treasury has the authority to do what you say. They would have to go and get that authority.

I sounded off this morning on some of the problems I think the Fed has had in conducting itself. Let me first touch on something akin to what you said. I think it's really important that the Fed show that it's competent. Right now in this country, there is an increasing feeling that the government can't do anything, can't even roll out a website. So it's important that it be competent, and

I think having a limited-purpose organization is the key to that competence. I think that's very important.

Second, with all due respect to transparency, I think the Fed speaks with about a dozen voices right now. People sound off all the time, and it's a little hard to figure out just what is the policy. Let me give an example. Bill Martin worked at the Fed quite a while, and I happened to know him for unrelated reasons. He had a squeaky little voice and he didn't speak a lot, but when he spoke, people listened. When I was secretary of the treasury, we had a lot of problems with the exchange markets, so I had a little committee that I appointed and I persuaded Bill to be on it. After I left office, I was put on it. Bill Martin was chairman of the Fed, and we had a meeting where Bill was talking about our currency: "We've said this about the dollar, we've said that about the dollar, and what should we say about the dollar?" There was dead silence. Then this squeaky little voice of Bill Martin says, "You should say less." I think there's something to be said for saying less. Remember Ted Williams: "Why ain't ya talking, Ted?" "I let my bat do the talking." The Fed has a big bat. Let it do the talking.

Then I think it's always important to remember the context in which actions are taken. I'll give two examples. In the early 1970s we had a big debate about wage and price controls. I lost that fight. On the other side was Arthur Burns. We put this into effect and the first thing that happened was a freeze. It was really effective and it scared the hell out of everybody because you knew the economy has got to be able to adjust. But I think in Arthur's mind he felt that "these things really work." The result was that you wound up with a looser monetary policy. In an odd way, you'd have to say wage and price controls caused inflation later on.

Then there's a completely different kind of issue, and that came up in the Paul Volcker period that's been spoken about. I think it's fair to say that the first thing Paul got involved in was the credit restriction business. It exploded. It was only a little later that he went to control the money supply. I remember the period very distinctly. Paul had been my under secretary when I was secretary of the treasury. I knew him very well and I knew Ronald Reagan very well. I organized his economic policies during the primaries and during the election campaign and afterwards. He was convinced, and we were all convinced—and Michael, I think you were a part of this—that we couldn't have a decent economy unless we got inflation under control. And the only way to do it was by what Paul was doing, so I made sure Paul knew that. Paul would tell you today that on quite a few occasions the press served up questions to the president, in essence inviting him to knock down Paul, but he never did, he never took the bait. People ran into the Oval Office all the time, saying, "Mr. President, Mr. President, it's going to cause a recession! We're going to lose seats in the midterm election!" Reagan basically took the view, "If not us, who? If not now, when?" So this period went on and it worked, but I don't think if Paul had been there as just chairman of the Fed that he could have handled it. You had to have a strong politician stand up to the reaction to the recession and the political implications.

I think I was reassured, Mary [Karr], by your comments about appointments and the idea that we don't need to be so concerned about regulatory capture, but I still worry. I think one of the answers is that we have this really complex Dodd-Frank, and all these banks have regulators by the dozens looking over their shoulders. It's a recipe for disaster. Why can't we have in place simpler, clearer regulations, like capital requirements and leverage? If you have them strongly in place, you don't need a million people. They will do the job, and you don't have potential for conflicts there.

I mentioned the incident this morning about calling banks in and making them take $25 billion when they didn't want it and basically threatening to regulate them out of existence if they didn't take it. That was a complete misuse of power. The Fed has a lot of power and it needs to be very careful how it uses it. Trust is the coin of the realm, and people can't be trusted with power if they use it improperly. So that's part of the confidence business that you were talking about. Be sure you behave in a way that is consistent with the idea that trust is the coin of the realm.

Thank you.

PART 3

Monetary Policy and the Independence Dilemma

John C. Williams

Recently there has been a great deal of commentary arguing that the Federal Reserve needs more oversight and greater transparency. This has culminated in a number of legislative proposals designed to constrain the Fed's freedom of action in monetary policy and other spheres. One prominent example is the bill proposed in the House of Representatives entitled the Federal Reserve Accountability and Transparency Act of 2014, or the FRAT Act for short. Much of the debate surrounds the Federal Reserve's policy actions during and following the global financial crisis and recession. But the deeper issue of oversight and independence of central banks in democratic societies is not new; on the contrary, it has been a contentious one for the past century. In the broader historical context, recent proposals are not unique to the current situation but instead represent the latest chapter in a long-running debate in the United States and around the globe.

I will delve into the question of central bank oversight and independence, examine some of the solutions that have been tried in the past but ultimately failed, and then turn to approaches that have proven more successful. I'll conclude by considering how the lessons from the past apply to the current debate about how to enhance the oversight and transparency of the Federal Reserve. Throughout, I will focus on monetary policy and not address other activities of central banks. Note that the views expressed here today are entirely my own, and do not necessarily reflect those of others in the Federal Reserve System.

The independence dilemma

Why has central bank oversight and transparency been so contentious? The independence dilemma stems from the enormous power central banks have to create money essentially out of thin air. Wielded judiciously, this power can foster economic prosperity and stability. However, it can also be misused as a short-term fix for governments to meet financing needs by printing money or to stimulate the economy before an election. Such misuse can undermine economic stability and fuel runaway inflation. The resulting longer-run damage may only be felt years or decades in the future, well outside usual political time frames.

To avoid the temptation of opportunistic money creation, modern governments have generally delegated the day-to-day operation of monetary policy to an independent central bank. This independence means that policymakers are free to focus on the technical aspects of their task, removed from direct political influence. This arrangement, however, creates a new problem: Who tells the central bank what to do, if not the government? Thus, the dilemma: successful monetary policy necessitates both an arm's-length relationship to the political process and oversight by elected officials. The search for balance at the horns of this predicament has been at the heart of central bank debates and reforms over the past century.

Two broad approaches have been taken to solve the quandary. In both cases, the overarching goal is the same: economic prosperity and stability. The difference is in the degree of operational latitude afforded the central bank. The first, more restrictive approach is to delegate an operational mandate stipulating that the central bank achieve a specific intermediate goal. The second approach is to delegate an overall economic goal, such as low inflation, and let the central bank determine how to best achieve its goal with the tools at its disposal.

Operational mandates

In the past, central banks were typically given an operational mandate. This choice reflected a strong desire to limit the discretionary power of central banks and to provide a nominal anchor, that is, a stable value of money. Operational mandates were thought to be highly predictable, accountable, and transparent, and able to provide the basis for longer-term economic stability, at the cost of short-term flexibility and discretion. However, as I will discuss in more detail, operational mandates have been beset by a string of failures rooted in this very lack of flexibility to deal with changing economic conditions and crises. After each failure, a new operational mandate framework has been introduced that, while an improvement over the prior one, still proved prone to breakdown under economic and political stress.

The classic example of an operational mandate is the gold standard. Under the gold standard, monetary policy is completely subordinate to the fixed price of gold at a legislated level. Many countries followed the gold standard before World War I and in the period between the wars. The gold standard represents the most extreme form of an operational mandate. The central bank has little freedom of action or decision and is therefore unable to take potentially harmful actions on its own—or, for that matter, *any* actions on its own.

History has shown that this inflexibility and the subservience of monetary policy to fluctuations in gold supply and demand contributed to economic crises and depressions. The gold standard's inability to cope with economic stress is reflected by its frequent curtailment during times of war and crisis. In fact, so often was it suspended that deviations from the gold standard routinely became the norm, rather than the exception. The inherent lack of flexibility in the money supply was blamed for contributing to the depth of the downturns experienced by many countries during the 1930s.[1]

The failure of the gold standard led to a new type of operational mandate, the fixed exchange rate regime. Under this system, the central bank is required to maintain the value of the domestic currency in relation to that of a foreign currency. As with the gold standard, predictability, accountability, and transparency were considered paramount virtues. The most famous example was the Bretton Woods system, in which foreign currencies were pegged to the US dollar. A fixed exchange rate system is somewhat less rigid than a gold standard and is far less subject to the particularities of gold supply and demand. Nonetheless, it puts a straitjacket on a central bank's ability to set monetary policy attuned to domestic economic conditions, since policy is beholden to the exchange-rate peg. As a result, monetary policy is less able to counter cyclical swings in the economy.

History has shown that fixed exchange rate systems at times perform poorly and are often abandoned during periods of severe economic stress or crisis. Although some economies have successfully operated with exchange-rate pegs, other regimes have not stood the test of time. For example, the Bretton Woods system collapsed in the early 1970s and the European Exchange Rate Mechanism faltered in the early 1990s.

The string of failures associated with the gold standard and fixed exchange rates led to other proposed operational mandates, including monetary targets. Monetary targeting is most often

1. Eichengreen 1992.

associated with Milton Friedman's proposal to have the money stock grow at a constant rate irrespective of economic conditions.[2] In theory, monetary targeting has the benefit of being predictable, accountable, and transparent, while providing a stronger automatic stabilizer for the economy than earlier, more rigid regimes. For example, if the economy heats up, demand for money balances rises, driving interest rates up, which slows the economy and reduces inflation pressures.

However, in practice, monetary targeting has proved an unreliable and overly restrictive framework. In particular, changes in the financial system have caused the relationship between money demand and the economy to shift in unexpected ways. As a result, a fixed growth rate of the money stock can have unpredictable implications for economic growth and inflation. Following on the theoretical insight of William Poole, in a world where money demand is hard to predict, it is preferable to use the interest rate as the primary policy instrument rather than money supply.[3] This is exactly what central banks around the world have done, leaving monetary targeting by the wayside.

Goal mandates

In light of the string of past failures of various forms of operational mandates, many countries have settled on a very different approach to deal with the issues of oversight and independence. Instead of stipulating an operational target, they set high-level economic goals and delegate to the central bank the authority to decide how to best achieve them. Under such a goal mandate, the central bank is held responsible for achieving its objectives and is typically required to regularly report on its progress and the steps

2. Friedman 1960.
3. Poole 1970.

it is taking. This framework stresses the predictability, accountability, and transparency of the main economic goals of policy, rather than operational actions.

An early entry in this category is the mandate under which the Federal Reserve has operated for the past thirty-eight years. The Federal Reserve Reform Act of 1977 states: "The Board of Governors of the Federal Reserve System and the Federal Open Market Committee shall maintain long run growth of the monetary and credit aggregates commensurate with the economy's long run potential to increase production, so as to promote effectively the goals of maximum employment, stable prices, and moderate long-term interest rates." Somewhat confusingly, this sentence combines elements of both operational and goal mandates. The operational mandate aspect is captured by the reference to long run growth of monetary and credit aggregates, hearkening to a monetary targeting regime. The goal mandate is specified as the ultimate objective of monetary policy. Later in this paragraph, the tension between the two approaches is resolved clearly in favor of the goal mandate: "Nothing in this Act shall be interpreted to require that such ranges of growth or diminution be achieved if the Board of Governors and the Federal Open Market Committee determine that they cannot or should not be achieved because of changing conditions." Although the description of the goals is left somewhat vague, the Federal Reserve filled in this gap by issuing a statement describing the longer-run goals and policy strategy in greater detail.[4]

The Act of 1977 also demanded a greater level of oversight and transparency regarding monetary policy. It stipulated that the Fed would consult with congressional committees at semiannual meetings concerning "objectives and plans with respect to the ranges of growth or diminution of monetary and credit aggregates for the

4. Board of Governors 2015.

upcoming twelve months, taking account of past and prospective developments in production, employment, and prices."[5] The Full Employment and Balanced Growth Act of 1978 added a requirement that the Fed issue semiannual reports to Congress in conjunction with these meetings. The semiannual meetings and reports continue to this day.

Other countries have taken the goal mandate framework considerably further. Some twenty-five years ago the Reserve Bank of New Zealand introduced a new goal mandate framework called inflation targeting.[6] Since then, dozens of countries have adopted some form of inflation targeting. The cornerstone of this approach is that the central bank—often in consultation and in formal agreement with the government—assumes responsibility for inflation being, on average, near a numerical target. It is important to note that, although the inflation goal is front and center, inflation-targeting central banks also recognize a role for stabilizing economic activity—what is often referred to as "flexible inflation targeting."

The inflation-targeting framework also features clear communication of the central bank's policy strategy and the rationale for its decisions, with the goal of enhancing the predictability of the central bank's actions and its accountability to the public. This is generally done in regular public reports with detailed analysis of the economic outlook and policy strategy and decisions.[7] Indeed, some governments require the head of the central bank to issue a public letter when the inflation goal is missed, explaining why the target was not achieved and what is being done to rectify the situation.[8]

5. Federal Reserve Reform Act of 1977.
6. Leiderman and Svensson 1995, Bernanke and Mishkin 1997, Bernanke et al. 1999, Kuttner 2004.
7. See, for example, Norges Bank 2014.
8. See, for example, Bank of England 2015.

As a testament to the effectiveness of this framework, countries with inflation goal mandates have generally kept inflation low and stable over the past few decades, even in the aftermath of the global financial crisis.[9]

Back to the future: Monetary policy rules as an operational mandate?

Although many countries have found that a goal mandate coupled with strong oversight and transparency works much better than past operational mandates, some commentators argue that the problem has not been with the notion of an operational mandate per se, but with how it has been implemented. They accept that the gold standard, fixed exchange rate, and monetary targeting are flawed, and argue that a more sophisticated operational mandate is needed—one that is more flexible at dealing with changing economic conditions but still puts a meaningful constraint on the central bank.

The latest proposed operational mandate is that the central bank should, under most circumstances, follow a fixed monetary policy rule such as the Taylor rule.[10] This is the basic idea underlying the FRAT Act. According to many standard monetary policy rules, the real (inflation-adjusted) federal funds rate depends on a few macroeconomic variables: specifically, the utilization gap—the difference between the level of economic activity and its normal, full-employment level; the inflation gap—the difference between the inflation rate and its target level; and the normal, or "natural," rate of interest. Like other operational mandates, this proposal places a high value on predictability, accountability, and transparency and aims to limit the discretionary decision-making of the central bank.

9. Williams 2014a.
10. Taylor 1993.

This approach has several advantages over previous operational mandate frameworks in terms of macroeconomic performance. First, a monetary policy rule makes clear the central bank's longer-term inflation goal, which is an integral part of the rule itself. This clarifies the communication of policy goals and actions. Second, a properly specified policy rule incorporates the fundamental principle ("Taylor principle") of monetary policy that the nominal interest rate needs to rise more than one-for-one with an increase in inflation as a necessary condition to achieve the desired level of inflation in the long run. Third, a policy rule incorporates systematic and predictable counter-cyclical responses to economic conditions consistent with economic theory and a wide range of economic models.[11]

Research has shown that a policy rule is likely to be superior to other operational mandates like the gold standard, fixed exchange rates, and monetary targeting.[12] In model simulations of typical economic fluctuations, an optimally designed monetary policy rule can come very close to the first-best achievable outcomes.[13] As a result, central banks around the world consult monetary policy rules in preparing forecasts, analyzing risk scenarios, and studying alternative policy strategies. At the Federal Reserve, monetary policy rules have been a regular feature of monetary policy analysis, briefings, and discussions for the past two decades.[14]

There is no question that monetary policy rules provide an invaluable tool for research and practical policy considerations at central banks. Nonetheless, before one rushes to institute a policy rule operational mandate, there are substantive issues and open questions that need to be addressed. Three are particularly relevant: the treatment of unobserved variables such as the natural

11. Taylor and Williams 2011.
12. Bryant, Hooper, and Mann 1993.
13. Levin, Wieland, and Williams 1999, 2003; Levin et al. 2006.
14. Williams 2014c.

rates of economic activity and interest; the zero lower bound on interest rates; and the specification of the rule itself.

An important element of most monetary policy rules is the dependence on unobservable measures of the normal, or "natural," levels of economic activity—such as real gross domestic product or the unemployment rate—and interest rates. In principle, these natural rates change over time in unpredictable ways and are therefore subject to considerable uncertainty.[15] Under a policy rule mandate, would the estimates of the natural rates be set by statute or by the central bank? Would they change over time as economic circumstances change or would they be fixed? These are not purely academic questions. Following the most recent recession, estimates of both the natural rate of output and interest have been subject to dramatic shifts, which would have sizable effects on the appropriate setting of policy according to standard monetary policy rules.[16] If the mandated policy rule uses outdated or inappropriate measures of natural rates, economic performance will suffer. On the other hand, allowing the central bank to freely choose natural rate measures would significantly loosen the constraint on policymaking. In the extreme, any deviation from the mandated rule could be defined away by a shift in the estimated natural rate.

A second issue is the zero lower bound on nominal interest rates that limits the ability to lower interest rates during periods of economic downturn or very low inflation relative to the prescription of a monetary policy rule. During the recent US recession, standard monetary policy rules prescribed negative nominal interest rates, but this was unattainable.[17] The Federal Reserve and other central banks turned to unconventional means to provide the missing monetary stimulus. These measures, including asset pur-

---

15. Orphanides and Williams 2002, Laubach and Williams 2003.
16. Williams 2014b, 2015.
17. Board of Governors 2009, Rudebusch 2009, Williams 2009.

chases and explicit forward policy guidance, are outside the realm of standard monetary policy rules. In such circumstances, which are very likely to occur again in the future, a policy rule mandate is silent. Moreover, research shows that the very presence of the zero lower bound argues for deviating from a standard policy rule around times when the constraint binds, as the central bank aims to make up for lost monetary stimulus.[18]

Third, although there has been a great deal of research about the properties of well-performing monetary policy rules, there is, as yet, no consensus about the best specification of such a rule. Different models imply different best rules. In addition, in the presence of the zero lower bound or uncertainty about natural rates, the best performing rules can be very different from those designed absent these features.[19] In those circumstances, mechanically following one policy rule designed to work well under one set of assumptions can yield very poor economic outcomes when those assumptions are violated.

Where do we go from here?

I have argued that the independence dilemma has been with us for a very long time. Despite the best intentions, attempts to solve it through an operational mandate have proven fruitless in the past. Although a policy rule operational mandate is unquestionably superior to past operational mandates, such an approach is subject to a number of issues and questions. First and foremost, what rule should the central bank follow? One lesson from the history of operational mandates is that what looks good in theory often fails to deliver when circumstances change in unpredictable ways. Particularly in situations of economic stress or crisis,

18. Reifschneider and Williams 2000.
19. Orphanides and Williams 2002, 2006, Reifschneider and Williams 2000.

operational mandates have proven to be ineffective and have often been abandoned.

Given the challenges for an operational mandate to succeed, a potentially more promising approach to address the independence dilemma may be to look to the experiences of inflation-targeting countries, where the principle of enhancing accountability and transparency within a goal mandate framework has proven to be very successful.

GENERAL DISCUSSION

JOHN WILLIAMS (ADDITIONAL COMMENT): Can I make one quick rejoinder? I think I have one minute left. I just want to explain, because I think I can hear Peter saying, "Well, here we go again, nineteen different policymakers and nineteen views." I don't think, and I was hoping that Arvind Krishnamurthy would be here, but I don't think the only argument for buying MBS was to affect credit to housing. I think that actually his research, a lot of other research has shown that the purchases of MBS actually did have bigger effects on other credit market rates than buying Treasury securities. And that's a legitimate debate among research economists. But I don't think it's fair, at least from my own perspective, to say, "We are buying MBS in order to boost housing." It's partly—at least my own view was—that MBS was shown to have a bigger effect on more general financial conditions and treasuries.

KEVIN WARSH: So, John Williams, you talked about the benefits of an inflation targeting regime. When Peter and I and many of us were at the Fed, before the more recent periods, we thought that there was a comfort zone for inflation, which we would broadly define between 1 and 2 percent. Would the inflation targeting regime, which we've now taken more precisely, because our ability presumably to measure inflation is to the tenth of the percent—our inflation target is now 2 percent. As best as I can recall from recent data, the core inflation rates, at least as measured by the Fed, are in the 1.5 or 1.6 percent range. Is it your judgment that there would be a material difference, the real economy, if the actual underlying core inflation were to converge with our target as opposed to being somewhere in the middle of our old-fashioned comfort zone?

WILLIAMS: I do feel that this is testimony . . . [Laughter.] So I think that the decision here is just really about being consistent over time. So what you were talking about is there was an unwritten consensus. So once a committee agreed to a 2 percent objective, and that's the middle of the objective, not a maximum, then I think that given that commitment and goal, I think that the view is on average we want to get 2 percent, but that doesn't mean any given year or other. But I do think we've learned from other countries, and I don't want to pick on them, but we've learned a lot from the experience in Japan over the last twenty-five years. When you communicate that, "Well, inflation, it's been really hard to get inflation higher, so let's just accept where it is," then inflation expectations can drift downwards. Of course, on the upside too, I agree, I make exactly the same point. If inflation were running high, I would argue we need to get it back down to the number we committed to. And I think that this issue about range versus number, I think numbers are important, I think that's what most countries have done. That said, we go through great pains in our one-pager—which, you know, Charlie really should be given a lot of credit for what he accomplished on getting the statement of long-run goals and strategy—in there, we go through great pains to emphasize that this is not month-to-month, quarter-to-quarter, even year-to-year, but it's a medium-run constant.

CHARLES PLOSSER: As John said, I was very involved in the effort to create the committee's statement on its long-term goals and objectives. Yet from a historical perspective, I can attest to the fact that there was considerable debate among us whether the inflation objective should be a point target or range. John was there and an active contributor on many points. I felt at the time that the number was better. But in retrospect, I think one of the things I didn't anticipate with the number, which I think turned out to be the case, is the precision with which both the public and the markets think we can control or even measure inflation. I think the point estimate has perhaps given a false degree of certainty and precision by which this can happen. So I think that you read the headlines: *Fed Significantly Below Its Target Yet Again!* And it's 1.5 or 2.5 instead of 2. The truth of the matter is: given our uncertainties and measurement challenges it is hard to consider such deviations as significant. So in retrospect, I think we should have given a little more thought to the issues, perhaps conveying more about the uncertainties and measurement challenges that actually exist. The way the ECB does it, which is 2 percent or just below, might be a better way. But it's an interesting conversation to have.

WILLIAMS: One thing I learned from reporters and other people is that if you give a range, they figure out very quickly on their iPhones what the midpoint of that range is.

PAUL TUCKER: An issue with the ECB's casting of its target is that it isn't clear whether the target is symmetric. The language suggests not, and I would say that this caused them difficulties, including political difficulties because: Why should unelected people decide whether the policy framework should be symmetric or asymmetric? There is a more general and deeper difficulty with a range rather than a point target, which is that in the deliberative discussion that Kevin wants to characterize monetary policy one cannot tell whether differences of view reflect different views on the outlook for the economy or different *personal* preferences about the steady-state rate of inflation. One can imagine circumstances where, in the dreadful expression, *the hawks* all appear to be in favor of 1 percent and *the doves* are all in favor of 2 percent, but none of them is actually revealing that. When the UK regime of central bank independence was being framed in 1997–98, we just wanted to take the objective off the table to avoid that kind of problem, as well as for the kind of democracy reasons that I was talking about earlier.

DAVID PAPELL: I want to expand a little bit on the Taylor rule and inflation targeting, maybe in the opposite direction. Suppose we have inflation targeting. And then inflation goes up. It will happen sometime. We may have forgotten about that. But what happens when inflation goes up? If the Fed doesn't raise the nominal interest rate more than point-for-point, inflation is going to stay up. So to have inflation targeting, you have adopted the first Taylor principle. Now what happens if you have a higher output gap, or unemployment goes up, or unemployment goes down, and you think there's some relation there with inflation? Well, now you have the second part of the Taylor rule. And you have the inflation target, so you have the third part of the Taylor rule. So what you have left is how you want to define the equilibrium real interest rate. So what I'm suggesting is that operationally, there may not be much difference between serious inflation targeting and some variant of the Taylor rule. I think the difference is that, if the Fed picks the coefficients and says what it's going to focus on, then it's really a question of the reporting. It's really a question of how it's explaining what it's doing more than a huge dichotomy between inflation targeting and a Taylor rule. And I think part of it is, using the buzzword for the day, the clarity rather than the transparency.

MICHAEL BOSKIN: I wanted to just add a few things to those that have been raised, in the parts that I've been able to attend, on the border of monetary and fiscal economics. In the case of tax reform, you wind up basically with three laws. Some people are operating under the old one, some under the new ones, and some under transition rules. You've got to pay attention to how quickly all that can happen.

But I think there's some interesting follow-up on what Charlie had to say about a new accord between the Treasury and the Fed, and the time limits, and what you can buy, and all that. I think it's really important—I'll just give you an example. When we did the savings and loans and third world money bank center bailouts in the early 1990s, in the end, they turned out to be good enough for government work. They weren't what we'd call necessarily textbook. But there were some principles embedded in them. The RTC (Resolution Trust Corporation) was set up to self-immolate. I was concerned about the risk it wouldn't, and so for that I got to co-lead the administration group that oversaw it. When we finally got them to sell the stuff in large blocks, rather than one at a time, it actually went quite smoothly. So I think the lesson there is there's at least an example of limited-time, orderly, rapid transition to private markets, etc. And I think you monetary economists might want to think a little bit about that, because these issues don't just arise in the monetary sphere.

On Brady bonds, we were getting a totally illiquid, in any sense of mark-to-market any time in the foreseeable future, close to worthless debt, because the Mexicans repudiated their debt and some of the other Latin American nations were about to. We created a liquid market in an alternative zero security, etc., and brokered agreements. So there were specific purposes. The reason I go into this is that in September of 2007, at a breakfast with Hank Paulson just before our corporate tax reform conference at the Treasury, I asked him what he was doing to get ready, if he needed to do any bailouts. And he just looked at me like it wasn't in his thinking. Then he asked me to go talk to Bob Steel, who was under secretary, and he at least took some notes, and I never heard from him again.

So I go through this because George mentioned the Treasury needs some authority, but the Treasury's going to need some expertise and some institutional procedure to be thinking about this across administrations. The treasury secretary comes and goes, and key officials come and go, more rapidly than they do at the Fed, by the way. You can argue whether the staffs change, too. You ought to think about actually how, if we did that, human beings would operate in this context. George has raised an important point that you wouldn't think of in this context, which has moved to a very odd form of government, which [is that] we don't have a cabinet system much anymore. We have czars in the White House, people can't get confirmed, therefore we don't always get good people, and George, I don't want to put words in your mouth, but I've often heard you say, "There are actually good people in the agencies who have that system, but everybody's just reporting to some twenty-eight-year-old czar in the White House, and that can't work." So I would just ask you to think some more about that, because I would worry that we could do that, and in the next crisis, the Treasury would be unprepared.

So I just think there's precedent for it. We've had a success- ful time with a limited self-immolation strategy in the previ- ous financial crisis. People tend to downplay it, but sized to today's economy, it was over a trillion dollars. So I think that's important.

I can't resist just saying, not only would you want to change it slowly, you'd also want to change it when we're measuring inflation differently, and have an understanding of what true inflation is. And a larger and larger fraction of the economy is becoming harder and harder to separate between nominal and real expenditures. On some of the biases that the commission I chaired pointed out, the BLS (Bureau of Labor Statistics) has changed some of its procedures, and its measured inflation is going up by half a percentage point slower than it would have otherwise. There's a lot of pressure to make some of the other recommendations. The PCE (personal consumption expendi- ture index) uses a Fisher Index, so you get some of the substitu- tion bias reduced at the upper levels. But all the stuff on quality change and new products really is a perplexing problem, and 2 percent inflation as we measure it today is very unlike what was being measured ten years ago. Over a quarter to a year, sure, but over years or a decade, probably not.

JOHN TAYLOR: A couple points on John Williams's thoughtful remarks. First, it's not inflation targeting versus rules-based strategy. As David was saying, you can find examples of inflation targeting countries which have a strategy to get there. And it works pretty well. You can find examples where there's an inflation target, or at least an implicit one, and the performance has not been so good, and I actually have to say, unfortunately that's the United States in recent years. Our performance over the last ten years is nothing to write home about: crisis, slow recovery, boom-bust. By way of comparison, both Greenspan and Volcker had a vaguer inflation target as Kevin was referring to. I think of it as about 1.5 percent, but they were not explicit numerically. But they also had kind of a strategy they were using. And you can document it with data and policy reaction functions, as best we can. And then somewhere around 2003 that strategy disappeared, or was changed, or something different happened, and the results have not been good. So I look at this experience and conclude that it's not just an inflation target. It's a strategy that goes with the inflation target. And even now it's worrisome that some of the very successful inflation targeting countries in emerging markets are, in effect, under a lot of pressure to do other things—macroprudential policy, even capital controls—going back to the bad old days before inflation targeting, when they were thinking about a million other things besides their inflation target. So that's worrisome.

Second, relating to the zero lower bound, it is very important, and—I thought our work showed this—that the interest rate instrument needs to be supplemented with a money growth instrument when you run into deflationary or hyper-inflationary situations—and in particular when you hit the zero bound.

Recall that early simulations with models were done with the zero bound in mind, usually setting the interest rate to 1 percent when the mathematical interest rate formula went below 1 percent. And it is certainly not inconsistent with an interest rate rule to use the "meta-rule" approach suggested by David Reifschneider and John Williams in their 1999 paper "Three Lessons for Monetary Policy in a Low Inflation Era," which seems to me very significant. So I think there are lots of ways to deal with this. It doesn't mean you throw out the whole ideas of rules or strategies for the instruments of monetary policy.

Also, there is now a debate about whether the zero bound is binding at all now. Why is the Fed still at zero, or between zero and 0.25 percent? There are lots of reasons why it already should be higher. It's a matter of choice of the central bank to be at that level. It's not necessarily a binding thing.

WILLIAMS: Can I respond briefly? I think, John, you're absolutely right, David's right, that in theory—this goes back to, I can't remember who made this point, maybe Mike made this point— that in rational expectations, where there's complete certainty, these all become, first of all, Mike Woodford and Ben McCallum and many people have shown these are all equivalent. Now we're just into semantics. So I think that this goes back to a question I raised with Carl's paper. It came up with a number of comments. What's the problem we're trying to solve? And that's what Carl's paper was really about. Let me try to specify what's the problem we're really dealing with. Is it a problem that the central bank has the wrong objective function? Is the problem that the central bank is not pursuing its own goals? Is the problem that the central bank is overly confident in its own ability to predict the future? So I think that we do have this problem that under the standard assumptions of our textbook models, none of these issues arise and this is a pointless conversation. We should go straight to the reception, because it's all the same rationalization expectations equilibrium. [Laughter.] Now that may well be optimal! But when I was thinking about this and reading everybody's reviews, what is the problem? Not just specifically today, but what was the problem that inflation targeting central banks of Canada, New Zealand, the United Kingdom, what were they trying to solve? And I think that in some of these cases, it was a very different problem, and they came to different solutions. And when I talk to my friends at the Bank of England over the years—I'll just mention Spencer Dale, because he was the one I used to have the lengthiest discussions with, and he said, "The main goal of monetary policy is to stabilize inflation and thereby create a solid nominal anchor, and the way you do that is you talk constantly, every day, 24/7, about inflation. You never talk about anything else. God forbid," he said, "you don't talk about your interest rate paths, or anything like that, you just focus on inflation. And once you've solved that kind of communication uncertainty/imperfect knowledge problem, you basically accomplish what a central bank can do." I'm not saying that he's necessarily right. But it is a different view of what the problem is, and what the right solution is, and I just think it's something to keep in mind when we have these discussions. And I agree 100 percent that being at a lower bound is a decision. You can't just say, "We're at the zero lower bound, therefore, the zero lower bound is a problem," because then we'll always be at the zero lower bound. [Laughter.]

PETER FISHER: John Taylor zeroed in on the idea that something changed in 2003. Having been in the asset management business for most years since then and, in my view, that's when the Federal Open Market Committee started targeting asset prices . . . no, they didn't say it as clearly then, although there was some verbiage in the early period. But Ben Bernanke's speeches, when he became chairman, are littered with asset prices, asset prices, asset prices. I think that's the conundrum the committee is in now: When do you stop targeting asset prices? The exit isn't about engineering the Fed funds market. That's a trivial issue. The effort is, once you've been targeting asset prices for seven years or longer, how do you stop? I think that's what is changing.

Now, to change gears a little bit, I wrote the legal brief that defended the constitutionality of the Federal Open Market Committee in the 1980s, when we actually got to Judge Harold Greene to uphold the constitutionality of the Reserve Bank presidents' seats on the FOMC. So, I've defended the constitutionality of Reserve Bank presidents. That's a different question from whether it's a wise thing to continue to defend. And there are plenty of central banks around the world that are independent of government, in which all the officials are appointed by the government. And I think that this is just something that has outlived its utility. The presidents of the Reserve Banks being appointed by their regional boards is something that's causing much more trouble than it's worth. That's a conclusion I've come to reluctantly.

I think they can be appointed by the US president. There's different ways to be appointed by government. I was appointed by the chancellor of the exchequer to the board of the FSA (Financial Services Authority); I never met the chancellor. I think I was pretty independent of the government. Technically, I was appointed by her majesty's government. But there's regulatory capture happening all over the regulatory apparatus in America that has nothing to do with the Reserve Bank presidents and it's time we removed this distraction.

TUCKER: Can I ask a question about this? There are two stages to this argument about the position of the regional Fed presidents. One is whether or not they should be appointed by elected representatives of the people. That's the debate we had earlier. If the national consensus on that question were to be "yes," then the second issue is whether the appointments should be made by a federal elected official, the president, subject to confirmation by the federal-level Senate or whether, alternatively, the appointments should be made by state-level elected representatives. I have been a bit surprised that that doesn't come up, given attitudes around the US to Washington government and politics and given the regional base of the various Fed presidents. In a nutshell, and truly without taking a substantive position, I'm struck that you're saying, "Make this all a Washington thing."

PETER FISHER: I'll be open-minded over whether we can come up with some other construct. But I think the days of having Reserve Bank presidents appointed by the boards of directors are over. The political cost of holding onto this vestige of independence is not worth the candle. The United States Senate is a pretty good representative of the country as a whole. And having the Senate confirm Reserve Bank presidents would be better than where we are.

ROBERT HODRICK: Monetary policy, as we've talked about it today, works through the interest rate and perhaps asset prices, and one of the chief asset prices that we haven't mentioned very much is the exchange rate. I was wondering to what extent we need to think about international coordination of monetary policy, and the fact that if we're following a Taylor rule that is just focusing on domestic inflation and the output gap, and other countries are running massive inflation, our currency is going to be massively appreciating and that's going to disadvantage our exporters and be good for the consumers and importers. Is that something we should be concerned about in designing appropriate monetary policy rules?

ANDREW LEVIN: I really like the speech that John Williams gave recently about policy rules. But as John Taylor has emphasized, there can't just be longer-run goals. There has to be a coherent policy strategy. And monetary policy is fundamentally a quantitative problem, which means that a strategy actually translates into what we would call a reaction function. That's all there is. We can use a model for the US economy, similar to the Totem model in Canada or the N.E.M.O. model in Norway; those models all seem to have fancy names. [Laughter.] And you can formulate a specific strategy using a model like that. Most inflation targeting central banks are effectively doing inflation forecast targeting, where they use a model with some judgmental adjustments and say, "With this policy path, we will get this trajectory for inflation and economic activity." But those models are essentially black boxes that are very difficult to explain to the public. Furthermore, the models oftentimes are simply wrong. In fact, you saw that in the charts that I showed earlier. Year after year for the past few years, those models—not just of the Fed, but professional forecasters' models—have been consistently wrong. And so my plea would be to say, we can do better in monetary policy by not just relying on models but also looking at benchmark rules. And I hope that's the spirit of this workshop: that it would be beneficial to bring benchmark rules into monetary policy discussions and into the FOMC's deliberations and communications, and not just rely on black boxes.

JOHN COCHRANE: I sense it's time to close. I want to close this conference with a short, cheery comment. Interest rates are zero, which Milton Friedman taught us was the optimal quantity of money. [Laughter.] Why are you laughing? He was exactly right.

Inflation is 1.5 percent and trending down, despite the Fed's best efforts. Congress asked for "price stability," and looks like we're getting it. What's to complain about that? Unemployment is back to normal. Growth is too slow, and employment is too low, but everyone concedes that the Fed can't do anything about long-term growth and structural problems.

Things could be a lot worse. Our benign situation doesn't mean what we've done today is useless. It means we have a little breathing space, time to get monetary policy right before the next crisis.

GEORGE SHULTZ: Welcome to California.

[Laughter.]

REFERENCES

Bank of England. 2015. "Letter from the Governor of the Bank of England to the Chancellor of the Exchequer, February 12, 2015," https://www.gov.uk/government/uploads/system/uploads/attachment_data/file/403346/Letter_from_the_Chancellor_to_the_Governor_12022015.pdf.

Bernanke, Ben S., Thomas Laubach, Frederic S. Mishkin, and Adam S. Posen. 1999. *Inflation Targeting: Lessons from the International Experience.* Princeton, NJ: Princeton University Press.

Bernanke, Ben S., and Frederic S. Mishkin. 1997. "Inflation Targeting: A New Framework for Monetary Policy?" *Journal of Economic Perspectives* 11, no. 2 (Spring): 97–116.

Board of Governors of the Federal Reserve System. 2009. "Monetary Policy Alternatives," June 18: 37, http://www.federalreserve.gov/monetary policy/files/FOMC20090624bluebook20090618.pdf.

Board of Governors of the Federal Reserve System. 2015. "Statement on Longer-Run Goals and Monetary Policy Strategy." Adopted January 24, 2012, amended January 27, 2015, http://www.federalreserve.gov/monetarypolicy/files/FOMC_LongerRunGoals.pdf.

Bryant, Ralph C., Peter Hooper, and Catherine L. Mann. 1993. *Evaluating Policy Regimes: New Research in Empirical Macroeconomics.* Washington, DC: Brookings Institution.

Eichengreen, Barry. 1992. *Golden Fetters: The Gold Standard and the Great Depression, 1919–1939.* New York: Oxford University Press.

Federal Reserve Accountability and Transparency Act of 2014, H.R. 5018, 113th Cong., https://www.congress.gov/bill/113th-congress/house-bill/5018.

Federal Reserve Reform Act of 1977. Pub. L. No. 95–188, 91 Stat. 1387, http://www.gpo.gov/fdsys/pkg/STATUTE-91/pdf/STATUTE-91-Pg1387.pdf.

Friedman, Milton. 1960. *A Program for Monetary Stability.* New York: Fordham University Press.

Full Employment and Balanced Growth Act of 1978, Pub. L. No. 95–523, 92 Stat. 1887, http://www.gpo.gov/fdsys/pkg/STATUTE-92/pdf/STATUTE-92-Pg1887.pdf.

Kuttner, Kenneth N. 2004. "A Snapshot of Inflation Targeting in its Adolescence." In *The Future of Inflation Targeting.* Edited by Christopher Kent and Simon Guttmann. Sydney: Reserve Bank of Australia: 6–42, http://www.rba.gov.au/publications/confs/2004/pdf/kuttner.pdf.

Laubach, Thomas, and John C. Williams. 2003. "Measuring the Natural Rate of Interest." *Review of Economics and Statistics* 85, no. 4: 1063–1070, http://www.mitpressjournals.org/doi/pdf/10.1162/00346530377 2815934.

Leiderman, Leonardo, and Lars E.O. Svensson, eds. 1995. *Inflation Targets.* London: Centre for Economic Policy Research.

Levin, Andrew T., Alexei Onatski, John C. Williams, and Noah Williams. 2006. "Monetary Policy under Uncertainty in Micro-founded Macroeconomic Models." *NBER Macroeconomics Annual 2005, vol. 20.* Cambridge, MA: MIT Press: 229–287.

Levin, Andrew T., Volker Wieland, and John C. Williams. 1999. "Robustness of Simple Monetary Policy Rules under Model Uncertainty." In *Monetary Policy Rules.* Edited by John Taylor. Chicago: University of Chicago Press: 263–299.

Levin, Andrew T., Volker Wieland, and John C. Williams. 2003. "The Performance of Forecast-Based Monetary Policy Rules under Model Uncertainty." *American Economic Review* 93, no. 3 (June): 622–645.

Norges Bank. 2014. *Monetary Policy Report with Financial Stability Assessment.* Oslo, September, http://static.norges-bank.no/pages/101366/monetary_policy_report_3_14.pdf.

Orphanides, Athanasios, and John C. Williams. 2002. "Robust Monetary Policy Rules with Unknown Natural Rates." *Brookings Papers on Economic Activity* 33, no. 2: 63–145.

Orphanides, Athanasios, and John C. Williams. 2006. "Monetary Policy with Imperfect Knowledge." *Journal of the European Economic Association* 4, no. 2–3 (April/May): 366–375.

Poole, William. 1970. "Optimal Choice of Monetary Policy Instruments in a Simple Stochastic Macro Model." *The Quarterly Journal of Economics* 84, no. 2 (May): 197–216.

Reifschneider, David, and John C. Williams. 2000. "Three Lessons for Monetary Policy in a Low-Inflation Era." *Journal of Money, Credit, & Banking* 32, no. 4: 936–966.

Rudebusch, Glenn D. 2009. "The Fed's Monetary Policy Response to the Current Crisis." *FRBSF Economic Letter* 2009–17 (May 22), http://www.frbsf.org/economic-research/publications/economic -letter/2009/may/fed-monetary-policy-crisis/.

Taylor, John B. 1993. "Discretion versus Policy Rules in Practice." *Carnegie-Rochester Conference Series on Public Policy* 39, no. 1 (December): 195–214.

Taylor, John B., and John C. Williams. 2011. "Simple and Robust Rules for Monetary Policy." In *Handbook of Monetary Economics,* vol. 3B. Edited by Benjamin Friedman and Michael Woodford. Amsterdam: North-Holland: 829–860.

Williams, John C. 2009. "Heeding Daedalus: Optimal Inflation and the Zero Lower Bound." *Brookings Papers on Economic Activity,* Fall: 1–37.

Williams, John C. 2014a. "Inflation Targeting and the Global Financial Crisis: Successes and Challenges." Presentation to the South African Reserve Bank Conference on "Fourteen Years of Inflation Targeting in South Africa and the Challenge of a Changing Mandate." Pretoria, South Africa, October 31, http://www.frbsf.org/our-district/ press/presidents-speeches/williams-speeches/2014/october/inflation -targeting-global-financial-crisis/.

Williams, John C. 2014b. "Monetary Policy at the Zero Lower Bound: Putting Theory into Practice." Working paper, Hutchins Center on Fiscal & Monetary Policy, Brookings Institution, January 16, http://www

.brookings.edu/~/media/research/files/papers/2014/01/16-monetary
-policy-zero-lower-bound/16-monetary-policy-zero-lower-bound
-williams.

Williams, John C. 2014c. "Policy Rules in Practice." *Journal of Economic Dynamics and Control* 49 (December): 151–153.

Williams, John C. 2015. "The Decline in the Natural Rate of Interest." Manuscript. March 2. http://www.frbsf.org/economic-research/economists/jwilliams/Williams_NABE_2015_natural_rate_FRBSF.pdf.

Central Bank Governance and Oversight Reform: A Policy Conference

May 21, 2015

Hoover Institution, Stanford University

This conference aims to consider central bank reforms relating to governance, oversight, and effectiveness. Since the Hoover Conference "Frames for Central Banking in the Next Century," held in May 2014, debates about central bank policy have intensified. This second conference will be in round-table format, with short opening presentations, a lead discussant, and general discussion. It will consider normalization of policy, recent changes in transparency, the expanded regulatory role of central banks, and bills that have been introduced to audit, impose specific reporting, reorganize, or place limits on the regulatory power of the central bank. Assessments of the costs and benefits of quantitative easing, negative interest rates. Competitive easing, and international spillovers will inform the discussion.

Thursday, May 21

8:30 AM   **Continental Breakfast**

9:00 AM   **How Can Central Banks Deliver Credible Commitment and Be "Emergency Institutions"?**
Paul Tucker, former deputy governor, Bank of England
Lead Discussant: John Cochrane, Hoover Institution
and University of Chicago

10:00 AM   **Coffee**

10:15 AM   **Policy Rule Legislation in Practice**
David Papell, University of Houston
Lead Discussant: Michael Dotsey, director of research,
            Federal Reserve Bank of Philadelphia

11:15   **Coffee**

11:30 AM   **Goals and Rules in Central Bank Design**
Carl Walsh, University of California, Santa Cruz
Lead Discussant: Andrew Levin, International Monetary
Fund and Dartmouth

12:30 PM   **Lunch**

1:30 PM   **Institutional Design: Deliberations, Decisions,
and Committee Dynamics**
Kevin Warsh, Hoover Institution
Lead Discussant: Peter Fisher, Center for Global
            Business and Government,
            Dartmouth, and BlackRock
            Investment Institute

2:30 PM   **Coffee**

2:45 PM   **Historical Reflections on the Governance of the Fed**
Michael Bordo, Rutgers University
Lead Discussant: Mary Karr, general counsel, Federal
            Reserve Bank of Saint Louis

3:45 PM   **Coffee**

4:00 PM   **Policy Panel on the Impact of Reform in Practice**
Charles Plosser, former president, Federal Reserve Bank
of Philadelphia
George Shultz, Hoover Institution and Stanford
University
John Williams, president, Federal Reserve Bank of San
Francisco

5:15 PM   **Adjourn**

6:00 PM   **Reception and Dinner**

About the Contributors

MICHAEL D. BORDO is a professor of economics and director of the Center for Monetary and Financial History at Rutgers University. He has held academic positions at the University of South Carolina and Carleton University in Ottawa, Canada. He has been a visiting professor at the University of California, Los Angeles, Carnegie Mellon University, Princeton University, Harvard University, and Cambridge University. He is a distinguished visiting fellow at the Hoover Institution and has been a visiting scholar at the International Monetary Fund; the Federal Reserve Banks of St. Louis, Cleveland, and Dallas; the Federal Reserve Board of Governors; the Bank of Canada; the Bank of England; and the Bank for International Settlement. He is a research associate of the National Bureau of Economic Research and a member of the Shadow Open Market Committee. He holds degrees from McGill University, the London School of Economics, and the University of Chicago.

JOHN H. COCHRANE is a senior fellow at the Hoover Institution and a research associate of the National Bureau of Economic Research. Before joining Hoover, he was a professor of finance at the University of Chicago Booth School of Business. He holds degrees from MIT and the University of California, Berkeley. He is the author of many academic articles on the effects of monetary policy, the relationship between deficits and inflation, risk and liquidity premiums in stock and bond markets, the volatility of exchange rates, the term structure of interest rates, the returns to venture capital, the relation between stock prices and investment, option pricing, health insurance, time-series econometrics, and other topics. He is the author of the popular textbook *Asset Pricing* and a co-author of *The Squam Lake Report*.

MICHAEL DOTSEY is senior vice president and director of research at the Federal Reserve Bank of Philadelphia. He earlier worked for the Federal Reserve Banks of New York and Richmond. Dotsey has served as a visiting scholar for the Bank of Japan, the Reserve Bank of Australia, the Reserve Bank of New Zealand, the Swiss National Bank, the Banco De Portugal, and the Bank of England. He was also a visiting associate professor at the University of Rochester and a visiting instructor at the Fuqua School of Business at Duke University. Dotsey is an associate editor for the *International Journal of Central Banking* and has published scholarly articles in leading economic journals, including the *American Economic Review*, the *Quarterly Journal of Economics*, the *Journal of Finance*, and the *Journal of Monetary Economics*. He holds degrees from the University of Rochester and the University of Chicago.

PETER R. FISHER is a senior fellow at the Center for Global Business and Government at the Tuck School of Business at Dartmouth, where he is also a senior lecturer. Fisher also serves as a senior director of the BlackRock Investment Institute. He is a member of the board of directors of AIG Inc., the Peterson Institute for International Economics, and the John F. Kennedy Library Foundation. He has previously served as head of BlackRock's fixed income portfolio management group and as chairman of BlackRock Asia. Before joining BlackRock in 2004, Fisher served as undersecretary of the US Treasury for domestic finance from 2001 to 2003. He also worked at the Federal Reserve Bank of New York from 1985 to 2001, concluding his service as executive vice president and manager of the Federal Reserve System Open Market Account. He holds degrees from Harvard College and Harvard Law School.

MARY H. KARR is senior vice president and general counsel of the Federal Reserve Bank of St. Louis, where she has responsibility for the bank's legal division, serves as ethics officer, and is secretary to the board of directors. She is also the executive sponsor of the bank's African American employee resource group. Previously, she was a partner with the St. Louis law firm of Peper, Martin, Jensen, Maichel and Hetlage, with her practice focused on mergers and acquisitions and securities law. Karr holds degrees from Washington University and the Washington University School of Law. She is a member of the Order of the Coif and served as notes and comments editor for the *Washington University Law Quarterly*. Karr also chairs the board of directors of the St. Louis Urban Debate League and is on the diversity committee of the St. Louis chapter of the Association of Corporate Counsel.

ANDREW LEVIN is a professor of economics at Dartmouth College. Before that, he was an adviser in the research department at the International Monetary Fund. He earned his PhD in economics at Stanford. He has been a staff member at the Federal Reserve Board and has had extensive interactions with many other central banks: as a consultant to the European Central Bank's inflation persistence network and to the Bank of Canada's external review of research; as co-editor of the *International Journal of Central Banking*; and as a visiting scholar at the Bank of Japan and the Dutch National Bank. He has provided technical assistance to the national banks of Albania and Macedonia and, most recently, the Bank of Ghana. Levin's research has been published in leading economic journals, including *American Economic Review, Journal of the European Economic Association, Journal of Monetary Economics,* and *Journal of Econometrics.*

ALEX NIKOLSKO-RZHEVSKYY is an associate professor of economics at Lehigh University, where he teaches graduate macroeconomics and econometrics and conducts research on monetary policy analysis. He holds degrees from the University of Houston and Odessa National University in Ukraine. Prior to joining Lehigh's faculty, Nikolsko-Rzhevskyy served as an assistant professor at the University of Memphis. His papers have been published in the *Journal of Monetary Economics, Journal of Money, Credit, & Banking,* and *Macroeconomic Dynamics.* He has been the recipient of several research grants and his research has been referred to by Congress, the *Wall Street Journal*, Bloomberg, and Forbes.

DAVID H. PAPELL is the Joel W. Sailors Endowed Professor and chair of the Department of Economics at the University of Houston, where he has taught since 1984. His fields of expertise are macroeconomics, international economics, and applied time-series econometrics. He previously taught at the University of Florida and has held visiting positions at the University of Pennsylvania, the University of Virginia, and the International Monetary Fund. He holds degrees from the University of Pennsylvania and Columbia University. He has published more than fifty articles in refereed journals and served as an associate editor for the *Journal of International Economics*, the *Journal of Money, Credit, & Banking*, and *Empirical Economics.*

CHARLES I. PLOSSER served as president and CEO of the Federal Reserve Bank of Philadelphia, retiring in 2015. Previously, he was the John M. Olin Distinguished Professor of Economics and Public Policy at the University of Rochester's Simon School of Business, where he also served as dean. He has been a visiting scholar at the Bank of England and is a research associate of the National Bureau of Economic Research. He is currently a visiting scholar at the Hoover Institution. Plosser served as co-editor of the *Journal of Monetary Economics* for two decades and co-chaired the Shadow Open Market Committee with Anna Schwartz. His research and teaching interests include monetary and fiscal policy, long-term economic growth, and banking and financial markets; his articles have appeared in numerous leading economic journals. He holds degrees from the University of Chicago and Vanderbilt University.

RUXANDRA PRODAN joined the Department of Economics at the University of Houston from the University of Alabama, where she served as an assistant professor of economics. She has taught courses in international finance, econometrics, and forecasting. Her research focuses on international finance, time series econometrics, and macroeconomics. Her research has been published in journals such as the *Journal of Money, Credit & Banking, Journal of Business and Economics Statistics, Economic Inquiry, International Journal of Forecasting, The B.E. Journal of Macroeconomics, Economic Modelling* and *Journal of Economic Dynamics and Control.*

GEORGE P. SHULTZ is the Thomas W. and Susan B. Ford Distinguished Fellow at the Hoover Institution. Among many other senior government and private-sector roles, he served as secretary of labor, director of the Office of Management and Budget, secretary of the treasury, and secretary of state. In January 1989 he was awarded the Medal of Freedom, the nation's highest civilian honor. Shultz rejoined Stanford University in 1989 as the Jack Steele Parker Professor of International Economics at the Graduate School of Business and as a distinguished fellow at the Hoover Institution. He chairs the Precourt Institute Energy Advisory Council at Stanford, the MIT Energy Initiative External Advisory Board, and the Hoover Institution's Shultz-Stephenson Task Force on Energy Policy. He is a distinguished fellow of the American Economic Association.

JOHN B. TAYLOR is the George P. Shultz Senior Fellow in Economics at the Hoover Institution and the Mary and Robert Raymond Professor of Economics at Stanford University. He chairs the Hoover Working Group on Economic Policy. An award-winning teacher and researcher specializing in macroeconomics, international economics, and monetary policy, he has served as a senior economist and member of the President's Council of Economic Advisers and as undersecretary of the treasury for international affairs. Taylor's book *Getting Off Track: How Government Actions and Interventions Caused, Prolonged, and Worsened the Financial Crisis* was one of the first on the financial crisis; he has since followed up writing or co-editing ten additional books on restoring economic growth and preventing future crises, including *First Principles: Five Keys to Restoring America's Prosperity*. Before joining the Stanford faculty in 1984, he held positions as a professor of economics at Princeton University and Columbia University.

PAUL TUCKER is chair of the Systemic Risk Council and a fellow at the Kennedy School of Government, Harvard University. (His paper was composed while he was also a fellow at the Harvard Business School.) He was deputy governor at the Bank of England from 2009 to October 2013, having joined the bank in 1980. He was a member of all of the Bank of England's statutory policy committees (the Monetary Policy Committee, Financial Policy Committee, and Prudential Regulatory Authority Board), and a member of the Court of Directors. Internationally, he was a member of the steering committee of the Group of Twenty Financial Stability Board and chaired its committee on the resolution of cross-border banks to solve the too-big-to-fail problem. He was a member of the board of directors of the Bank for International Settlements and was chair of the Basel Committee for Payment and Settlement Systems. He is a visiting fellow of Nuffield College, Oxford, and a governor of the Ditchley Foundation.

CARL E. WALSH is a distinguished professor of economics at the University of California, Santa Cruz, where he has been on the faculty since 1987. He holds degrees from the University of California, Berkeley. His research focuses on issues in monetary economics, central banking, and monetary policy. His previous positions include faculty appointments at Auckland University, New Zealand, and Princeton University. He is a former senior economist at the Federal Reserve Bank of San Francisco and has been a visiting scholar at the Federal Reserve Banks of Kansas City, Philadelphia, and San Francisco, as well as at the Federal Reserve Board. He has taught intensive courses on monetary theory and policy for several national central banks and universities, as well as for the International Monetary Fund. His editorial positions have included the *Journal of Money, Credit, & Banking, International Journal of Central Banking*, and *American Economic Review*.

KEVIN M. WARSH is the Shepard Family Distinguished Visiting Fellow in Economics at Stanford University's Hoover Institution and lecturer at Stanford's Graduate School of Business. He has served as a member of the Board of Governors of the Federal Reserve System; the Fed's representative to the Group of Twenty; and the board's emissary to emerging and advanced economies in Asia. He was administrative governor, managing and overseeing the board's operations, personnel, and financial performance. Earlier, Warsh served as special assistant for economic policy to the president and as executive secretary of the White House National Economic Council. Previously, he was a member of the mergers & acquisitions department at Morgan Stanley & Co. in New York, serving as vice president and executive director. He holds degrees from Stanford and Harvard Law School.

JOHN C. WILLIAMS is president and chief executive officer of the Federal Reserve Bank of San Francisco. He was previously the executive vice president and director of research for the San Francisco Fed and, before that, an economist at the Board of Governors of the Federal Reserve System. He also served as senior economist at the White House Council of Economic Advisers and as a lecturer at Stanford's Graduate School of Business. Williams currently serves as the managing editor of the *International Journal of Central Banking* and was previously the associate editor of the *American Economic Review*. His research focuses on monetary policy under uncertainty, innovation, productivity, and business cycles. He holds degrees from Stanford, the London School of Economics, and the University of California, Berkeley.

About the Hoover Institution's Working Group on Economic Policy

The Working Group on Economic Policy brings together experts on economic and financial policy at the Hoover Institution to study key developments in the U.S. and global economies, examine their interactions, and develop specific policy proposals.

For twenty-five years starting in the early 1980s, the United States economy experienced an unprecedented economic boom. Economic expansions were stronger and longer than in the past. Recessions were shorter, shallower, and less frequent. GDP doubled and household net worth increased by 250 percent in real terms. Forty-seven million jobs were created.

This quarter-century boom strengthened as its length increased. Productivity growth surged by one full percentage point per year in the United States, creating an additional $9 trillion of goods and services that would never have existed. And the long boom went global with emerging market countries from Asia to Latin America to Africa experiencing the enormous improvements in both economic growth and economic stability.

Economic policies that place greater reliance on the principles of free markets, price stability, and flexibility have been the key to these successes. Recently, however, several powerful new economic forces have begun to change the economic landscape, and these principles are being challenged with far-reaching implications for U.S. economic policy, both domestic and international. A financial crisis flared up in 2007 and turned into a severe panic in 2008 leading to the Great Recession. How we interpret and react to these forces—and in particular whether proven policy principles prevail going forward—will determine whether strong economic growth and stability returns and again continues to spread and improve more people's lives or whether the economy stalls and stagnates.

Our Working Group organizes seminars and conferences, prepares policy papers and other publications, and serves as a resource for policymakers and interested members of the public.

Current members of this working group include Michael J. Boskin, John F. Cogan, Darrell Duffie, Simon Gleeson, Joseph A. Grundfest, John A. Gunn, Richard J. Herring, Tom Huertas, Thomas Jackson, Charles B. Johnson, Emily C. Kapur, William F. Kroener III, Monika Piazzesi, John F. Powers, Martin Schneider, Kenneth E. Scott, John Shoven, George P. Shultz, David Skeel, Kimberly Anne Summe, and John B. Taylor (chair).

Working Group on Economic Policy—Associated Publications
Many of the writings associated with this working group will be published by the Hoover Institution Press or other publishers. Materials published to date, or in production, are listed below. Books that are part of the Working Group on Economic Policy's Resolution Project are marked with an asterisk.

Central Bank Governance and Oversight Reform
Edited by John H. Cochrane and John B. Taylor

Inequality and Economic Policy: Essays in Honor of Gary Becker
Edited by Tom Church, Chris Miller, and John B. Taylor

Making Failure Feasible: How Bankruptcy Reform Can End "Too Big to Fail"*
Edited by Kenneth E. Scott, Thomas H. Jackson, and John B. Taylor

Across the Great Divide: New Perspectives on the Financial Crisis
Edited by Martin Neil Baily and John B. Taylor

Bankruptcy Not Bailout: A Special Chapter 14*
Edited by Kenneth E. Scott and John B. Taylor

Government Policies and the Delayed Economic Recovery
Edited by Lee E. Ohanian, John B. Taylor, and Ian J. Wright

Why Capitalism?
Allan H. Meltzer

First Principles: Five Keys to Restoring America's Prosperity
John B. Taylor

Ending Government Bailouts as We Know Them*
Edited by Kenneth E. Scott, George P. Shultz, and John B. Taylor

How Big Banks Fail: And What to Do about It*
Darrell Duffie

The Squam Lake Report: Fixing the Financial System
Darrell Duffie et al.

Getting Off Track: How Government Actions and Interventions Caused, Prolonged, and Worsened the Financial Crisis
John B. Taylor

The Road Ahead for the Fed
Edited by John B. Taylor and John D. Ciorciari

Putting Our House in Order: A Guide to Social Security and Health Care Reform
George P. Shultz and John B. Shoven

Index

accountability
  aspect, of rules, 97, 111–22
  central bank independence and, 112–22, 255–64
  central bank reforms for, 116, 122
  individual *vs.* group, xiv–xv, 194, 196, 198
  inflation targeting and, 109, 117n13
  to lower social loss, 124
  in simple model goal-based and rule-based regimes, 123
  of stewardship, 10, 41
  transparent communication, of monetary policy strategy, xvii, 6, 10, 41, 257
active listening, 180
AEA. *See* American Economic Association
aggregate demand shocks, xiii, 3, 127, 131–32, 134–35, 156
aggregate supply shocks, xiii, 156
AIG, 46, 256, 262
Aldrich Plan, 234
  on nationwide branch banking, 223n3
  for regional central bank system, defeat of, 223
Aldrich-Vreeland Act (1908)
  National Reserve Association network creation, 222
  NMC establishment, 223
Alesina, Alberto, 10n3, 115n8
Alvarez, Scott, 197
American Economic Association (AEA), 260
"An Appreciation of the Fed's Twelve Banks" (Plosser), 246
asset price targeting, by FOMC, 287–88
asset purchases and sales, by Fed, xvi, 262
  restrictions on, xvii, 255, 256, 257, 261
asset values fall, liquidity premia and, 42
Athey, Susan, 118n14
Atkeson, Andrew, 118n1
Audit the Fed legislation. *See* Federal Reserve Accountability and Transparency Act

Bade, Robin, 115n8
Bagehot, Walter, 8
Bagehot rules
  bank runs and, 42
  central bank constraints by, 33
  criticism of, ix, 42
  fraudulent preference and, 37
  illiquidity, insolvency and, 8, 33
Bai, Jushan, 64
bailouts, xvi, 16, 32
  AIG, 46, 256, 262
  Bear Stearns, 32, 46, 49–50, 201, 256, 262
  congressional sanction and, 16
  constraints on, 33–34
  Continental Illinois, 233n8
  fiscal policy decisions, xvii, 263
  of individual financial institutions, 256
  of insolvent financial firms, 221, 234
  JP Morgan, 49, 262
  just this once, 31
  under LOLR, 44–45
  Penn Central, 51, 233n8
  solvency, 1, 14, 28, 33
Balls, Ed, 211
Bank for International Settlements, 26
Bank of Canada, 236
Bank of England, 100, 101, 183, 236, 287
  committees of mixed membership, 44
  independence in, 211
  permission for liquidity support, 18
  on private-sector purchases and credit, 19, 19n9
  on QE against government bonds, 19
Bank of Japan, 236
bank runs, 31, 33, 35, 42, 43
bankers, viii, xvi, 32, 241, 245
Banking Act (1935), 229
  Fed Board replaced with BOG, of Federal Reserve System, 230

bankruptcy
  Lehman Brothers, 32, 45–48, 50
  Penn Central, 51, 233n8
  resolution regime for, viii, 8, 33
Banque de France, 236
Barabas, Jason, 177–78, 181
Baring, Francis, 5
Barro, Robert J., 114n5, 116n9, 118, 164
base drift, 98, 117, 117n12
Bayes, Thomas, 194, 195
Bayesian candor, for decision-making,
  195–96, 200
Bayesian methods, for sticky prices and
  wages, 137
Bean, Charlie, 101
Bear Stearns, 32, 46, 49–50, 201, 256, 262
Beige Book, 236
Belongia, Michael, 238n12
Bernanke, Ben, 61, 77, 82, 188, 201, 205, 208,
  246, 287–88
Billi, Roberto M., 111n2
Blinder, Alan, 55, 181, 181n5, 182n6
BLS. *See* Bureau of Labor Statistics
Board of Directors, 230
  Dodd-Frank Act, on voting procedures
    change, 221, 234
  Reserve Banks selection process, xvi,
    241–42
Board of Governors (BOG), 85, 192, 272
  Dodd-Frank Act giving power to, xv, 234
  FOMC members of, 187
  international economic policy, 230
  LOLR facilities approval by, 44, 45, 46
  regional banks conflict with, xv, 246–47
  Reserve Bank presidents appointment
    and dismissal, 221, 224, 236, 241,
    245–46
  Reserve Bank relations, 231–33, 240–41
  shift of power from Reserve Banks, xv,
    230, 234, 235
  state of economy meetings, 193
Bordo, Michael, xv–xvi, 221–38
Brady bonds, 283
Bretton Woods system, 231, 233, 270
Broaddus, J. Alfred, 233
Brown, Gordon, 211
Brunner, Karl, 228
Bryan, Malcom, 232n7
Buchanan, James, 7
Bullard, Jim, 239
Bundesbank, 236, 247
Bureau of Labor Statistics (BLS), 284
Burgess-Riefler-Strong doctrine., 228
Burns, Arthur, 51, 205, 232, 265

Calomiris, Charles, 40
Calvo model of price adjustment, 124, 132
Canzoneri, Matthew B., 118, 118n14, 164
Carney, Mark, 174
Casares, Miguel, 137
CBO. *See* Congressional Budget Office
central bank constraints, viii, ix, 9–11, 34, 39
  on asset purchase and interventions, xvii,
    255, 256, 257, 261
  by Bagehot rules, 33
  of fiscal risks, 32–33
  government lending on government's
    direction, 9
  MCC component, viii, 8, 33
central bank degrees of freedom
  maximalist conception, 4–5
  minimalist conception, of Goodfriend, 4,
    13, 27
central bank design precepts
  ex ante clarity regarding boundaries
    reached, 10, 11, 14, 18, 31, 263
  legislature setting powers and objectives,
    9–10, 11
  operating principles stated to guide discre-
    tion, 10, 11, 12
  transparency for accountability of steward-
    ship, xvii, 6, 10, 41, 257
central bank independence
  dilemma of, 268–69
  fiscal constitution for, 28
  inflation relationships, viii, 115n8
  loss of government control, 5–6
  policy rule legislation and, 83–84
  political imperative, 6
  transparency, 116n10
central bank independence, accountability
  and, 112–22, 255–64
  assets purchased or sold restrictions, xvii,
    255, 256, 257, 261
  Fed monetary policy strategy description,
    263–64
  FOMC mandate vagueness, 257–59
  monetary policy mandate narrowed, 257
  political control and interference, 257
  political independence, 256
  price stability single mandate for Fed, 261
  public expectation of economic resolu-
    tion, 260
  separation between government spending
    and currency printed, xvi, 256, 268
  transparent communication on monetary
    policy strategy, xvii, 6, 10, 41, 257
central bank reforms, 150
  for accountability, 116, 122

for instrument independence, 116
types of, 121–22, 122t
central banks, 115, 118–19
clear objectives and standards for stability, 29
consolidated state balance sheet management by, 3–5, 23, 27
constructed as regime, based on general principles, 24
as de facto multiple-mission agencies, 7, 10, 10n3
decisions, executive branch private support of, 22, 45, 156
elected officials influence on decisions of, 157
as emergency institution, vii–viii, 1–53
fiscal carve-out operations, 27, 29
Hamiltonian objection and, 21–23
individual *vs.* group accountability, xiv–xv, 194, 196, 198
inferior economic results from, 25–26
inflation control, 161–62
lending to insolvent firms, ix, 13–14, 37–38
LOLR flexible operation function, 1, 13, 15, 28–29
as market-maker of last resort, viii, 13
as MCC, 5–9
monetary policy systematic operation function, 1–2, 28–29
non-banks lending, viii, 13, 234, 236
performance measures, xiii, 109–66, 114n6, 133f, 140t
purchasing power and fiat currency value maintained by, 255
rule-based policy, in normal times, viii, 2, 28–29, 276
short-term interest rate, xv, 12, 198
solvency assessments, 14
state-contingent contracts to, 17–18
transparency, 6, 158, 264–67
unelected bankers, 5, 10, 13, 16, 18, 20–21
See also credible commitment or emergency institutions
Chen, Han, 137
Chicago plan credit focus, 39
Chicago Reserve Bank, 225, 226, 228, 238n12
Clarida, Richard, 111–12, 127, 143
Cochrane, John H., vii–xviii, 31–36, 39, 40
cognitive conflict, 180
commitment technologies, democracy choice of, 11
committee designs
comparison of, 184t
optimal, 176f, 182, 183t, 185, 188

committees
dynamics, in institutional design, 181–82, 185–87
FOMC evaluation, of dynamics of, 187–93
inquiry *vs.* advocacy balance, xiii, 178–81, 186
members, role strengthening, 12
of mixed membership, in Bank of England, 44
MPC evaluation, of dynamics of, 185–87
See also monetary policy committee
communication
on deviation reasons, 89
Fed quarterly monetary policy reports, 56, 63, 65, 89–90, 93, 215
of FOMC monetary policy strategy, 96, 161, 206, 258, 263, 290
inflation targeting framework and, 273
technology, 35, 43
transparency and, xi, xiii, xvii, 109, 155, 202, 204, 206, 215, 263
competency, of government, xvii, 264–65
Congress
on bailouts sanction, by Feds, 16
Taylor rule bills in, 2
See also legislature
Congressional Budget Office (CBO), 70n7, 158
estimates of potential GDP, 59, 69–70
output gaps, 69, 70n7, 75, 76f, 77, 77f, 78, 78f, 79, 79f, 80f
consolidated state balance sheet
central banks' degrees of freedom and, 4–5, 13, 27
central bank's role in management of, 3–5, 23, 27
government liability and asset structure, 3
constrained discretion, 12, 146, 163, 261, 269, 274
Consumer Price Index (CPI), 60, 61, 75, 75f
Consumer Protection Agency, 237n11
Conti-Brown, Peter, 221, 235
Continental Illinois bailout, 233n8
cost shocks, xii, 126, 127, 130, 143
volatility of, 132, 133, 134, 150
Council of Economic Advisers, 51
CPI. *See* Consumer Price Index
credible commitment or emergency institutions, of central banks, 1–53
central banks constraints, viii, ix, xvii, 8, 9–11, 32–34, 39, 255–57, 261
Cochrane comments on, 31–36
consolidated state balance sheet management, 3–5, 23, 27

credible commitment or emergency institutions (*continued*)
discussion on, 37–53
emergency powers and emergency institutions, ix, 16–18
executive branch cooperation with central banks, ix, 23–24, 29
fiscal authority strategic interaction with, 25–28
Hamiltonian objection and, 21–23
joined-up regimes under MCC, 24–25, 29–30, 35
LOLR regime defined, viii, 13–15
macroeconomic demand management emergencies, 18–21
majoritarian control loss disadvantage, 5
MCC, 5–9
normal times rule-like behavior, viii, 2, 28–29, 276
regime boundaries, 15–16
regimes needed, ix, 11
systematic policy for, 1–2
welfare advantages of, 5
credit, 43, 233
Bank of England on, 19, 19n9
central banks involvement with, 7
Chicago plan focus on, 39
constraint, 39, 265
market rates, 279
MPC examination of condition of, 40–41
restriction, Bolcker and, 265–66
-to-GDP ratio, 154
See also money-credit constitution
credit allocation policy, xvi, 39, 256, 263
credit policy, xvi, 221, 224, 226
emergencies in macroeconomic demand management, 18–21
Fed growing use of, 234
critical thinking, 179
Croushore, Dean, 66
Cukierman, Alex, 115n8
Curdia, Vasco, 137
Currie, Lauchlin, 229
Cutting, Bronson, 39

Dale, Spencer, 287
de facto multiple-mission agencies, central bank as, 7, 10, 10n3
Debelle, Guy, 116
decision-making, sound
consensus and, 206–7
deliberation in, 176f, 177–81
external factors for, 176
high-quality inputs, 176f

internal factors for, 176
optimal committee design, 176f, 182, 183t, 185, 188
prerequisites for, 175–76, 176f
decision-making attributes
Bayesian candor, 195–96, 200
individual *vs.* group accountability, xiv–xv, 194, 196, 198
single objective/multiple constraints, 195, 197–200, 216
delegation
in goal-based and rule-based regimes, 11, 125–26
of policy function, in independent agencies, 9
deliberation, in sound decision-making, 176f
Barabas on, 177–78, 181
Fishkin on, 180–81
Garvin and Roberto on, 178–79
identification of, through inquiry *vs.* adequacy, 178–81
Schonhardt-Bailey on, 178
demand shocks, xiii, 131–35
volatility of, 132, 147, 150
See also aggregate demand shocks
design
institutional, xiii, 173–221, 176n3
monetary policy committee features of, 182–85
optimal committee, 176f, 182, 183t, 185, 188
design precepts
of central bank, xvii, 6, 9–12, 14, 18, 31, 41, 257, 263
of independent agencies, 9–10
detrending, 58, 60
HP, 67, 67f, 74n10
linear, 59, 67, 67f, 68, 68n6, 74n10, 81
output gaps, 68, 73
quadratic, 59, 67, 67f, 68, 68n6, 74n10, 81
deviations
communication on reasons for, 89
extended periods of substantial, x, 59–60, 62, 74
of federal funds rate, 110
during Great Inflation, 59–60, 72, 74
of modified Taylor rule, 60, 74, 81
of original Taylor rule, 59–60, 72, 81
policy rule, 57, 57n3, 58, 63–66, 91–92
policy rule legislation, from 1954–2015 and, 59–60, 71–72, 74
policy rule legislation, from 1991–2015 and, 75, 75n12
policy rule legislation and, 61–66

from Reference Policy Rule, of FRAT bill, 128–29
during Volcker disinflation, 60, 72
Dimon, Jamie, 49
Directive Policy Rule, of FRAT bill, 55–56, 57, 119–20
discount rates
Fed use of, 225
set by Reserve Banks, 224
discretion, xii–xiii, 64, 82, 110n1, 111, 118, 155, 257
by Fed, on FOMC mandate interpretation, 258–59
limiting, 12, 119, 121, 146, 163, 261, 269, 274
operating principles stated to guide, 10, 11, 12
rules *vs.*, 57, 58, 92, 98–99, 118n14, 194, 198
discretionary policy, viii, ix, xvii, 62, 97, 125, 146, 164
distortions from, 113–14
inflation bias resulting from, 114, 114n5, 153
optimal, 124–26, 142, 143
dissent
in FOMC, xiv, xv, 188, 190, 205, 206–7, 214, 217–18, 232
by Reserve Bank presidents, 188, 232
distortionary shocks, 113, 126, 127, 129–30, 140, 143
volatility of, 133, 134
distortions, from discretionary policy, 113–14
distributions
as monetary policy goal, 11
prior and posterior, in estimated model with sticky prices and wages, 138t
Dodd-Frank Act, 7, 33
Board of Directors voting procedures change, 221, 234
BOG given power by, xv, 234
complexity of, 266
Consumer Protection Agency creation by, 237n11
on Fed chairman, of Financial Stability Oversight Council, 236
on Fed innovation permission from treasury secretary, ix, 18, 18n8, 234
on Fed LOLR policy, 2–3, 221
Fed power increased by, 238
lending to non-bank financial institutions prohibition, 234
local boards power weakened, xv, 221, 234

on Reserve Bank presidents appointment, 234, 241
Dotsey, Michael
on monetary policy reports role, 89–90
on monitoring independent agencies, 88–89
outcome-based rule analysis, 84–88
policy rule legislation comments, 83–90
DSGE (dynamic stochastic general equilibrium) model with sticky prices and wages, 151
Dutton, Jane E., 177
dynamic stochastic general equilibrium. *See* DSGE

ECB. *See* European Central Bank
Eccles, Marriner, 229–30
Eccles Plan of 1935, 235
effective federal funds rate, 138, 138n24
Eichengreen, Barry, 228
elasticity, of wage inflation, 136–37
emergencies, in macroeconomic demand management, 18–21
private-sector purchases and credit, 19, 19n9
QE against government bonds, 19
emergency decisions, by executive branch, 16–17, 21–22
emergency institutions, ix
central banks as, vii–viii, 1–53
emergency LOLR operations, 20
emergency powers, 18
by executive branch, in financial crisis, 16–17, 23, 29
precept, of central banks, 10, 10n3
unelected central bankers role, 16, 20–21
equations
Euler, 124, 125, 130, 136–37
for Taylor rule, 63–64
equilibrium real rate of interest, 80f, 151, 156
equity-financed banking system, x, 36
Erceg, Christopher, 135, 137, 141–42
estimated model with sticky prices and wages, 143t, 145f, 145t, 166
Bayesian methods, 137
Casares, Moreno, Vazquez and, 137
Chen, Curdia, Ferrero and, 137
Clarida, Gali, Gertler and, 143
elasticity of wage inflation, 136–37
Erceg, Henderson, Levin and, 135, 137, 141–42
estimation, 137–38
estimation period, 138n24
extensions and conclusions, 150–54

estimated model with sticky prices and wages
(*continued*)
marginal utility of consumption, 136
prior and posterior distributions, 138t
results, 142–49
social loss and, 148f, 149f
welfare measures, 139–42, 140t
estimated Taylor rule, 57
estimates of potential GDP, by CBO, 59,
69–70
Euler equation, 124, 125
on marginal utility of consumption, 136
on price and wage inflation, 136–37
shocks and, 130
European Central Bank (ECB), 183, 281
price stability mandate, 173
restrictions, 261
staff forecast of, 215
European Exchange Rate Mechanism, 270
ex ante clarity, by central banks, 10, 11, 14,
18, 31, 263
ex ante process, with majoritarian credentials, 23
ex post outturns, 14, 31
exchange rate, 102, 122t, 289, 290
fixed, xviii, 270, 274, 275
executive branch, 18
cooperation with central banks, ix,
23–24, 29
emergency decisions by, 16–17, 21–22
exceptional power during financial crisis,
16–17, 23, 29
inflation tax and, 6
private support of central bank decisions,
22, 45, 156
Reserve Bank presidents appointments, 45,
49, 221, 236–37, 288, 289
sanctions on ventures, by unelected central
bankers, 18
expansionary policies, 113
external factors, for sound decision-making,
176

FDIC. *See* Federal Deposit Insurance
Corporation
Fed. *See* Federal Reserve
Federal Advisory Council, 242
Federal Deposit Insurance Corporation
(FDIC), 229, 230n5
federal funds rate, 55, 58–60, 63–66, 69–75,
69f, 81
deviations of, 110
effective, 138, 138n24
estimated Taylor rule description of, 57

during Great Inflation, 74
inflation-adjusted, 274
lags of, 93
modified Taylor rule description of, 57
original Taylor rule description of, 57
outcome-based rule and, 85–86, 85f, 86f,
92–93
Reference Policy Rule as, 120
in Summary of Economic Projections,
159
during Volcker disinflation, 74
Federal Open Market Committee (FOMC),
US, xiii, 174, 233–34
asset price targeting, 287–88
committee dynamics evaluation, 187–93
communication, of monetary policy strategy, 96, 161, 206, 258, 263, 290
constitutionality of, 288
decision-making process improvement,
248
dissent in, xiv, xv, 188, 190, 205, 206–7,
214, 217–18, 232
forecasts by Summary of Economic Projections, 159
FRAT bill on, 119–20
Hansen, McMahon, and Prat on transcripts of, 191, 192
institutional design, 187–93
mandate vagueness, 257–59
on maximum sustainable employment,
158, 258–59
Meade and Stasavage on transcript policy
of, 190
members of, 187, 188
MPC compared to, xiv, 175
press conferences for transparency, 205–6
public transcripts of, xiv, 92, 190–91
Reserve Bank presidents information and
opinions, 236
Reserve Bank presidents vote, 230
rookie status members, 192
Schonhardt-Bailey on transcripts of,
190–91
Senate bill on, 56, 63, 65
SEP of, 159, 259
on SOMA return to all-treasuries portfolio, 262
Statement on Longer-Run Goals and
Policy Strategy, 158–59
Federal Reserve (Fed)
assets purchase and sales, xvi, xvii, 255,
256, 257, 261, 262
BOG LOLR facilities approval, 44, 45, 46
Conti-Brown proposed reforms, 235

credit policy, 224, 234
Dodd-Frank Act on power increase of, 238
financial stability goal, 237
fiscal stability objectives, 7
goals and objectives, 197–98, 257–58
governance study, by GAO, 243, 244
Great Contraction caused by, 228, 229
Great Depression and, 226–27
inflation after WWI, 225
international comparisons to, 247–48
large-scale MBS purchases, 262
maximum sustainable employment mandate, 158, 173
mismanagement of financial crisis, of 2007–2008, 221
mistakes of theory, xvi, 239–40
monetary aggregates targets, 97–98
Monetary Policy Report by, 65
monetary policy rule and, x, 274–77
monetary policy strategy description, 263–64
open market operations, 4, 225, 226, 227, 229, 255
Paul call for abolition of, 235, 240
personality- and individual-driven decisions, 44
policymaking improvements by St. Louis Reserve Bank, 236
price stability mandate, xvii, 6, 116, 173, 261, 290
public announcement, on monetary growth targets, 116–17
quarterly monetary policy reports, 56, 63, 65, 89–90, 93, 215
short-term interest rates to fund WWI, 224–25
SIFIs supervision and regulation by, 235n10
SOMA restrictions, 261–62
staff forecast of, 203, 210–12, 215
strong staff model of, 209
Taylor rule compliance, xi, 125n20
Treasury accord with, xvii, 263, 282–83
treasury secretary permission for innovation, ix, 18, 18n8, 234
as WWII engine of inflation, 231
See also Board of Directors; Board of Governors; Reserve Banks
Federal Reserve Accountability and Transparency Act (FRAT Act) proposed legislation, 2014 (House bill) (Audit the Fed legislation), 2, 81, 83
Blinder and Meltzer on, 55
Directive Policy Rule, 55–56, 57, 119–20

Fed testimony before congressional committee, 63, 65
on Intermediate Policy Inputs, 119
Reference Policy Rule, 56, 119–20, 128–29
on Taylor rule as operational mandate, 274
Yellen on, 55, 120
Federal Reserve Act (1913), 251
Banking Act reform of, 229
BOG authority to lend, 45
Conti-Brown, on unconstitutionality of, 235
Glass-Steagall Act reform of, 229
nationwide branch banking, 223n3
single objective and three goals of, 197–98
Federal Reserve Bank of St. Louis, 232–33, 236
Federal Reserve governance history, xv, 221
BOG Reserve Bank relations: 1951–2006, 231–33, 240–41
conflict in early years, 226–28
discount rates use, 225
discussion, 243–51
early years: 1914–1935, 224–29
Fed reform, 229–31
federal reserve system establishment, 222–24, 230
financial crisis, of 2007–2008 and beyond, 16–17, 233–36
Fisher, R., proposed reforms, 235n10
Karr comments on, 239–42
lessons from history, 236–38
mistakes of theory, xvi, 239–40
OMIC disbanded, 227
OMPC created, 227
open market operations, 4, 225, 226, 227, 229, 255
recent criticism of, 256
Federal Reserve Reform Act of 1977
Fed oversight and transparency demand, 272–73
goal mandate, 272
federal reserve system establishment, 222–24, 230
Federal Reserve Treasury Accord, of March 1951, 231
Ferrero, Andrea, 137
fiat money regimes, 255
financial crisis
contemporary policy response, 34
executive branch emergency powers during, 16–17, 23, 29
LOLR role in, 2
moral hazard and, ix, 31–35
pre-commitment problem and, viii–ix, 31

financial crisis, of 2007–2008
  BOG discount window extension to non-banks, 234
  Bretton Woods-era swap network and, 233
  Fed credit policy concern, 234
  Fed mismanagement criticisms, 221
  Financial Crisis Inquiry Report, of 2010 after, 234
  FOMC and New York Reserve Bank management of, 233–34
  global, 16–17
  non-bank financial intermediaries bailouts, 234
Financial Crisis Inquiry Report, of 2010, 234
Financial Regulatory Improvement Act proposed legislation, 2015 (Senate bill), 57, 81
Fed quarterly report to Congress, on FOMC decisions, 56, 63, 65
Financial Services Authority (FSA), 47, 288
financial stability goal, of Fed, 237
Financial Stability Oversight Council, xv, 236
financial system
  government debt crisis influence on, 35–36
  political system and, 40
fiscal authority, strategic interaction with, 25–28
fiscal carve-out operations, 27, 29
fiscal policy
  bailouts, xvii, 263
  risks, 32–33
  stability objectives, 7
Fischer, Stanley, 116
Fisher, Peter, 194–99, 257–58
Fisher, Richard, xvi, 234, 235n10
Fishkin, James, 180–81
fixed exchange rates, xviii, 270, 274, 275
flexible operation function, of central banks, 1, 13, 28–29
flexible rule-based regime, 118
FOIA. See Freedom of Information Act
FOMC. See Federal Open Market Committee
forecasts, 159, 188, 189, 196, 207, 275
  of central bank, 198
  difficulty of, 14
  by FOMC Summary of Economic Projections, 159
  GDP, 70, 70n7
  Greenbook inflation, 66, 72, 77
  inflation, 58, 61, 66, 72, 77, 84, 101, 290
  of liquidity, in LOLR policy, 14
  monetary policy committee, 40–41
  out-of-sample, 92, 93
  rules and, 97

staff, 203, 211–12, 215
forward-looking Phillips curve, xii, 124, 233
fractional-reserve banking, 24, 27
  money as exchangeable and, 42–43
  politics and, 42
  social benefits, of liquidity insurance, 6
  society and, 2, 35
Fragile by Design (Haber and Calomiris), 40
Francis, Darryl, 232
FRAT Act. See Federal Reserve Accountability and Transparency Act
fraudulent preference, Bagehot rule and, 37
Freedom of Information Act (FOIA), 248–49
Friedman, Milton, 37, 38, 40, 225–28, 230–32, 260, 271, 290
FSA. See Financial Services Authority
Fuhrer, Jeff C., 89
Full Employment and Balanced Growth Act (1978), 232, 273
  on Fed money growth targets, 117

Gali, Jordi, 111–12, 127, 135, 138, 143
GAO. See Government Accountability Office
Garvin, David A., 178–79, 186
GDP. See gross domestic product
Geithner, Timothy, 201
General Theory (Keynes), 229
George, Eddie, 100
Gertler, Mark, 111–12, 127, 143
Giannoni, Marc P., 83–84, 88, 91
Glass, Carter, 230, 235
Glass-Steagall Act, 229
global financial crisis, of 2007–2009, 16–17
global liquidity crisis, prevention of, 233–34
goal mandates, xviii, 271–74
  Federal Reserve Reform Act of 1977 and, 272
  Full Employment and Balanced Growth Act of 1978, 273
  inflation targeting framework, 273, 279
  RBNZ framework of, 273
goal-based regimes
  delegation, 11, 125–26
  demand shocks under, xiii, 134
  goals assignment, 126–28
  inflation and, 125n19
  inflation targeting, 152
  jointly optimal rule-based regimes and, 131–34, 133f
  simple model of, 112, 123, 125–35, 133f, 150–52, 165
goal-based rules
  instrument-based rules vs., xii, 10–11, 112, 121–22, 122t, 162–63

performance of, 123–24
gold standard, 6, 8, 162, 224, 226, 228
  as operational mandate, xviii, 269–70
  Paul on return to, 235
Goodfriend, Marvin, 4
Gordon, David B., 114n5, 116n9, 118, 164
government
  aggregate demand interventions by, 4
  bonds, 19
  central bank lending, on direction of, 9
  competency of, xvii, 264–65
  constraints, monetary policy influence
    on, 115
  control loss, central bank independence
    and, 5–6
  credit allocation policy involvement, 39
  debt crisis, financial system influenced by,
    35–36
  deposits guaranteed, bank runs and, 31
  -guaranteed, MBS, ix, 19
  liability and asset structure, 3
  -provided banknotes and interest-paying
    money, 36
  spending, separation from currency
    printed, xvi, 256, 268
Government Accountability Office (GAO)
  Fed governance study by, 243, 244
  monetary policy audits, 257
Government in the Sunshine Act, xiv, 192, 202
Great Contraction, of 1929–1933, 222
  Fed cause of, 228, 229
  final panic of, 227–28
Great Depression, 37
  Fed and, 226–27
  Strong's policy leading to, 226
Great Inflation, 62, 229, 231, 233, 236, 237,
  240
  federal funds rate during, 74
  modified Taylor rule negative deviations,
    60, 74
  negative deviations during, 59–60, 72, 74
  original Taylor rule negative deviations
    during, 59, 60, 72
Great Moderation, 233, 236
  modified Taylor rule and, 60, 74
  original Taylor rule during, 60, 72
Great Recession, 62, 68
Great Society, of Johnson, 232
Greenbook inflation forecasts, 66, 72, 77
Greenspan, Alan, 188, 190, 205, 208, 244–45,
  285
Greider, William, 244n13
gross domestic product (GDP), 49, 59, 69–70,
  70n7, 154

group *vs.* individual accountability, xiv–xv,
  194, 196, 198
groupthink, xvi, 182, 196, 203–4
  consensus decision-making and, 206–7
  Sibert on, 185
Groupthink theory, of Janis, 177

Haber, Stephen, 40
Hambrick, Donald C., 177
Hansen, Stephen, 191, 192
Harlow, Bryce, 51
Harrison, George, 227
Hayes, Alfred, 231
Helms, Dick, 199
Henderson, Dale W., 135, 137, 141–42
Hodrick-Prescott (HP) detrending, 67, 67f,
  74n10
Hoenig, Thomas, xvi, 234
Holmstrom, Bengt, 10n3
Hoover, Hubert, 226
Hoskins, W. Lee, 233
House bill. *See* Federal Reserve Accountability
  and Transparency Act
HP. *See* Hodrick-Prescott
Humphrey-Hawkins Full Employment Act
  (1978). *See* Full Employment and
  Balanced Growth Act (1978)

Ilbas, Pelin, 88, 89, 111, 153
illiquid loans, viii, 13, 33
illiquidity, 283
  insolvency compared to, viii–ix, 8, 33,
    40, 262
IMF. *See* International Monetary Fund
independence dilemma, xviii, 268–69, 277
independent agencies
  constraints and principles, 9–11
  design precepts, 9–10
  monitoring of, 88–89
  multiple missions of, 7, 10, 10n3
  policy function delegation, 9
individual *vs.* group accountability, xiv–xv,
  194, 196, 198
inertial rule, with lags, xi, 91–92
inflation, xii, 216–17, 274, 280
  after WWI, 225
  central bank independence relationship
    with, viii, 115n8
  central banks control of, 161–62
  elasticity of wage, 136–37
  Fed as agent of, during WWII, 231
  goal-based regimes and, 125n19
  output gaps and, 91, 111, 125n19, 126, 128,
    129, 150, 158, 289

inflation (*continued*)
  price and wage, 136–37
  rate, used in Taylor rule, xi, 66
  tax, executive branch and, 6
  variability, 130
inflation bias, from discretionary policies,
    114, 114n5, 153
inflation forecasts, 58, 61, 66, 72, 77, 84, 101,
    290
inflation shocks, 103, 111, 112
inflation targeting, xviii, 98, 161–62, 165,
    285, 290
  accountability and, 109, 117n13
  component, of MCC, viii, 8, 33
  framework, 273, 279
  in goal-based regimes, 152
  by Reserve Bank of New Zealand Act,
    109, 161
  rule, optimal, xii, 84, 112, 130, 156,
    157–58
  Taylor rule and, 163, 281–82
inquiry *vs.* advocacy balance, xiii, 181
  active listening, 180
  constructive conflict, not personal, 180
  critical thinking and assumption testing,
    179
  deliberation of multiple alternatives, 179
  Garvin and Roberto on, 178–79, 186
  open and balanced information sharing,
    179
insolvency, illiquidity compared to, viii–ix, 8,
    33, 40, 262
insolvent firms, viii, 221, 234
  bank runs and, 33
  central banks lending to, ix, 13–14,
    37–38
  liquidity assistance and, 37–38
institutional design, 219–21
  committee dynamics, 181–82, 185–87
  decision-making and organizational suc-
    cess, 176–78, 176f, 206–7
  discussion, 199–218
  Fisher, P., comments on, 194–98
  FOMC committee dynamics evaluation,
    187–89
  FOMC transcripts and academic research
    evaluation, 189–93
  inquiry *vs.* advocacy, xiii, 178–81, 186
  institutional setting and, 173–74
  institutions success, 175–76
  Mellahi and Wilkinson on, 176, 176n3
  MPC design features, 182–85
  MPC evaluation, 185–87
  MPC success, 181–82

instrument-based rules
  complex, 121
  goal-based rules *vs.*, xii, 10–11, 112, 121–
    22, 122t, 162–63
interest rate, 289
  equilibrium real, 80f, 151, 156
  instrument, 131, 271
  natural, xviii, 274, 276
  rule, optimal, 103, 130, 151
  See also nominal interest rate; short-term
    interest rates; zero lower bound inter-
    est rates
Intermediate Policy Inputs, FRAT bill on, 119
International Monetary Fund (IMF), 158
intertemporal substitution relation, xii, 136
Ireland, Peter, 238n12

Jackson, Andrew, 222
Janis, Irving L., 177
Johns, D. C., 232n7
Johnson, Lyndon, 52, 232
Jones, Homer, 232
Jordan, Jerry, 233
JP Morgan, 49, 262
just this once bailouts, 31
Justiniano, Alejandro, 92, 93

Karr, Mary, 239–42
Kehoe, Patrick J., 118n14
King, Mervyn, 101
Koenig, Evan, 70
Kohn, Donald L., 61, 77, 82, 203
Kotlikoff, Larry, 38
  credit constraints and, 39
  mutual funds intermediation, 39
Krishnamurthy, Arvind, 279
Kydland, Finn E., 114n5

labor markets
  monetary policy relationship with, 259
  monopolistic competition in, 113
Lacker, Jeffrey, xvi, 234
lagged funds rate, xi, 65, 66, 91
Laubach, Thomas, 62, 79
Lazar, Nomi, 22
  on exceptional executive power, 17
  legislation, x, 58
  on central bank rules, 118–19
  on central bank's short-term interest rate,
    12
  on Fed structural reorganization, 239
  lending sanction, 9
  on solvency and liquidity support, 15
  See also policy rule legislation

legislature
  decision-making procedures, of independent agencies set by, 10
  Hamiltonian objection and, 21–23
  in-crisis decisions, 20
  independent agency purposes, objectives, powers set by, 9–10, 11
Lehman Brothers, 32, 45–48, 50
lender of last resort (LOLR) policy, xviii, 8, 31, 238, 262
  bailouts under, 44–45
  BOG facility approval, 44, 45, 46
  Dodd-Frank on, 2–3, 221
  financial crisis role, 2
  flexible operation function, of central banks, 1, 13, 15, 28–29
  forecasting liquidity, 14
  insolvent firms and, 38
  liquidity reinsurance policy, vii, viii, 2, 6, 13, 14, 37–38
  minimalist conception and, 4, 13
  moral hazard and, 233n8
  non-bank lending, 13
  regime definition, viii, 13–16
  systematic, viii, 237
  transparent communication strategy, 41
Levin, Andrew, 65, 121, 135, 137, 141–42
  comments on rules *vs.* goal model, 155–60
linear detrending, 59, 67, 67f, 68, 68n6, 74n10, 81
liquidity premia, asset values fall and, 42
liquidity reinsurance policy, vii, viii, 2, 13, 14
  fractional-reserve banking and, 6
  insolvent firms and, 37–38
liquidity-support operations, 14–15
  Dodd-Frank on treasury secretary permission for, 18, 18n8
  insolvent firms and, 37–38
local boards power weakened, by Dodd-Frank Act, xv, 221, 234
LOLR. *See* lender of last resort

macroeconomic demand management, emergencies in, 18–21
Maier, Philip, 182, 185–86
marginal utility of consumption, 136
market-maker of last resort, central banks as, viii, 13
mark-to-market test, 41
Martin, William McChesney, 205, 231, 265
Mason, Phyllis A., 177
maximalist conception, of central bank, 4–5
maximum sustainable employment mandate, 158, 173, 258–59

MBS. *See* mortgage-backed securities
MCC. *See* money-credit constitution
McCallum, Ben, 157, 162, 286
McMahon, Michael, 191, 192
Meade, Ellen E., 190
measures
  incorporated in policy rule legislation, 63n4
  output gap, xi, 66, 67, 67f, 85, 85n16
  performance, of central banks, xiii, 109–66, 114n6, 133f, 140t
  unobservable, in monetary policy rule, 276
  welfare, in estimated model with sticky prices and wages, 139–42, 140t
Mellahi, Kamel, 176, 176n3
Meltzer, Allan, 37, 55, 62, 228–29
Milgrom, Paul, 10n3
Mill, John Stuart, 177
Miller, Adolph, 226
minimalist conception, of Goodfriend, 27
  aggregate demand interventions by government, 4
  central bank restriction to open market operations, 4
  elected policymakers and, 4
  on LOLR, 4, 13
modern quantity theory views, of Friedman, 232
modified Taylor rule, 57, 59, 74n10, 81
  deviations, 74, 81
  during Great Moderation, 60, 74
  negative deviations during Great Inflation, 60, 74
  from 1954–2015, 73–74, 73f
  with real-time CBO output gaps and PCE inflation: 1991–2015, 75, 76f, 78–79, 79f
  during Volcker disinflation, 60, 74
  Yellen on, 61–62, 64, 64n5, 78
monetary aggregates, 97–98, 116, 117, 119, 131, 162, 232
monetary easing, aggressive, 26
monetary growth targets, public announcement on, 116–17
monetary policy
  asset prices and, 287–89
  distortions from discretionary policy, 113–14
  distributional goal of, 11
  expansionary policies and, 113
  government constraints influenced by, 115
  labor market relationship with, 259
  loss function, 111n3
  mandate, narrowed, 257
  nominal interest rate as instrument of, 126

monetary policy (*continued*)
  normal-times, viii, 2, 28–29, 276
  operating principles for, 10, 11, 12, 99–100
  optimal, xiii, 66, 78, 83, 95, 114n5, 131, 156, 164
  output, of short-term interest rates, xv, 12, 198
  political pressures on, 111, 112–13, 115
  public prediction of outcomes of, 97
  reports, role of, 89
  systematic operation function, of central banks, 1–2, 28–29
  transparent communication strategy, xvii, 6, 10, 41, 257
monetary policy, independence and
  future and, 277–78
  goal mandates, 271–74, 279
  independence dilemma, xviii, 268–69, 277
  operational mandates, 268–71
  rules as operational mandate, 274–77
monetary policy committee
  benefits and costs of, 182
  Blinder and Morgan on, 181, 181n5, 182n6
  design features, 182–85
  forecasts, 40–41
  Maier on, 182
  Schonhardt-Bailey on process of, 183–84
  Sibert on, 182
  success, 181–82
Monetary Policy Committee (MPC), UK, 174, 186n8
  committee dynamics evaluation, 185–87
  on credit condition examination, 40–41
  FOMC compared to, xiv, 175
  institutional design and, 181–87
  internal and external members, 185
  Maier on, 185–86
  QE decision by, 19, 24
Monetary Policy Report, by Fed, 65
monetary policy rule
  Fed and, x, 274–77
  lack of consensus on, 277
  as operational mandate, 274–77
  unobservable measures dependence, 276
  ZLB interest rates, xvi, 152, 152n27, 256, 276–77, 285–86, 287
monetary targets, xviii, 270–71
money as exchangeable, fractional-reserve banking and, 42–43
money growth targets, Full Employment Act on, 117
money-credit constitution (MCC), ix–x, 5–9
  bankrupt banks resolution regime component, viii, 8, 33

central bank constraints component, viii, 8, 33
  inflation targeting component, viii, 8, 33
  joined-up regimes under, 24–25, 29–30, 35
  liquidity reinsurance regime component, viii, 8, 33
  nominal anchor cohesion with, 8, 24
  price stability maintenance, 6
  private banks reserves requirement, viii, 8, 33
monopolistic competition, in labor markets, 113
Moore, George, 89
moral hazard, viii, 7, 45, 52, 53, 77
  financial crisis and, ix, 31–35
  in LOLR policy, 233n8
Moreno, Antonio, 137
Morgan, John, 181, 181n5
mortgage-backed securities (MBS), 259
  Fed purchase of, xvi, 256, 279
  government-guaranteed, ix, 19
MPC. *See* Monetary Policy Committee
multiple constraints, for decision-making, 195, 197–200, 216
multiple-mission central banks, 7, 10, 10n3
mutual funds, 34
  financial intermediation, 39

narrow banking, 38–39
National Banking Act, 241
National Bureau of Economic Research (NBER), 67
National Monetary Commission (NMC), 223
National Reserve Association network, 222
nationwide branch banking, 223n3, 251
NBER. *See* National Bureau of Economic Research
negative deviations, during Great Inflation, 59–60, 72, 74
N.E.M.O. *See* Norges Bank's DSGE model
New York Fed, 49
  close connection to Wall Street, 221, 234, 246
  criticism of, after 2007–2008 financial crisis, xv, 234
  presidential selection process at, 245
New York Reserve Bank, 6, 226
  bailout execution, 46
  conflict of interest safeguards for, 237
  gold reserves depletion, 228
  open market operations of, 227
  president appointment with Senate approval, 221, 235

new-Keynesian model, 87
  forward-looking Phillips curve, xii, 124, 233
  inflation shocks, 103, 111, 112
  intertemporal substitution relation, xii, 136
  monopolistic competition in goods and/or labor markets, 113
  of sticky prices and wages, 135–54, 138n24, 138t, 140t, 143f, 145t, 148f, 149f
Neyapti, Bilin, 115n8
Nikolsko-Rzhevskyy, Alex, x–xi, 55–90
NMC. *See* National Monetary Commission
nominal anchor, 1, 267, 269
  MCC cohesion with, 8, 24
  no monetary financing by, 13–14
nominal income policies, 110
  Billi on, 111n2
nominal interest rate, 63, 111n2, 111n3, 137, 276, 282
  as monetary policy instrument, 126
  ZLB, 151, 152, 152n27, 285–86, 287
non-bank lending, viii, 13, 234, 236
  Dodd-Frank Act prohibition on, 234
noninertial rules, 91–92
Norges Bank's DSGE model (N.E.M.O), 111n3
normal-times monetary policy, viii, 2, 28–29, 276

objectives
  by central banks, for stability, 29
  of Fed, 257–58
  Fed fiscal stability, 7
  legislature setting of central bank, 9–10, 11
  output, 144, 145f, 146, 148, 149f
  single, for decision-making, 195, 197–200, 216
Office of Management and Budget, 51
Okun's Law, during recessions, 59, 68
OMIC. *See* Open Market Investment Committee
OMPC. *See* Open Market Policy Committee
On Liberty (Mill), 177
Open Market Investment Committee (OMIC), 225–26, 227
open market operations, 4, 225, 226, 227, 229, 255
Open Market Policy Committee (OMPC), 227
  becomes FOMC, 229
operating principles, for monetary policy, 10, 11, 12, 99–100
operational mandates, 268, 278
  fixed exchange rates, xviii, 270, 274, 275

gold standard, xviii, 269–70
  monetary targets, xviii, 270–71
  rules as, 274–77
optimal committee design, 176f, 182, 183t, 185, 188
optimal discretionary policy, 125–26, 142, 143
optimal goal- and rule-based regimes, 131–34, 133f
optimal inflation targeting rule, xii, 84, 112, 130, 156, 157–58
optimal instrument rule, 121
optimal interest rate rule, 103, 130, 151
optimal monetary policy, xiii, 66, 78, 83, 95, 114n5, 131, 156, 164
optimal rule, xii, 33, 84, 88–89, 91, 101, 131, 151, 164–65
Organisation for Economic Co-operation and Development, 158
organizational failure, internal management and
  Hambrick and Mason's Upper Echelon theory, 177
  Janis's Groupthink theory, 177
  Staw, Sandelands, and Dutton's Threat Rigidity Effect theory, 177
original Taylor rule, 57, 64, 74n10
  Bernanke on, 61, 77
  deviations, 81
  during Great Moderation, 60, 72
  Kohn on, 61, 77
  Laubach and Williams on, 62
  negative deviations during Great Inflation, 59, 60, 72
  negative deviations from 2001, 60
  from 1954 to 1974 with deviations, 59–60
  from 1954 to 2015, 71f
  Poole and Taylor on, 60–61
  positive deviations during Volcker disinflation, 60, 72
  with real-time CBO output gaps, PCE inflation and time-varying equilibrium real interest rates: 1991–2015, 80f
  with real-time CBO output gaps and PCE inflation: 1991–2015, 75, 76f, 78–79, 79f
  with real-time CBO output gaps and CPI inflation: 1994–2015, 75, 76nf
  with real-time CBO output gaps and core PCE inflation: 1996–2015, 77–78, 78f
  with real-time CBO output gaps and CPI inflation: 1999–2015, 77, 77f
  Reference Policy Rule, of FRAT bill as, 56, 119–20
  rules-based eras, 64
  Yellen on, 62

Orphanides, Athanasios, 66, 93
outcome-based rule
    Dotsey analysis of, 84–88
    federal funds rate and, 85–86, 85f, 86f,
        92–93
    loss functions, 86–87, 87f
out-of-sample forecasts, 92, 93
output, xii, xiii
    of monetary policy, of short-term interest
        rates, xv, 12, 198
    objective, 144, 145f, 146, 148, 149f
output gaps, 56–62, 282
    CBO, 69, 70n7, 75, 76f, 77, 77f, 78, 78f, 79,
        79f, 80f
    detrended, 68, 73
    growth rate, 63n4, 111n2
    inflation and, 91, 111, 125n19, 126, 128,
        129, 150, 158, 289
    measures, xi, 66, 67, 67f, 85, 85n16
    real-time data on, 67, 67f, 68, 71, 75, 76f,
        77–79, 77f, 78f, 79f, 80f, 81, 158
Overend and Gurney Crisis (1866), 38

Panic of 1907, 222
Papell, David, x–xi, 55–90
Parkin, Michael, 115n8
Paul, Ron, 235, 240
Paulson, Hank, 283
PCE. *See* Personal Consumption Expenditure
Penn Central, 51, 233n8
Perron, Pierre, 64
Personal Consumption Expenditure (PCE),
    60, 61, 75, 75f, 284
Pettit, Philip, 10n3
Philadelphia Reserve Bank, 49, 59
Plosser, Charles, xvi, xvi–xvii, 234, 246,
    255–64
policy robustness role, 111
policy rule deviations, 57, 57n3, 63–66,
    91–92
    Bai, Perron, and Qu on, 64
    legislation definition, 58
policy rule legislation, x, 55–103, 163
    central bank independence and, 83–84
    deviations from, 61–62, 63–66
    discussion, 91–103
    Dotsey comments on, 83–90
    FRAT bill, 2, 55–57, 63, 65, 83, 119–20,
        128–29, 274
    inertial and noninertial rules, 91–92
    measurements incorporated in, 63n4
    real-time data, 59, 66–70
    Senate bill, 56, 57, 63, 65, 81
    Taylor rule problems, 65–66

policy rule legislation, from 1954–2015,
    70–74, 71f
    CBO estimates of potential GDP, 59, 69–70
    CPI and PCE during, 60, 61
    linear detrending until 1973, 59
    negative deviations during Great Inflation,
        59–60, 72, 74
    original Taylor rule from 1954 to 1974,
        with deviations, 59–60
    Philadelphia real-time GDP data, after
        1991, 49
    positive deviations during Volcker disinfla-
        tion, 60, 72
    quadratic detrending after 1973, 59
    real GDP from Philadelphia Fed, on infla-
        tion and output gap, 59
    real-time data on GDP deflator, on infla-
        tion and output gap, 59
    sustained deviations, 71–72
policy rule legislation, from 1991–2015, 75–80
    CPI and PCE during, 75, 75f
    deviations, 75, 75n12
    Wu and Xia (forthcoming) rates, 59, 69,
        69f, 75
Policy Targets Agreement, 115
political pressures, on monetary policy, 111,
    112–13, 115
politics, 40
    central bank independence and, 6, 256,
        257
    fractional-reserve banking and, 42
Poole, William, 60–61, 75, 82, 131–32, 271
Posen, Adam, 19n9, 115n8
positive deviations, during Volcker disinfla-
    tion, 60, 72
Posner, Eric, 17
Prat, Andrea, 191, 192
pre-commitment problem, viii–ix, 31
Prescott, Edward C., 114n5
price stability mandate, xvii, 6, 116, 173, 261,
    290
price-level targeting, 111n2
private banking system
    MCC, on reserves requirement, viii, 8, 33
    stability of, 7
private-sector purchase and credit, by Bank of
    England, 19, 19n9
Prodan, Ruxandra, x–xi, 55–90
public
    announcement, on monetary growth
        targets, 116–17
    economic resolution expectation, 260
    monetary policy outcomes prediction, 97
public transcripts, 200, 201, 204, 210, 214

of FOMC, xiv, 92, 190–91
transparency role, 191, 202, 212–13

QE. *See* quantitative easing
Qu, Zhongjun, 64
quadratic detrending, 59, 67, 67f, 68, 68n6,
  74n10, 81
quantitative easing (QE), 19, 24

RBNZ. *See* Reserve Bank of New Zealand
Reagan, Ronald, 266
real-time data, 59, 66–70
  on inflation and output gap, from 1965–
    2013, 57
  on output gap, 67, 67f, 68, 71, 75, 76f,
    77–79, 77f, 78f, 79f, 80f, 81, 158
Real-Time Data Set for Macroeconomists
  (RTDSM), 66, 70
recession, in 1936–1937, 231
reference policy rule, 147f, 148f, 151, 152
Reference Policy Rule, of FRAT bill
  deviation from, 128–29
  as federal funds rate, 120
  as original Taylor rule, 56, 119–20
regimes
  boundaries of, 15–16
  contingency planning in, 17
  delegated responsibilities and powers, 11
  flexible rule-based, 118
  joined up, under MCC, 24–25, 29–30, 35
  LOLR, viii, 13–16
  for monetary stability broadly defined, 3
  need for, ix, 11, 31
  principles to guide, 20
  See also goal-based regimes; rule-based
    regimes; simple model goal-based and
    rule-based regimes
regional banks. *See* Reserve Banks
Reifschneider, David, 286
Reserve Bank of New Zealand (RBNZ), 183,
  273
Reserve Bank of New Zealand Act (1989)
  central bank and political pressures, 115
  central bank instrument independence
    by, 116
  central bank reforms, 150
  elected government and central bank con-
    tract, 115
  on inflation targeting, 109, 161
  with Policy Targets Agreement, 115
Reserve Bank presidents, 230
  BOG appointment and dismissal, 221, 224,
    236, 241, 245–46
  constitutionality of, 288

dissent, 188, 232
Dodd-Frank Act on appointment of, 234,
  241
economist staff support, 188
executive branch appointments with
  Senate confirmation, 45, 49, 221, 235,
  236–37, 288, 289
FOMC information and opinions by, 236
on large-scale asset purchases, xvi, 262
as political appointees, 257
regional board appointment, 288, 289
Reserve Banks
  BOG conflict with, xv, 246–47
  Chicago, 225, 226, 228, 238n12
  Cleveland, 233
  Conti-Brown's proposed reforms, 235
  Dallas, 234
  director selection process, xvi, 241–42
  discount rates set by, 224
  execution of lending action by, 46
  Federal, of St. Louis, 232–33, 236
  Friedman and Simon's plans for, 37
  Governors' Conference, in 1921, 225
  groupthink, xvi, 206–7
  Kansas City, 234
  LOLR approval, 44, 45, 46
  member banks ownership of, xv, 224
  Minneapolis, 233
  New York, 6, 46, 221, 226, 227, 228, 235, 237
  OMIC set up by, 225–26
  Philadelphia, 49, 59, 234
  powers, 240–41
  RBNZ, 183, 273
  Richmond, 233, 234
  shift of power to BOG, xv, 230, 234, 235
Resolution Trust Corporation (RTC), 283
Richardson, Henry, 195
Roberto, Michael A., 178–79, 186
Rogoff, Kenneth, 127, 139, 153
Roisland, Oistein, 88, 89, 111, 153
rookie status members, of FOMC, 192
Roosevelt, Franklin Delano, 222, 227–28
RTC. *See* Resolution Trust Corporation
RTDSM. *See* Real-Time Data Set for
  Macroeconomists
Rudebusch, Glenn, 64, 89, 121
rule-based regimes, 150, 238
  delegation, 11, 125–26
  demand shocks and, xiii, 134–35
  jointly optimal goal-based regimes and,
    131–34, 133f
  performance of, 123–24
  rules assignment, 128–31
  simple model of, 112

rules
  accountability aspect of, 97, 111–22
  -based reforms, Fed's discretion limited
    by, 119
  discretion *vs.*, 57, 58, 92, 98–99, 118n14,
    194, 198
  forecasts and, 97
  as operational mandate, 274–77
  optimal, xii, 33, 84, 88–89, 91, 101, 131,
    151, 164–65
  public prediction of monetary policy out-
    comes, 97
  simple, xi, 111
  variables and, 102
rules *vs.* goal model, of central bank perfor-
    mance measures, 109–66
  delegation in, 124–26
  discussion on, 161–66
  estimated model with sticky prices and
    wages, 135–54
  estimation, 137–38
  extensions and conclusions, 150–54
  Fed offset of aggregate demand shocks,
    xiii, 134–35
  goal-based and rule-based regimes perfor-
    mance, 123–24
  goals assignment, 126–28
  independence and accountability,
    112–22
  jointly optimal goal- and rule-based
    regimes, 131–34, 133f
  Levin comments on, 155–60
  results, 142–49
  rules assignment, 128–31
  simple model conclusions, 134–35
  welfare measures, 139–42, 140t
runs. *See* bank runs

Sandelands, Lance E., 177
Schmidt, Helmut, 51
Schmitt, Carl, 16, 22
Schonhardt-Bailey, Cheryl, 178, 183–84,
    190–91
Schwartz, Anna J., 225–26, 227, 228,
    230–31
Secrets of the Temple (Greider), 244, 244n13
Senate bill. *See* Financial Regulatory Improve-
    ment Act
SEP. *See* Summary of Economic Projections
serially uncorrelated shocks, 129
shadow rate, Wu and Xia (forthcoming rates),
    59, 69, 69f, 75
Shelby bill, 221

shocks, 163–64
  aggregate demand, xiii, 3, 127, 131–32,
    134–35, 156
  aggregate supply, xiii, 156
  cost, xii, 126, 127, 130, 132, 133, 134, 143,
    150
  demand, xiii, 131–35, 132, 147, 150
  distortionary, 113, 126, 127, 129–30, 133,
    134, 140, 143
  Euler equation and, 130
  inflation, 103, 111, 112
  serially uncorrelated, 129
short-term interest rates
  of Fed, to fund WWI, 224–25
  legislation on central bank's, 12
  monetary policy output and, xv, 12, 198
Shultz, George, xvii, xviii, 161, 264–67
Sibert, Anne, 182, 184, 185
SIFIs. *See* systematically important financial
    institutions
Simons, Henry, 37, 38, 40
simple model goal-based and rule-based
    regimes, 112, 150, 151–52, 165
  accountability and flexibility, 123
  conclusions from, 134–35
  delegation, 125–26
  goal assignment, 126–28
  jointly optimal goal- and rule-based
    regimes, 131–34, 133f
  rules assignment, 128–31
simple rules, xi, 111
single objective/multiple constraints, in
    decision-making, 195, 197–200, 216
social loss, 111, 127, 129, 144, 147f
  central bank accountability to lower, 124
  estimated model with sticky prices and
    wages and, 148f, 149f
social welfare function, xii, 121n16, 125,
    139–42, 143–44, 157
  alternative welfare measures, 140t
  distortionary shocks to lower, 126
society
  fractional-reserve banking and, 2, 35
  on liquidity reinsurance to banks, 2
solvency
  bailouts, 1, 14, 28, 33
  central banks assessment of, 14
  liquidity support and, 14–15
SOMA. *See* System Open Market Account
Sproul, Allan, 231
staff forecasts, 203, 210–12, 215
Stark, Tom, 66
Stasavage, David, 190

Statement on Longer-Run Goals and Policy
Strategy, of FOMC, 158–59
Staw, Barry M., 177
Steel, Bob, 283
Stigler, George, 49
stocks, 43, 102
central bank purchase of, during financial
crisis, ix, 165
strategic interaction, with fiscal authority,
25–28
Strong, Benjamin, 225–26, 227, 228
substance *vs.* process, 194
Summary of Economic Projections (SEP), of
FOMC
on forecasts, 159
on maximum employment mandate, 259
Summers, Lawrence, 115n8
Sunshine Act. *See* Government in the
Sunshine Act
Sveen, Tommy, 88, 89, 111, 153
Svensson, Lars E. O., 89, 157
System Open Market Account (SOMA), Fed
restrictions and, 261–62
systematic LOLR policy, viii, 237
systematic operation function, of central
banks, 1–2, 28–29
systematically important financial institutions
(SIFIs)
Fed supervision and regulation, 235n10
non-bank financial entities as, 236

Tabellini, Guido, 10n3
Taft-Hartley, 52
TARP. *See* Troubled Asset Relief Program
Taylor, John B., vii–xviii, 60–61, 62, 75, 82,
118
on FRAT bill, 120
Taylor rule, xviii
bills, in Congress, 2
debate, 12
equations for, 63–64
estimated, federal funds rate description,
57
extended periods of substantial deviation,
x, 59–60, 62, 74
Fed compliance with, xi, 125n20
inflation rate used in, xi, 66
inflation target, 163, 281–82
lagged funds rate and, xi, 65, 66, 91
legislation on short-term interest rate, by
central bank, 12
modified, federal funds rate description, 57
monetary policy operating principles, 12

original, federal funds rate description, 57
Orphanides on, 66
output gap measurement, xi, 66, 67, 67f
policy rule legislation problems with,
65–66
proposed operational mandate, 274
Reference Policy Rule as original, 56,
119–20
RTDSM and, 66
See also modified Taylor rule; original
Taylor rule
Threat Rigidity Effect theory, of Staw, Sande-
lands, and Dutton, 177
"Three Lessons for Monetary Policy in a
Low Inflation Era" (Reifschneider and
Williams), 286
Tillmann, Peter, 111, 112
Tirole, Jean, 118
transparency, 244
central bank independence and, 116n10
central banks and, 6, 158, 264–67
communication and, xi, xiii, xvii, 109, 155,
202, 204, 206, 215, 263
FOMC press conferences, 205–6
public transcripts role, 191, 202, 212–13
*Transparency and the Bank of England's Mone-
tary Policy Committee*, 174
Treasury, 284
authority for, 264
Bear Stearns bailout by, 32, 40, 46, 49–50,
201, 256, 262
Fed accord with, xvii, 263, 282–83
secretary, Dodd-Frank Act on permission
from, ix, 18, 18n8, 234
Troubled Asset Relief Program (TARP), 32
Tucker, Paul, vii–x, 1–30, 10n3, 13n4

unelected central bankers, 5, 10, 13
emergency powers role, 16, 20–21
executive branch sanctions on ventures
by, 18
unit banking system, 230n5, 251
Upper Echelon theory, of Hambrick and
Mason, 177

Vazquez, Jesus, 137
Vermeule, Adrian, 17
vertical Phillips curve, 233
Vestin, David, 111n2
volatility
of cost shocks, 132, 133, 134, 150
of demand shocks, 132, 147, 150
of distortionary shocks, 133, 134

Volcker, Paul, 7, 34, 205, 208, 233, 246,
    265–66, 285
Volcker disinflation, x, 62
    modified Taylor rule and, 60, 74
    original Taylor rule positive deviations
    during, 60, 72

wage inflation, elasticity of, 136–37
wages. *See* estimated model with sticky prices
    and wages
Wall Street
    conflict of interest with Fed, 234
    New York Fed close connection to, 221,
    234, 246
Wall Street Crash, in October 1929, 227
Walsh, Carl E., xi–xiii, 87, 88, 89, 109–54,
    111n2, 118n14, 126
Warburg, Paul, 223
Warsh, Kevin, xiii–xiv, 173–93
Webb, Steven B., 115n8
welfare
    advantages of, 5
    measures, in estimated model with sticky
    prices and wages, 139–42, 140t
    See also social welfare function
Wheelock, David, 228, 240

Wieland, Volker, 65, 121
Wilkinson, Adrian, 176, 176n3
Willes, Mark H., 233
Williams, John, xviii, 62, 65, 79, 93, 121,
    267–78, 286
World War I (WWI)
    Fed inflation after, 225
    Fed short-term interest rates to fund,
    224–25
World War II (WWII), Fed as engine of
    inflation during, 231
Wu, Cynthia Jing, 59, 69, 69f, 75
Wu and Xia (forthcoming) rates, 59, 69, 6
    9f, 75
WWI. *See* World War I
WWII. *See* World War II

Xia, Fan Dora, 59, 69, 69f, 75

Yellen, Janet, 69, 82, 110n1, 246
    on FRAT bill, 55, 120
    on modified Taylor rule, 61–62, 64,
    64n5, 78

zero lower bound (ZLB) interest rates, xvi,
    152, 152n27, 256, 276–77, 285–86, 287

CPSIA information can be obtained at www.ICGtesting.com
Printed in the USA
BVOW08*0121020416

442668BV00001B/1/P